DIRTY LOOKS

DIRTY LOOKS

Women, Pornography, Power

Edited by
PAMELA CHURCH GIBSON and ROMA GIBSON

BFI PUBLISHING

First published in 1993 by the
British Film Institute
21 Stephen Street
London W1P 1PL

British Library Cataloguing-in-Publication Data.
A catalogue record for this book is available from the British Library

ISBN 0-85170-403-4
0-85170-404-2 pbk

Cover design by Andrew Barron
Cover photograph by Grace Lau

Set by Goodfellow & Egan Photosetting Ltd, Cambridge
and printed in Great Britain by
The Trinity Press, Worcester

Contents

Acknowledgments

The editors are grateful to the following friends and colleagues for offering support, materials, information and ideas:

Karen Alexander, Celia Britton, Pam Cook, Barry Curtis, James Donald, Andrew Gibson, John Hill, Mary McIntosh, Claire Pajakowska, Constance Penley, John O. Thompson, Ginette Vincendeau, Lola Young, Michele Wallace and David Wilson.

At the BFI thanks are due to Ed Buscombe, Dawn King, Colin MacCabe and John Smoker.

Grace Lau deserves a special mention for her untiring commitment to the project and for introducing us to a broad spectrum of artists and cultural activists.

Above all, our thanks go to Paul Willemen for his invaluable comments and assistance throughout the project.

Notes on Contributors

Carol J. Clover is Professor of Scandinavian and Rhetoric at the University of California, Berkeley. She teaches medieval studies and film, and her most recent book is *Men, Women and Chain Saws: Gender in the Modern Horror Film* (Princeton University Press and the British Film Institute: 1992).

Bette Gordon is a film-maker, lecturer and writer living and working in New York City. Her early short films have won numerous awards worldwide and her first feature, *Variety*, was shown in cinemas and film festivals throughout the world. She has directed episodic television for Laurel Entertainment (*Tales of the Darkside, Monsters*) and is shortly to direct for HBO Television a film dealing with prostitution. She is a professor at Hofstra University and at Columbia University's Graduate Film Division.

Karyn Kay is an independent film-maker and writer. She was scriptwriter and associate producer of *Call Me*, an erotic thriller directed by Solace Mitchell, which won the award for best screenplay at the 1988 Mystery Film Festival in Catolica, Italy. She has written for television and has recently teamed up again with Mitchell on another erotic thriller, *Forbidden*. She wrote *Women and Cinema: A Critical Anthology* (E.P. Dutton) and wrote *Myrna Loy* (Pyramid Press). She teaches screenwriting and film theory at Fordham University.

Laura Kipnis is a video artist and critic. A collection of her essays and videoscripts, *Ecstasy Unlimited: On Sex, Capital, Gender and Aesthetics*, was recently published by the University of Minnesota Press. She teaches in the Radio-TV-Film Department at Northwestern University.

Gertrud Koch is Professor in Film Studies at the Ruhr University, Bochum and has lectured widely in Europe and in the US. She has published on the work of Herbert Marcuse, Siegfried Kracauer, representation and sexual difference and the visual construction of Jewishness. She is co-publisher of the journals *Babylon – Beitrage zur Judischen Gegenwart* and *Frauen und Film*.

Liz Kotz is a New York-based critic and curator who has written on film, video and visual arts for *Artforum, Art in America, Afterimage*, and other publications. She is a graduate student in Comparative Literature at Columbia University in New York, and is co-editing an anthology of lesbian writing with poet Eileen Myles for *Semiotext(e)*.

Grace Lau is a freelance photographer living and working in London. She is the house photographer for *Skin Two* and her work has been featured in numerous other magazines and publications in Europe. Her photographs have been exhibited in several group shows and she has had her own exhibition at the Submarine Gallery in London. She has recently founded a workshop with three other radical women photographers.

Anne McClintock teaches gender and cultural studies at Columbia University, New York. She has written *Maids, Maps and Mines. Gender and Imperialism in Victorian Britain and South Africa* (forthcoming, 1992), and is working on a book about women and the sex industry (to be published by Jonathan Cape).

Lynda Nead is lecturer in the History of Art Department at Birkbeck College, London. She is author of *Myths of Sexuality: Representations of Women in Victorian Britain* (Blackwell, 1988) and *The Female Nude: Art, Obscenity and Sexuality* (Routledge, 1992).

Lynne Segal teaches Psychology at Middlesex University and is a member of the *Feminist Review* collective. Her previous works include *Is the Future Female?: Troubled Thoughts on Contemporary Feminism* (Virago, 1987), *Slow Motion: Changing Masculinities, Changing Men* (Virago, 1990) and *Sex Exposed: Sexuality & the Pornography Debate* with Mary McIntosh (eds) (Virago, 1992).

Chris Straayer is an Assistant Professor in the Department of Cinema Studies at New York University. Her book, *Deviant Spectatorship/Gay and Lesbian Discourses/Film and Video*, will be published by Columbia University Press.

Maureen Turim is Professor of Film Studies in the English Department of the University of Florida. Author of *Flashbacks in Film: Memory and History* (New York: Routledge) and *Abstraction in Avant-Garde Films* (Ann Arbor: UMI Research Press), she has also published articles on a wide range of theoretical, historical and aesthetic issues in cinema. She is now completing her next book, *The Films of Oshima: Images of a Japanese Iconoclast*.

Jennifer Wicke is Associate Professor of Comparative Literature at New York University where she teaches literature, theory, film and cultural studies. She is the author of *Advertising Fictions: Literature, Advertisement, and Social Reading* (Columbia University Press, 1988) and of the forthcoming *The Politics of Feminist Theory* (Basil Blackwell). Her current project is a study of gender, modernity and consumption.

Linda Williams teaches film and Women's Studies at the University of California, Irvine. She wrote *Hard Core: Power, Pleasure and the Frenzy of the Visible* (Berkeley: University of California Press, 1989 and London: Pandora, 1990) and *Figures of Desire: A Theory and Analysis of Surrealist Film* (University of Illinois Press, 1981; reprinted by University of California Press, 1991).

CAROL J. CLOVER

Introduction

For better or worse, pornography has become the feminist issue of the decade. Sexual matters in general have moved from the shadow to the light of day – not just 'vanilla sex' (the separate denomination of which is itself telling), but homosexuality, sadomasochism, sex crimes (rape, child molestation, incest), erotic bondage, masturbation, bestiality, and so on. Pornography is part and parcel of the larger drift. But pornography is also different, set apart by its status as a second-order practice or a fantasy of practices rather than itself a 'practice'. Because pornography is representation and representation is amenable to interpretation, the logic goes, pornography offers a kind of key or master text to the practices that it portrays and that flood our daily news and entertainment. Read pornography right and you will understand those practices. Read pornography right and you will understand rape.

All this hinges, of course, on what 'right reading' might be, and it is on this point that feminism has split down the middle. For those on the anti-censorship side, pornography is a *meaningful text about* the sexual acts it represents. For those on the censorship side (conspicuously Robin Morgan, Catharine MacKinnon, and Andrea Dworkin), it is the *enabling theory of* the acts it represents: a charter for action, or, in Morgan's lapidary formulation, the claim that pornography is the theory and rape the practice. This is not a minor quibble. It hits our most basic sense of how to understand culture, what to do to improve our place in it, and with whom (the Moral Right or the American Civil Liberties Union) to throw in our political lot.

This volume stands on the anti-censorship side of the fence. Because the censorship position is commonly taken, by the media and the public, to be the feminist position, it has seemed all the more urgent for those of us on the other side to speak up. The essays in this volume vary greatly in what they have to say about pornography, but they are all animated by the spirit of dissent, and they all refuse a scheme that discounts dissenters as complicit with male domination. Pornography may be a 'meaningful text', but that is not to say that its meaning is transparent. Even in the case of a single, apparently simple image, 'real' or 'true' meanings are hard to come by. It is one thing to feel offended by that image, as a person and as a woman, but quite another to claim that it is transparently harmful. And pornography does not in any case devolve on one image, or one kind of image, infinitely duplicated ('rape'). It comprises a great variety of images and scenarios, many of which fall outside the standard scheme of male-female relations, many of which contradict one another, and many of which have little to do with women (as in the case of gay male or male transvestite pornography, for example) or even with men (lesbian pornography).

Consider, for example, porn's fondness for dominatrix scenarios – images in which men are shown as the slaves and sexual servants of women. In practice, to judge from the accounts of sex workers, 'by far the most common service paid for by men in heterosexual S/M is the extravagant display of submission'. So writes Anne McClintock in an essay on the subculture of sadomasochism. Certainly this image, and this practice, pose problems for any monolithic understanding of pornography. It is not just that the usual positions are reversed; it is that the reversal – particularly when the subordinate male is dressed as a girl or woman – opens up the possibility that at least some male consumers at least some of the time are not uniformly 'identified' (the term is a tricky one) with the male-dominant role, but rather are aligned with what convention and the social unconcious designate as the powerless or effeminate position – the object, not the subject, of rape. Is it possible that even in the standard set-up (overpowering male, cringing female), male spectators may engage, at some level, not only with the dominant but with the submissive part? And what do we make of transvestite or 'she-male' pornography and self-portraiture, forms in which, as Laura Kipnis reminds us, there are no women, but which speak plainly to the desire to be feminine and arguably female as well?

Then there is the figure of Annie Sprinkle. Two essays – one by Linda Williams, one by Chris Straayer – explore the political significance of the woman who has worked (in chronological order) as masseuse, prostitute, burlesque and live sex-show performer, sex magazine writer, porn actress, porn director, and, most recently, avant-garde performance artist in her show *Post-Post Porn Modernist*. It is not only that Sprinkle's parodic relation to the business of sex and her spectacular and spectacularly public orgasms confound our notions of what it is porn actresses are and do. It is that Sprinkle herself, Sprinkle the phenomenon, obliges us to ask, as Williams notes, why we have drawn such a firm line between obscene pornography on the one hand and legitimate art on the other, and whether there might not be some political value, in terms of women's agency, of opening the categories up to each other (themes developed along other lines by Kipnis, Liz Kotz and Lynda Nead). Sprinkle is clearly unusual. Other accounts of porn actresses and sex performers are less happy, and Maureen Turim's essay on the Asian traffic in pornography reminds us just how heavily social traditions and economics can weigh on women. But however special, Sprinkle's case stands as an object lesson – not because she has transcended the sex industry, but, on the contrary, because she stands so squarely within it and has insisted with such humour and integrity on its being acknowledged as the context of her own performance art. She has stayed with, and unabashedly inhabits, her own pornographic body.

The pornographic body: this is the heart of the matter. Although our systems of censorship and our production codes concern themselves with the status of bodies 'up there' (on the photograph, on the canvas or screen), what is really at stake is the body 'down here', the body of the viewer. Pornography's shame lies in the fact that it has one simple, unequivocal intention: to excite its consumer. We are in general suspicious of forms (including music and dance forms) that aim themselves so directly at the body, and it is no surprise that the other two film genres that do so (horror, which is meant to speed the pulse and prompt screams, and melodrama, which is meant to jerk tears) are also consigned to the lower reaches of the status scale. In fact, as Lynda Nead, Jennifer Wicke and Laura Kipnis remind us, the debate on pornography is always linked, however covertly, with the debate on high and low culture. What is erotica (that favoured category of pro-censorship feminism) but a category that moves us less, a form that, as Nead says, 'allows the viewer to be aroused but within the purified, contemplative mode of high culture'? For Wicke, the association of pornography with mass culture and erotica with art is crucial to an understanding of the popularity of pornography in the academy. Pornography, she writes, 'is a secret sharer in the canon debate, and a hidden partner of the high art/mass culture conflict that rages beyond the perimeters of the canon'.

There *is* something awesome about the way that pornography can move our bodies, even when we don't want it to and even if we don't approve of the images that make it happen. (If the unconscious were a politically correct place, it would not need to be unconscious.) No wonder we fear pornography's effects, given its power to override or short-circuit our sense of propriety. The question is whether these effects translate into real-life behaviour – whether, again, porn is rightly read as a charter for action. For pro-censorship feminists, as for much of the general public, the answer is yes, and over the last couple of decades social researchers have devised increasingly clever experiments to prove the connection. The jury is still out, according to Lynne Segal's survey and analysis of evidence. So long has it been out, in fact, that we may consider the case to be in a kind of default. The only lesson to be drawn from the evidence is that there is no lesson: 'It is never possible, whatever the image, to isolate it, fix its meaning and predict some inevitable pattern of response, independently from assessing its wider representational context and the particular recreational, educational or social context in which it is being received'. Both Segal and Williams speak eloquently of the political consequences of the 'harm'-driven movement to censor pornography: it falls heavily on marginal or minority sexualities (conspicuously homosexuality); it shifts the blame for real sexual harm from the perpetrator to the pornographer ('porn made me do it'); and it deflects attention from what are surely the far more influential 'gender messages' of the daily mainstream (billboards, magazine ads, sports events, film and television entertainment, etc.). It scapegoats, in a word.

There is no doubt that the great bulk of pornography has been and remains created by and for men. But is that to say that its meanings can be so neatly reduced to the symbolic organisation of a phallocentric world? Photographer Grace Lau and film-makers Bette Gordon and Karyn Kay (*Variety* and *Call Me*) give intriguing accounts of how they as women negotiate their way in the world of hardcore, and Liz Kotz shows how two women media artists (Lutz Bacher and Abigail Child) explore and appropriate the terms and forms of pornographic representation. For Gertrud Koch, the porn film's welter of real bodies and genitals must always exceed its organising phallocentric fictions, and part of the pleasure for even the male viewer, but surely the female one, must lie in the 'details of a quivering world of objects' that elude the 'abstract, generalising mania of male perception'.

Koch's vision of pornography as producing something it can never contain, a 'shadow realm' that lies beyond symbolic systems, is a deeply utopian one. Not all the contributors to this volume would go that far, but they all share the conviction that there is no single 'right reading' of pornography, and that even the most standard forms of heterosexual pornography confess a deeply complicated relation to women and femininity, to men and masculinity, and to the terms of sexual difference that order our everyday lives. Above all, they share the conviction that to make sexually explicit material take the fall for, say, the battery of women on Super Bowl Sunday is simply and terribly beside the point.

LYNNE SEGAL

Does Pornography Cause Violence?

The Search for Evidence

The conviction that pornography causes sexual violence is what motivates much of the contemporary campaigning for legislation against it – at least by feminists. In the latest British collection produced by Catherine Itzin in order to strengthen anti-pornography initiatives and legislation in the UK, we read repeatedly of the consistent and conclusive links between pornography and violence. Pornography, Itzin asserts, is 'a crucial element', causing violence against women and children and male dominance generally (Itzin, 1992, p. 412). The link here, the earlier publication by *Everywoman* had announced, 'is considerably stronger than that for cigarette smoking and cancer' (*Everywoman*, 1988, p. 5). 'I doubt that anybody disputes the data,' the psychologist Edward Donnerstein, a leading figure in pornography research, declared at public hearings in the USA in 1983, thereby hoping to help secure the implementation of new anti-pornography legislation in the state of Minneapolis, known as the Minneapolis Ordinance (*Everywoman*, 1988, p. 22). It is odd, then, that it should be Donnerstein and his fellow researchers who themselves dispute the data.

In their more scholarly writings, these psychologists indicate that whether or not their laboratory reports of links between pornography and violence tell us anything at all 'about real-world aggression, such as rape, is still a matter for considerable debate.' Indeed they even, rather disingenuously, complain now that their research has been misunderstood and misused by anti-pornographers to strengthen censorship laws (Donnerstein *et al.*, 1987, p. 174). Given the passion and anger poured into the pornography debate, however, not to mention Donnerstein's own former readiness for public testimony, this is hardly surprising. Today, at a time of ever greater alarm over the extent of men's violence against women and children – much of it sexual violence – pornography, for many, serves as its most appropriate metaphor or symbol. It is this which makes it one of the most fiercely contested moral issues of our time, conceptually and politically.

When first used in the 1860s to describe the photography of prostitutes, 'pornography' was defined as sexually explicit, and therefore obscene or lewd words or images intended to provoke sexual excitement, but its meaning has never been fixed. Today, however, disagreements over both its definition and its significance are deeper than ever – disagreements flowing inevitably from the contrasting political positions which exist around pornography. Before we consider the psychological research on the effects of pornography, and the use made of it, some knowledge of the competing political and moral arguments which feed into the debates is therefore necessary.

Definitions and Convictions

It is now customary to identify three distinct positions on pornography: *liberal, moral right* and *feminist*. The liberal position, manifest in the North American *Presidential Commission* of 1970 or, in a more qualified way, in the British *Williams Report* of 1979, offers a non-evaluative definition of pornography, as sexually explicit material designed for sexual arousal. It argues that there is no scientific evidence for pornography causing harm in society, and therefore no sound reasons for banning or taking other forms of action against it. While pornography may offend many women and men, it brings harmless pleasure to others. The Williams Report aimed to limit the *public* display of pornography in the interests of those who might find it offensive. This position, clearly, explicitly calls upon the support of existing empirical research.

The position of the Moral Right in Britain, of Mary Whitehouse and the Festival of Light, outlined in the *Longford Report* of 1972, assumes a different definition of the pornographic, as representations of sex removed from what is believed to be its legitimate function and context: 'a symptom of preoccupation with sex which is unrelated to its purpose' (Longford, 1972, p. 205). Pornography is a threat to traditional family values because sex exists for procreation and should be confined to marriage. In line with this approach, censorship in Britain during the 1950s and early 1960s was mainly targeted at any public display of the naked body or of premarital or extramarital sex. Then as now, the Moral Right also sought to suppress information on birth control, abortion and sex education in schools, while demanding rigid censorship of any type of sexually explicit material designed for arousal and pleasure, condemning in particular 'perverse' and homosexual imagery as threatening family life and creating general social and moral decay.

This was the position which grew in strength throughout the 1980s, assisted both by sexual panics around AIDS and the increasing, though piecemeal, tightening up of censorship legislation under the Thatcher government. In these years, the Local Government (Miscellaneous Provisions) Act of 1982, which provided guidelines to local councils for controlling the licensing of 'sex establishments' and their cinematic materials, replaced the Williams Report's emphasis on harm with a condemnation of material intended to stimulate 'sexual activity' or 'acts of force or restraint which are associated with sexual activity' or images which portray 'genital organs or urinary or excretory functions'. Two years later, the Video

Recordings Act went further, again with stipulations not just against violence, but against explicit sexual images of genitalia, excretory functions and acts of sex (Merck, 1992, p. 50). The Moral Right, however, has little interest in whether research offers any evidence for links between pornography and violence, believing it to be common sense that imagery or writing designed primarily for titillation is offensive and dangerous, and leads to sexual decadence and crime.

The *feminist* critique of pornography, in contrast, addresses the sexism and exploitation of women represented in mainstream pornographic material – which is frequently also racist. Pin-ups, pornography, advertising, textbooks and religious beliefs and imagery, all – with spray gun and paint – were declared 'offensive to women'. It is from *within* this position, however, that some of the most passionate battles have been waged in recent years, especially over the evidence for the 'harm' of pornography. It is widely thought that feminists have uniformly understood pornography as abusive to women and an incitement to violence against them. And certainly all feminists criticise the mythologies mediated through mainstream pornography, at least in its heterosexual versions, which represent women as passive, perpetually desiring bodies – or bits of bodies – ubiquitously available for men's insatiable sexual appetites. Produced and consumed primarily by men, standard pornography would seem to mock standard feminist attempts to express a woman-centred sexuality, liberated from male-centred discourses and practices.

But there is more than one argument about pornography within feminism from which conflicting conclusions have been drawn. In the 1970s feminists did not seek legal restrictions on pornography, or treat pornography as uniquely symbolic of male dominance. With the state and the judiciary so comprehensively controlled by men, obscenity laws were known to have always served to suppress the work, if not jail the organisers, of those fighting for women's own control of their fertility and sexuality. Objecting to all forms of sexist representation, feminists set out to subvert a whole cultural landscape which, whether in selling carpet-sweepers, collecting census information or uncovering women's crotches, placed women as the subordinate sex. Representatively, Ruth Wallsgrove, then working for *Spare Rib*, declared in 1977: 'I believe we should not agitate for more laws against pornography, but should rather stand up together and say what we feel about it, and what we feel about our own sexuality, and force men to re-examine their own attitudes to sex and women implicit in their consumption of porn' (Wallsgrove, 1977, p. 65).

This type of feminist emphasis on women's need to assert their own sexual needs and desires, however, came by the end of the 1970s to be overshadowed by, and entangled with, feminist concern with the issue of male violence. It was the popular writing of Robin Morgan and Susan Brownmiller in the USA in the mid-1970s which first made a definitive connection between pornography and male violence: 'Pornography is the Theory, Rape is the Practice' (Segal, 1987 and 1990). With male sexuality here seen as indistinguishable from male violence, with male violence here presented as the key to male dominance, and with pornography portrayed as the symbolic proof of the connection between the two, anti-pornography campaigning was soon to become emblematic of this strand of feminism. It redefined 'pornography' once again, as material which depicts violence against women, and is in itself violence against women.

Andrea Dworkin's *Pornography: Men Possessing Women* remains the single most influential text proclaiming this particular feminist view of pornography, in which 'pornography' lies not only behind all forms of female oppression, but behind exploitation, murder and brutality throughout human history (Dworkin, 1981). Following through such logic to draft model feminist anti-pornography legislation – the Minneapolis Ordinance – Andrea Dworkin and Catharine MacKinnon define pornography as 'the graphic sexually explicit subordination of women through pictures or words' (MacKinnon, 1987, p. 176). Armed with this definition, they propose that any individual should be able to use the courts to seek financial redress against the producers or distributors of sexually explicit material if they can show that it has caused them 'harm'. The question of proof of harm thus lies at the heart of feminist anti-pornography campaigning.

And yet, despite the growth and strength of the feminist anti-pornography movement during the 1980s, particularly in the United States and in Britain (where we have seen the emergence of the 'Campaign against Pornography' and a similar 'Campaign against Pornography and Censorship'), some feminists (represented in Britain by Feminists Against Censorship) passionately reject its analysis and related practice. They see it as a complete mistake to reduce the dominance of sexism and misogyny in our culture to sexuality and its representations. They believe that men's cultural contempt for and sexualisation of women long predated the growth of commercial pornography, and is a product of the relative powerlessness of women as a sex. Narrowing the focus on women's subordination to the explicitly sexual, they argue, downplays the sexism and misogyny at work within all our most respectable social institutions and practices, whether judicial, legal, familial, occupational, religious, scientific or cultural.

More dangerously (in today's conservative political climate), they fear that we risk terminating women's evolving exploration of our sexuality and pleasure by forming alliances with, instead of strongly combating, the conservative anti-pornography crusade. These are alliances which Dworkin and MacKinnon have unhesitatingly pursued in the US, collaborating almost exclusively with the extreme right: Presbyterian minister Mayor Hudnut III in Indianapolis; anti-ERA, anti-feminist, Republican conservative Bealah Coughenour in Minneapolis; far right preacher Greg Dixon; and of course the pro-family, anti-feminist Reagan appointee responsible for removing funds from Women's Refuges, Edwin Meese (Duggan, 1986, p. 63). Blanket condemnation of pornography, its critics stress, discourages us all from facing up to women's own sexual fears and infantile fantasies, which are by no means free from guilt, anxiety, shame, contradiction, and eroticisation of power on display in men's pornographic productions. What women need, according to feminists opposed to anti-pornography crusades, is not more censorship but more sexually explicit material produced by and for women, more open and honest discussion of all sexual issues, alongside the struggle against women's general subordinate economic and social status.

These then are currently the *four* (rather than three) distinct political positions on pornography. The question which for many is still seen as crucial, however, especially for those uncertain how to define and react to pornography, is whether pornographic images *are* responsible for inciting men's violence against women. Which position, if any, does existing empirical research, or other types of evidence, support?

Early Research on Pornography and its Effects

The liberal arguments which lay behind the relaxations in censorship in Britain and the USA in the 1970s seemed to win out then precisely because they were based almost entirely upon research, or what was seen as scientific evidence. There had been little systematic study of the effects of pornography before the US Commission on Obscenity and Pornography of 1970, which was set up in part to undertake new psychological research and report on existing literature. The conclusions from all the new and existing studies at that time were nearly unanimous in the view that pornography had no harmful effects on its consumers.

There can be few things more contested, even from within its own theoretical framework, than the relevance of the controlled and contrived social-psychological laboratory experiment to human action in the world at large. However, it was from within such research that many of the conclusions of policy-makers and campaigners around pornography have been and are still drawn. Considering the impact of pornographic material on sexual arousal and behaviour, the studies of the 1970s reported that a large proportion of adult males and females did find sexually explicit material arousing; men tended to display more arousal in response to films and photographs, women to written material. Heterosexual people were more aroused by heterosexual material, and homosexual males by homosexual material. Despite repeated exposure to slides showing highly 'deviant' sexual activity, subjects showed no tendency to copy such practices. (For better or worse, those habitually practising 'missionary sex' remained untempted by the titillating representations of its alternatives!) Those with less guilt, and more liberal attitudes to sexuality, found pornographic material more arousing. The greater the exposure to sexually arousing material, however, the less the arousal. And the greater the exposure to such material, the more liberal and tolerant of it consumers became.

These studies thus reported *no* antisocial changes in sexual behaviour after short or long exposure to sexually explicit material (Byrne and Lamberth, 1970; Davis and Braucht, 1970; Mann *et al.*, 1970; Kutchinsky, 1973; and Mosher, 1970). At this time, only one study looked at the effects of exposure to pornography on aggressive behaviour (performatively defined as willingness to administer electric shocks to another person to assist learning). This study by Tannenbaum (in Donnerstein *et al.*, 1987) found that exposure to highly arousing erotica did lead to increased shock levels being administered to another person (the experimenter's stooge or 'confederate') who had earlier angered the subject. However, Tannenbaum found that the same material also led to more positive behaviour towards the stooge if the previous interaction had been friendly.

Other studies undertaken by this Commission also supported the liberal position on pornography. Those investigating the connections between pornography and sex crimes in the US, for example, reported no correlation between pornographic consumption and juvenile crimes in general, while studies of convicted rapists found them to have had *less* exposure to pornography during adolescence, and also less recent exposure to pornography than the control group (Goldstein *et al.*, 1970; Walker, in Goldstein *et al.*, 1970; Johnson *et al.*, 1970). (Interestingly, and tellingly for later reports from people working with sex offenders to the 1985 Minneapolis hearings, the rapists themselves, though having access to pornography later than the general population, were nevertheless inclined to blame pornography for their crimes.)

The Commission also looked at empirical research by Kutchinsky from Denmark, which had removed all legal prohibitions between 1967 and 1969. Here again they found a *negative* correlation between access to pornography and sex crimes (Kutchinsky, 1973). The quite significant reductions in sex crimes reported over that same period convinced the Commission that access to pornography did not increase the rate of sexual crimes. Subsequent work (Kant and Goldstein, 1978) also confirmed that sex offenders had less exposure to pornography, both as teenagers and as adults. (Although it does not invalidate these findings, we do, however, need to be aware that rape is very often not reported, and rapists – especially if they are white and apparently 'respectable' – very often escape conviction. This means that those who are reported and successfully convicted are only a minority of rapists, and perhaps an atypical minority.)

The psychological and sociological research of the late 1960s and early 1970s which, by and large, concluded that there was *no* connection between pornographic consumption and either change in sexual practices or an increase in sexual violence, was always rejected as irrelevant by the Moral Right in both the US and Britain. As US newspaper columnist James Kilpatrick declared: 'Common sense is a better guide than laboratory experiments; and common sense tells us pornography is bound to contribute to sexual crime. ...It seems ludicrous to argue "bad" books do not promote bad behaviour' (in Donnerstein *et al.*, 1987, p. 1). More significantly, in terms of subsequent research, these studies were conducted just before the emergence of the feminist critique of pornography, which at first stressed its significance as part of our culture of sexism and misogyny and later, for some, stressed its role in directly causing violence against women, in being in itself violence against women. On the latter view, pornography becomes *the* source of myths about women's sexuality, teaching men that women enjoy being raped or sexually coerced. This feminist critique has helped spark off the new psychological research of the 1980s, which is currently being used by those seeking new legal restrictions on pornography.

Updating the Research on Pornography

Whereas in the 1960s and early 1970s studies of pornography had been concerned to look at the effects of pornography – seen as sexually explicit material – on men's general sexual practices or antisocial behaviour, by the late 70s the emphasis had shifted to the more specific study of men's violence against, or calloused and contemptuous attitudes towards, women. Feminists could indeed rightly claim it as a victory that whereas once the concern about pornography was mainly over its effects upon those who consumed it, today the concern is mainly over its effects upon those who are represented by it. Another reason for this shift, however, was the belief, encouraged by feminist writers like Dworkin, that pornography had become, and would continue to become, ever more violent – because of its assumed 'addictive' nature. This was the belief, for example, repeated throughout the Minneapolis and the subsequent, and similar, Meese Commission in the US. There is no evidence, however, to support it.

One study (Malamuth and Spinner, 1980) found that violent images in *Playboy* and *Penthouse* did increase from 1 to 5 per cent between 1973 and 1977 but a more recent US study (Scott, 1985) on such imagery in *Playboy* between 1954 and 1983 found a *decline* after 1977, with well under 1 per cent of material containing violent imagery – suggesting that the feminist critique is having some effect. Nor was there any increase in violent sexual imagery in 'adult' videos, according to a US study covering the years 1979 to 1983 (Donnerstein *et al.*, 1987, p. 67). In most pornography, it would seem – unlike in certain other genres of representation like horror and 'slasher' movies – violent imagery is rare. One recent New York survey reported between 3.3 and 4.7 per cent of violent imagery in a random sample of pornographic films, and another found 7 per cent of s/m or bondage imagery with women submissive in pornographic magazines, but 9 per cent with men submissive (Howitt and Cumberbatch, 1990, pp. 7–8). While it seems to be a myth that violent imagery in pornography has in fact been increasing, experiments on its possible effects have undoubtedly increased. The best summary of this newer research of the 1980s, most of it conducted in the US, can be found in Donnerstein, Linz and Penrod's book, *The Question of Pornography: Research Findings and Policy Implications* (1987).

Showing some awareness of the diverse and shifting definitions of the 'pornographic', the authors distinguish different types of pornography before seeking to detect its effects. First, and in line with previous studies, they reported a multitude of laboratory experiments, all of which failed to find any increase – following exposure to *non-violent* or soft-core pornographic material – in men's aggressive or general antisocial behaviour, either towards other men or towards women. Indeed some of the experiments suggested that exposure to non-violent pornography lowers aggression levels and increases subjects' sociability, measured by their willingness to reward a confederate of the experimenter (with money) after such exposure, and their failure to increase their aggressiveness when angered after viewing such material. Exposure to this type of pornography did not alter subjects' attitudes towards rape.

Next, the authors looked at the research on what they defined as non-violent but degrading images of women (depictions of women as sexually promiscuous and insatiable, even in the face of men's callousness and contempt). For example, Check in 1985 (in Donnerstein, 1987) showed male subjects a film clip of a woman doctor being verbally abused and sexually harassed by a male, who, once she catches sight of his penis, is desperately eager for and enjoys instant sex. Following such exposure, Check claimed, his subjects were more likely to say that they might commit rape – if they could get away with it. Linz, on the other hand, also in 1985 (in Donnerstein, 1987), found that subjects watching a similar film narrative, *Debbie Does Dallas*, but seeing it in its entirety rather than in brief excerpts, exhibited no significant increase in their acceptance of calloused attitudes about rape, nor any increased likelihood to view women as sexual objects or to condone the actions of rapists and judge the victims of rape narratives as more responsible for their own assault. Donnerstein, Linz and Penrod therefore argued that no definite conclusions could be drawn about non-violent but degrading images of women (Donnerstein *et al.*, 1987).

Their main concern, however, was to explore the effects of pornographic material which depicts violence against women. Those familiar with Dworkin's or MacKinnon's frequent linking of pornography and the Holocaust ('Dachau brought into the bedroom and celebrated', Dworkin, 1981, p. 69) may be surprised that men in general list violence as the least titillating aspect of pornography, react to it with distress rather than pleasure, and have become less, rather than more, tolerant towards violent pornography. But, drawing upon their own research and that of Malamuth, Check and others, they did conclude that exposure to violent pornography (for example, depictions of rape) does increase sexual arousal in *some* men, especially if the victim is shown as 'enjoying' the rape. And a few subjects, those who say that they might commit a rape if they could get away with it, showed the same arousal even when the victim was seen to be suffering. Some researchers suggest, therefore, that arousal to sadistic material might provide a good predictor of men's proclivity to rape.

The main finding which Donnerstein, Linz and Penrod wanted to emphasise, therefore, was that exposure to aggressive pornography can not only arouse some men, but might in some cases, in particular contexts, alter certain men's attitudes and behaviour towards women. Specifically, such exposure can produce more calloused attitudes towards women and greater acceptance of rape myths which downplay or dismiss the significance of rape. Malamuth and Donnerstein report, for example, that exposing male college students to sexually violent films in which a woman is raped but also portrayed as 'enjoying' it causes subjects, who have also been provoked by insults from a female 'confederate' of the experimenter, to score higher on a Rape Acceptance Scale (Donnerstein *et al.*, 1987). From other experiments which asked men whether they might commit rape if guaranteed they would not be caught, Malamuth and Check suggested that the negative effects they reported from exposure to violent pornography may only occur if men are already predisposed to consider sexual violence towards women. Donnerstein, Linz and Penrod therefore conclude that the calloused attitudes to rape, which may in certain cases follow exposure to violent pornography, may not so much be *caused* by the exposure to pornography as strengthened by it (Donnerstein *et al.*, 1987).

They further suggest, from experiments using imagery which is not sexually explicit but involves violence against women, that it is the violence, rather than the sexual explicitness, which is mainly responsible for any increase in aggressiveness and calloused attitudes in men following exposure to violent pornography. And this in turn means, as they indicate, that we should worry more about material which is not pornographic at all but which contains images of violence against women – from soap operas to popular commercially released films.

Psychologists Fall Out Over Experimental Research

There are nevertheless problems with the conclusions Donnerstein, Linz and Penrod draw from their survey of the psychological research on pornography in the 1980s – some of which the authors themselves admit. These problems stem from the intrinsic weaknesses of any such laboratory experiments. The highly artificial conditions in which psychologists produce their results may not involve behaviour which is in any way generalisable. So, for instance, the tests of arousal have been criticised by Canadian psychologist Thelma McCormack because the subjects' own reports of sexual arousal may be unreliable, and the apparatus used to measure tumescence (expansion of the penis) may itself stimulate arousal (McCormack, 1985).

There is the additional problem of the failure of these experiments even to consider the complex question of the relationship between fantasy and reality, between psychic arousal and behaviour. They assume some direct causal relation between arousal to sado-masochistic fantasy and the seeking out of such engagements in reality, when we know, for instance, from the surveys of Nancy Friday, Shere Hite and Thelma McCormack (and others) that such fantasy is commonly used by both women and men to enhance sexual arousal – particularly masochistic fantasy (Friday, 1973; Hite, 1976). It would be absurd to suggest that most of us therefore happily accept the existence of rape, let alone that we desire to be raped. So arousal to sexual fantasy which includes images of violence would seem, contrary to the expectations of these psychologists, to be a particularly poor predictor of behaviour.

Similarly, the laboratory measures for increases in violent behaviour following exposure to violent pornography may also have little correspondence with subjects' likelihood to resort to real violence outside the laboratory. The measure most often used is the subject's willingness to act in complicity with the experimenter in apparently delivering an electric shock to the experimenter's 'confederate' for failure in some task, usually after having also been provoked in some way by this same confederate. But the validity of this test of aggressive behaviour will depend upon the laboratory behaviour having the same *meaning* for the subject as aggression in other situations – which seems most unlikely. (Donnerstein, Linz and Penrod themselves admit, as I have indicated, that laboratory 'aggression' may be unrepresentative of aggressive behaviour outside the laboratory.) There is also the danger, as in all psychological experiments, that subjects may 'wise up to the game', attempting to guess and confirm the experimenter's hypotheses – this is the now well-known 'experimenter demand effect'.

The extremely simplified and totally artificial nature of these experiments would seem to cast doubt on their usefulness in considering the shifting and complex meanings attached to events and behaviour in real life. Donnerstein, Linz and Penrod, for example, report that if, following exposure to rape narratives where the victim was depicted as 'enjoying' the rape, experimenters debriefed the subjects by pointing out that of course rape was always a terrible thing, then not only did subjects not show increased acceptance of rape myths or greater callousness towards women, but instead they displayed greater sensitivity about sexist material and a heightened *rejection* of rape myths. This effect, moreover, continued even many months after the original exposure to violent pornography followed by the debriefing, suggesting that the critical consumption of such material, for example in sex education classes, could prove useful.

As I have mentioned, the main finding of these recent experiments into men's reactions to depictions of sexual cruelty is that the usual response is one of anxiety and depression, of revulsion rather than of arousal (whether self-report or tumescence is the data being recorded). And in the smaller number of cases where arousal to sexual violence is reported, Donnerstein and Malamuth now themselves admit that they are not quite sure how to interpret their positive finding. As the psychologist C.W. Sherif points out, experimenters have always assumed that any male arousal must occur through the subject's identification with the male aggressor, but of course it could be that the subject identifies with the female victim (Sherif, 1980). These are some of the reasons why it is less than clear whether the recent experiments on violent pornography can establish that access to such material does in fact cause greater violence against women. Probably all they *can* establish is a weak effect in a very few people under carefully controlled experimental conditions.

It is because such findings, if we do accept their applicability, do not apply to the vast bulk of commercial pornography, either in the US or Britain, that newer research has sought more to implicate 'standard' non-violent pornography in producing negative attitudes and behaviour towards women. James Weaver is the psychologist now most popular with the feminist anti-pornography campaigners. And it is Weaver's recent research that Catherine Itzin includes in her bulky collection of essays which aims to clear up all the misunderstandings and confusions surrounding the troubled topic of pornography, and to provide an up-to-date 'comprehensive and exhaustive' coverage (see Itzin, 1992, p. 9). Ironically, however, Weaver's work serves only to mock Itzin's opening references to the clear and consistent empirical evidence of links between pornography and violence. Weaver's research, in fact, overturns almost all previous research implicating only images of sexually explicit violence with more calloused attitudes in the laboratory from men towards women. His own data 'proves' that exposure to *any* sexually explicit images, but *especially* to 'consensual and female-instigated sex', produces the most calloused responses from *both men and women*!

Such research, were we to treat it with any seriousness in formulating legislation or educational and cultural policies, would of course only support the positions and strategies of the Moral Right, who have always been deeply horrified by the idea of women as sexually assertive, autonomous and entitled to sex on their own terms. It could be used not only to suggest that any type of sex education is dangerous, but to demand that we be particularly vigilant in protecting women and men from any representations of female control or empowerment in sexual situations. Since these are just the images and discourses some feminists, myself included, are trying hard to produce, the implications here are frightening indeed (Segal, 1992).

What we might more seriously conclude from all this experimental muddle, however, which provides anything but clear and consistent proof of anything at all, is not really so hard to see. *It is never possible, whatever the image, to isolate it, to fix its meaning and predict some inevitable pattern of response, independently from assessing its wider representational context and the particular recreational, educational or social context in which it is being received.* Men together can, and regularly do, pornographise any image at all – from the Arab woman in her chador to any coding of anything as male and female (nuts and bolts, for example) – while the most apparently 'violent' images of S & M pornography may be used in only the most consensual and caring encounters between two people. Context really does matter. This may help to explain why inconsistency is the *only* consistency to emerge from empirical research which ignores both the semiotic and the social context of images of sexual explicitness, as the most recent Home Office report on pornography commissioned in the UK concluded: 'Inconsistencies emerge between very similar studies and many interpretations of these have reached almost opposite conclusions' (Howitt and Cumberbatch, 1990, p. 94).

Personal Testimony of Harm

Some anti-pornography feminists who are more aware of both the inconsistency and the possible irrelevance of the experimental proof of pornography's harms have preferred to call upon the testimony of women's own experience of the harm they feel pornography has caused them. A typical example is the evidence provided by one woman at the Minneapolis public hearings. There she described how, after reading *Playboy, Penthouse* and *Forum,* her husband developed an interest in group sex, took her to various pornographic institutions and even invited a friend into their marital bed. To prevent any further group situations occurring, which she found very painful, this woman had agreed to act out in private scenarios depicting bondage and the different sex acts which her husband wanted her to perform, even though she found them all very humiliating (*Everywoman,* 1988, p. 68). It was only after learning karate and beginning to travel on her own that she felt strong enough to leave her husband. This is indeed moving testimony, but surely all along there was only one suitable solution to any such woman's distress: having the power and the confidence to leave a man who forced her into actions she wished to avoid, and who showed no concern at all for her own wishes. Pornography is not the problem here, nor its elimination the solution.

Another type of gruesome evidence frequently used by anti-pornography feminists to establish links between pornography and violence draws upon the myth of the 'snuff movie', first circulated in New York in 1975 about underground films supposedly coming from Latin America in which women were murdered on camera as they apparently reached a sexual climax. On investigation such movies, like the classic *Snuff* itself, released in the US in 1976, have always turned out to be a variant of the 'slasher' film, using the special effects of the horror genre and thus distinct from what is seen as the genre of pornography (Williams, 1990, pp. 189-95). There is, however, also the personal testimony of some former sex workers, exemplified by that of Linda 'Lovelace'/Marchiano. In her book *Ordeal,* Linda Marchiano has described how she was coerced, bullied and beaten by her husband, Chuck Traynor, into working as a porn actress. (Interestingly, although she was coerced into sex work by a violent husband, the book actually describes how it was her success as a porn actress in *Deep Throat* which gave her the confidence to leave her husband, remarry and start campaigning against pornography. See McClintock, 1992.)

The more general problem here is that other sex workers complain bitterly about what they see as the false and hypocritical victimisation of them by anti-pornography feminists, whose campaigns they believe would, if successful, serve only to worsen their pay and working conditions and increase the stigmatisation of their work (Delacoste and Alexander, 1988). (I am not referring here, of course, to the production of child pornography, which is illegal, along with other forms of exploitation of children.) Some sex workers declare that they choose and like the work they do, and the control they believe it gives them over their lives. Indeed, it has been suggested that the feminist anti-pornography campaign itself primarily reflects the privileges of largely white, middle-class women who, not being as exploited as many other women, can self-servingly present the issue of women's sexual objectification by men as the principal source of oppression of all women (Freccero, 1992).

Whether it is from abused women or abused sex workers, however, what we hear when we do hear or read women's testimony against pornography or the pornography industry is stories of women coercively pressurised into sex, or sexual display, which they do not want – from straight, to oral, anal, bondage and group sex. But we should be more than foolish if we saw the harm we heard about as residing in the pornographic images themselves, or in the possibility of enacting them (all, without any doubt, practices which certain women as well as men freely choose), and not in the men's (or possibly, although very rarely in heterosexual encounters, women's) abuse of power. The harm, it is important to be clear about, is contained not in the explicitly sexual material, but in the social context which deprives a woman (or sometimes a man) of her (or his) ability to reject any unwanted sexual activity – whether with husband, lover, parent, relative, friend, acquaintance or stranger. And this is one fundamental reason feminists opposed to anti-pornography campaigning are so distressed at each attempt to bring in some new version of the Minneapolis Ordinance, like the so-called Pornography Victims' Compensation Act first introduced into the US Senate in 1989 and cropping up again in New York in 1992, or Itzin's own proposals taken up by MPs like Dawn Primarolo in Britain.

It is not just that these bills, quite contrary to the self-deceiving rhetoric of their advocates (Itzin and Dworkin claim to be 'absolutely opposed to censorship in every form'), would suppress sexual and erotic materials by opening up the threat of quite unprecedented levels of censorship through harassing lawsuits and financial penalties against producers, distributors, booksellers, writers, photographers and movie-makers. It is also that, again quite contrary to the stated goals of their supporters, such legislative proposals cost nothing and do nothing to provide real remedies against men's violence. State funding for women's refuges; anti-sexist, anti-violence educational initiatives; and, above all, empowering women more fundamentally through improved job prospects, housing and welfare facilities, would seem to be the only effective ways of enabling women to avoid violence.

Instead, however, the idea that pornographic material causes men's violence tends to excuse the behaviour of the men who are sexually coercive and violent, by removing the blame on to pornography. Men who rape, murder and commit other violent sex crimes against women, children or other men may (or may not) have an interest in violent pornography. However, as overviews of all the available empirical data suggest, the evidence does not point to pornography as a cause of their behaviour (Howitt and Cumberbatch, 1990, p. 94). When Itzin, along with so many of the authors in her collection, weirdly but repeatedly cite as 'evidence' for pornography's harm the final testimony of serial killer Ted Bundy before his execution, they surely do more to expose rather than to support their argument. Today both the rapist and, even more hypocritically, tabloid wisdom have learnt to lay the blame for sex crimes on 'pornography' (whereas once, with the same certainty, they would lay the blame on 'mothers').

Meanwhile, although Dworkin, MacKinnon, Itzin and their supporters continue to argue that it is pornography which violates women's civil rights by increasing discrimination against them, studies in the US and Europe have tended to reverse the picture. In the US it is in states with a preponderance of Southern Baptists (followers of leading anti-pornography campaigner Jerry Falwell) that the highest levels of social, political and economic inequality between women and men can be found – despite the lowest circulation of pornography (Baron, 1990). Indeed, Larry Baron discovered a positive correlation between equal opportunities for women in employment, education and politics and higher rates of pornography, which he attributed to the greater social tolerance generally in states which provided such opportunities. Such findings are consistent with those from Europe, where we find far higher levels of economic, political and other indices of gender equality in Sweden and Denmark compared with either the US or Britain, and lower levels of violence against women – coupled with more liberal attitudes towards pornography (Kutchinsky, 1990). Baron's survey, interestingly, also found that gender inequality correlated with the presence and extent of *legitimate* use of violence in a state (as measured by the numbers of people trained to work in the military, corporal punishment in schools, government use of violence as in the death penalty), as well as with mass-media preferences for violence, as in circulation rates of *Guns and Ammo*).

Beyond Pornography

It is time for feminists, and their supporters, who want to act against men's greater use of violence and sexual coercion, and their continuing social dominance, to abandon the search for some spurious causal link with 'pornography' – however we define it. Most men are, as they always have been, quite capable of using violence without the assistance of pornography. We are, it is true, ubiquitously surrounded by images and discourses which represent women as passive, fetishised objects, and men as active, controlling agents, devoid of weakness, passivity or any type of 'femininity'. They saturate all scientific and cultural discourses of the last hundred years – from sexology, embryology and psychoanalysis to literary and visual genres, high and low – and they construct the dominant images of masculinity to which so many men, inevitably, fail to match up. Women provide the most available scapegoats for the perceived shame and anxiety this causes them.

Men don't need pornography to encounter these 'facts' of crude and coercive, promiscuous male sexualities, or helpless and yielding, nurturing female sensitivities. The anxious mirrorings of these narratives of male transcendence and female passivity (as well as occasional challenges to them) are, it is true, on offer in the culturally marginal and generally disparaged genre of 'pornography'. Women (or men) may well choose to pull down or deface the sexist pin-ups or pornography which men together may use to create their own exclusionary space or to taunt the women around them. (Some women have preferred to paste up their own images of penile display, which usually brings down the pin-ups.) There is a variety of tactics we can use to discredit, mock or remove images we find offensive from the personal and public spaces of our lives. It is a battle which has only just begun. But there is no compelling reason to focus upon sexually explicit material alone, unless as feminists we do wish to throw in our lot with the initiatives and goals of the Moral Right.

In the end, anti-pornography campaigns, feminist or not, can only enlist today, as they invariably enlisted before, guilt and anxiety around sex, as well as lifetimes of confusion in our personal experiences of sexual arousal and activity. In contrast, campaigns which get to the heart of men's violence and sadism towards women must enlist the widest possible resources to empower women socially to seek only the types of sexual encounters they choose, and to empower women sexually to explore openly their own interests and pleasures. We do need the space to produce our own sexually explicit narratives and images of female desire and sensuous engagement, if we are even to begin to embark upon that journey. And there are certain to be people who will feel harmed and provoked by our attempts. Let us hope they are not empowered to prevent us: like the Canadian courts whose new 'feminist' anti-pornography legislation was recently used against two lesbian magazines, or the leading anti-pornographer Jesse Helms in the US, launching his investigation of Post-Porn Modernist Annie Sprinkle as she performs on stage in California to promote women's active, pleasurable and spiritual enjoyment of their sexuality.

Note: This essay is a substantially extended and reworked version of an article which appeared in *Feminist Review*, no. 36, Autumn 1990.

Works Cited

Baron, L. 'Pornography and gender equality: An Empirical Analysis', *Journal of Sex Research*, vol. 27 no. 3, 1990.

Byrne, D. and Lamberth, J. 'The effect of erotic stimuli on sex arousal, evaluative responses, and subsequent behavior', *Technical Reports of the Commission on Obscenity and Pornography*, vol. 8 (Washington: US Government Printing Office, 1970).

Chester, G. and Dickey, J. *Feminism and Censorship: The Current Debate* (London: Prism Press, 1988).

Davis, K.E. and Braught, N. 'Exposure to pornography, character and sexual deviance', *Technical Reports of the Commission on Obscenity and Pornography*, vol. 7, 1970.

Delacoste, F. and Alexander, P. (eds.). *Sex Work: Writings by Women in the Sex Industry* (London: Virago, 1988).
Donnerstein, E., Linz, D. and Penrod, S. *The Question of Pornography: Research Findings and Policy Implications* (London: Collier Macmillan, 1987).
Duggan, L. 'Censorship in the Name of Feminism' in *Caught Looking* (New York: Caught Looking Inc., 1986).
Dworkin, A. *Pornography: Men Possessing Women* (London: Women's Press, 1981).
Freccero, C. 'Notes of a Post Sex-War Theorizer' in Hirsch, M. and Fox Keller, E. (eds.), *Conflicts in Feminism* (London: Routledge, 1991).
Friday, N. *My Secret Garden* (New York: Trident, 1973).
Goldstein, *et al.* 'Exposure to pornography and sexual behaviour in deviant and normal groups', *Technical Reports of the Commission on Obscenity and Pornography*, vol. 7, 1970.
Hite, S. *The Hite Report* (New York: Dell, 1976).
Howitt, D. and Cumberbatch, G. *Pornography: impacts and influences* (London: Home Office Research and Planning Unit, 1990).
Itzin, C. (ed.). *Pornography: Women, Violence and Civil Liberties* (Oxford: Oxford University Press, 1992).
Johnson, W.T. *et al.* 'Sex offenders' experience with erotica', *Technical Reports of the Commission on Obscenity and Pornography*, 1970.
Kant, H.S. and Goldstein, M.J. 'Pornography and its effects' in Savitz, D. and Johnson, J. (eds.), *Crime in Society* (New York: Wiley, 1978).
Kutchinsky, B. 'The effect of easy availability of pornography on the incidence of sex crimes: The Danish experience', *Journal of Social Issues*, no. 29, 1973.
Kutchinsky, B. 'Pornography and rape: Theory and practice? Evidence from Crime Data in Four Countries where Pornography is easily Available', *International Journal of Law and Society*, vol. 13 no. 4, 1990.
Longford. *Pornography: The Longford Report* (London: Coronet, 1972).
McClintock, A. 'Gonad the Barbarian and the Venus Flytrap' in Segal, L. and McIntosh, M. (eds.), *Sex Exposed: Sexuality and the Pornography Debate* (London: Virago, 1992) .
McCormack, T. 'Making Sense of the Research on Pornography' in Burstyn, V. (ed.), *Women Against Censorship* (Vancouver, Douglas & McIntyre, 1985).
MacKinnon, Catharine. *Feminism Unmodified: Discourses on Life and Law* (Cambridge, Mass.: Harvard University Press, 1987).
Malamuth, N. and Spinner, E. 'A longitudinal content analysis of sexual violence in the best selling erotica magazines', *Journal of Sex Research*, no. 16, 1980.
Mann, J. *et al.* 'Effects of erotic films on sexual behaviour of married couples', *Technical Report of the Commission on Obscenity and Pornography*, vol. 8, 1970.
Merck, M. 'From Minneapolis to Westminster' in Segal, L. and McIntosh, M. (eds.), *Sex Exposed: Sexuality and the Pornography Debate*, 1992.
Mosher, D. 'Sex callousness towards women', *Technical Reports of the Commission on Obscenity and Pornography*, vol. 7, 1970.
Scott, D.A. 'Pornography and its effects on family, community, and culture', *Family Policy Insights*, vol. 4 no. 2, March 1985.
Segal, L. *Is the Future Female: Troubled Thoughts on Contemporary Feminism* (London: Virago, 1987).
Segal, L. *Slow Motion: Changing Masculinities, Changing Men* (London: Virago, 1990).
Segal, L. and McIntosh, M. (eds.). *Sex Exposed: Sexuality and the Pornography Debate* (London: Virago, 1992).
Segal, L. 'Sweet Sorrows, Painful Pleasures: Pornography and the Perils of Heterosexual Desire' in Segal and McIntosh, *Sex Exposed*, 1992.
Sherif, C.W. 'Comment on Ethical Issues in Malamuth, Heim and Feshbach's "Sexual Responsiveness of College Students to Rape Depictions: Inhibitory and Disinhibitory Effects"', *Journal of Personality and Social Psychology*, vol. 38 no. 3, 1980.
Wallsgrove, R. 'Pornography: Between the Devil and the True Blue Whitehouse', *Spare Rib*, no. 65, December 1977.

Weaver, J. 'The Social Science and Psychological Research Evidence: Perceptual and Behavioural Consequences of Exposure to Pornography', in Itzin (ed.), *Pornography: Women, Violence and Civil Liberties*.
Williams, L. *Hard Core: Power, Pleasure and the 'Frenzy of the Visible'* (London: Pandora, 1990).

GERTRUD KOCH

The Body's Shadow Realm

On the History of Pornographic Films: Cinema in Brothels, Brothels in Cinema, Cinema in Place of Brothels

The history of film is also the history of its limitations, supervision, regimentation, judicial constraint, and examination of norms. Reviewing chronologies of film history, we see the extent of the censor's alarm system, which would monitor the flow of cinematographic production, classified and catalogued into acceptable and unacceptable areas:

> According to a police directive, censorship cards will be instituted and censorship jurisdiction will be transferred to the chief of police of each of Berlin's police precincts. (20 May 1908)[1]
>
> All members of the Seventh District Court appeared at Berlin police headquarters for the screening of a film which has caused a public scandal. This is the first judicial review of a film in Germany. (12 December 1909)
>
> In March, the People's Institute of New York and Dr Charles Sprague Smith established the 'National Board of Censorship' as a film review board. (1902)[2]
>
> In Sweden, film censorship is instituted at the request of the film industry. (1911)
>
> According to a German municipal ordinance, every film must be submitted for certification to the appropriate precinct office twenty-four hours before public screening. (1911)[3]
>
> Through the founding of the Hays organisation's 'Motion Picture Producers and Distributors of America', the American film industry sets up a form of voluntary self-regulation. (1922)[4]

Although these historians do not mention the rules then in effect for banning a film as offensive, we know from another source that the censorship authorities collected pornographic films:

For the most part, the supervising authorities, the police, know about this class of films, films fated to lead a humble and obscure life. We define pornographic films as the cinematic depiction in an obscene form of whatever concerns sexual life, and these include just about everything human fantasy can possibly invent in the area of sexuality. The films pass directly from the producer to the consumer, thus steering clear of the censor, and with good reason. Nevertheless, the police archives are filled with films such as chance and vigilance have brought their way.[5]

Even though the invention of cinema was soon followed by institutionalised censorship, pornographic films still had time to become widespread. Unencumbered by censorship, which wasn't established until 1908, film pornography was already in full bloom in Germany by 1904. Short pornographic films – of up to a minute in length – furthered the technical development already seen in photographic pornography in such apparatuses as the stereoscope and mutascope. By 1904, such films had grown to four acts and ran twenty minutes. Early pornographic movies thus kept pace with most of cinema's developments, which raises the questions: what kind of aesthetic development did this genre undergo? can we in fact even speak of a genre? and what would define its particular aesthetic?

To answer these questions we have to look to the few available sources describing early pornographic films and their modes of reception:

In most cases, these sotadic films were screened in private societies or in men's clubs founded for this purpose. In Germany, the entry price ranged from ten to thirty marks. The distribution of tickets was handled by prostitutes, pimps, cafe waiters, barbers, and other persons in contact with the clientele, who knew they could earn a tidy profit by marking up the price. Since these vendors usually knew their clientele and their preferences, there was little danger of coming into conflict with the police.[6]

For the most part, pornographic films were bought and screened by brothels, which hoped to entice customers with filmic come-ons while also earning money by charging for the screenings. At first, the pleasure offered by pornographic films was expensive, reserved for the well-to-do customers who frequented such establishments in European metropolises from Paris to Moscow. Abroad, both Buenos Aires and Cairo offered international tourists the opportunity to visit pornographic cinemas. In *Die Schaubühne*, Kurt Tucholsky describes an experience in a porn house in Berlin:

Nobody spoke out loud, since everyone was a bit anxious; they only murmured. The screen turned white; a fragile, mottled silver-white light appeared, trembling. It began. But everyone laughed, myself included. We had expected something bizarre and extravagant. We saw a meow-kitty and a woof-doggy romping on the screen. Maybe the exporter had tacked the scene on to fool the police – who knows? The film ran without music, rattling monotonously; it was gloomy and not very pleasant. . . .

Things remained *gemütlich* in the cinema. We didn't realise that even Tristan and Isolde would seem ridiculous in this setting, or that Romeo and Juliet, viewed impartially from another planet, would seem a comic and straightlaced affair.

No, nothing of the sort among the patrons. The only reason they didn't play cards was because it was too dark. An atmosphere of healthy and hearty pleasure prevailed. You had to say to yourself – all this phony business – at least here you knew. . . . The ending was so obscure that when it was over everyone thought there was more to come – it just goes to show, that's how it is with sex. The men stood around feeling self-conscious and embarrassed, remarking on the lack of values here and in general. And then we pushed through narrow passageways into an adjoining establishment where the music was loud and shrill, and everyone was strangely quiet and excited. I heard later that the proprietor had ordered twenty call girls.[7]

The atmosphere of this occasion in Berlin – with the camaraderie of male bonding, uneasy and secret arousal, and forced jocularity – was apparently not unique. Norbert Jacques provides an illustration from Buenos Aires, one that enriches the steamy Berlin-beer flavour with sado-masochistically tinged exotic stereotypes:

One night in Caracas, walking along the harbour wall where the long, low Platte River steamers slept, I reached a point beyond the criminal quarter. An odd but impressive scaffolding stopped me in my tracks. . . . While I was looking up into its towering height, I saw a boat under me with a light, tied to the harbour wall. A man on the boat called out something to me. This man and I were totally alone there. He rushed up to me and pointed across the harbour, saying: 'Isla Maciel!' and blurted out in an international language, 'Cinematografo. Nina, deitsch, frances, englishmen, amor, dirty cinematographico!'. . . A large arc lamp radiated harshly over a sinister-looking shack on the other side.

The man rowed me over there past the ships. . . . I came to a lonely trail, and one hundred metres up ahead of me was the glaring arc lamp. . . . On my left was a hedge; on the right, an impenetrable gloom of dirty shacks and dark corners; and on both sides, the breath of sudden, quick, raw, silent criminality. . . . I came to the house with the arc lamp. A large sign declared: 'Cinematografo para hombres solo'. The scene at its best! Before I went in, two local police at the door searched my pockets. It was like a scene out of a detective yarn.

The show was in progress. It was a large hall with a gallery running around the sides. A screen hung from the ceiling, on which the cine-

> matographic theatre played out its scenes. ... While stupid pricks chased each other around up there, women roamed among the guests. They were mostly Germans. The dregs of the world's brothels....
>
> It was so stupid, so unbelievably dull and absurd, these idiotic, tired and insolent wenches and the pretend vices on the screen overhead, which were supposed to enflame the customers' passions. It was all so insane, so nonsensically perverse. Here is this modern technical device, lighting up the faces of men staring up out of the darkness, acting as a pacesetter for a cat house, by speeding up the nervous, excited procession to the rooms. Men and hookers disappeared noisily and quickly up the dark steps.[8]

It seems that in viewing pornographic films one has to overcome a certain kind of shyness. Which has nothing to do with the legal or moral condemnation of pornography, nor with the obvious reason for pornographic films being suited to the brothel. Even today, when pornographic films are shown in public theatres and no longer connected to the business of a brothel, a palpable sense of shame still attaches to the experience, which cannot be fully explained by the few remaining moral taboos. The same atmosphere of uneasiness and shame, excitement and repulsion is also revealed in historical documents encountered in more recent reports. Günter Kunert, for example, describes a visit to a porn house as follows:

> Kino Rondell. Silent men in darkness. No women. No throat-clearing. No coughing. Not even the proverbial pin drop could be heard. A gathering of the living dead, so it seems, sitting on folding chairs, always two at a table, whose greasy top has a list of drinks lit up from underneath, and a call bell. ...
>
> A trailer for next week's feature is playing: a fat, ageing 'Herr Robert', whose voice lags behind the picture, snaps his fingers out of sync, followed by quick cuts of more or less (mostly more) naked girls parading across the screen in more or less (mostly less) seductive poses, displaying out-of-proportion bodies and faces radiating an aura of stupidity.
>
> Now a brandy! No one orders. No one smokes. No one breathes louder or heavier. In front of the rows of seats the celluloid nymphs twist and turn and seem more alive than the live audience, which, later, after the feature – a Danish production on the complexities and peculiarities of sex – leaves the Kino Rondell as silently as they had occupied it: without a laugh, without audible approval or disapproval.
>
> A kind of erotic phantom fades away quickly and quietly, condemned to take on corporeal existence once again, when the bell sounds for the next performance.[9]

If the porn cinema clientele is made up of human beings who act like zombies, voyeuristic pleasure in these cinemas clearly must have something in common with the secrecy of the peeping tom. The voyeur likes to look, but doesn't like to be seen. Displeasure in the porn house apparently results from the displeasure in being seen while looking. Where the connection between 'cinema and brothel' still exists, and a 'modern technical device' acts as a 'pacesetter' for cat houses, then this displeasure and this shame in erotic relations will be channelled into 'healthy and hearty pleasure'. Pornographic films fulfil this function still, not only as a kind of G-rated masturbatory cinema, but also in brothels and prostitution. Along with this type, however, another type of pornographic film has developed which has no other intention, no other purpose than that of satisfying voyeuristic desire. In these films, the specialised sense of sight, regarded in the other type of pornographic cinema as fulfilling a subordinate function in foreplay, asserts its autonomy as isolated, unadulterated voyeuristic pleasure.

Only by assuming such a specialised mode of viewing can we explain the tremendous success of public pornographic movie houses, in spite of the displeasure they inflict on the zombie-like voyeur. The language of our age of visual culture, in which the active subjugating eye wins out over the passive receptive sense organs, such as the ears, finds an apt metaphor in the recent divorce of cinema from brothel, pornography from prostitution. Since the workplace has long since demanded nothing more of the body than keeping a watchful eye on the control board, perhaps the private peep-show booth will soon offer the porn theatre visitor a serviceable leisure-time retreat. It may be that over the history of pornographic cinema the films themselves have not changed so much as the organisation of the senses. It may be that films' effects are more directly related to the social environments in which the films are presented than to the films' form and content. In other words, the audience's sexual orientation defines the way the product is consumed.

Although it is not certain whether pornographic films for heterosexuals are, aesthetically speaking, better or worse than those for homosexuals, they obviously encompass different modes of reception and consumption. Kurt Tucholsky described audience response in the days when the business of heterosexual pornography was still linked to prostitution: 'Shouts, encouragements, grunts, applause, and rooting cheers rang out. Somebody compares his own private ecstasy. There was a lot of noise and yelling'.[10]

Brendan Gill rediscovered a similar scene in a New York porn theatre in the 1970s: 'A large portion of the audience at both heterosexual and homosexual blue movies is Oriental. Unlike white males, Oriental males come into the theatre by two's and three's and talk and laugh freely throughout the course of the program.'[11] Gill also describes a connection between gay porn theatres and erotic practice that is hardly ever encountered in public heterosexual porn houses:

> For the homosexual, it is the accepted thing that the theatre is there to be cruised in; this is one of the advantages he has purchased with his expensive ticket of admission. ... Far from sitting slumped motionless in one's chair, one moves about at will, sizing up possibilities. Often there

will be found standing at the back of the theatre two or three young men, any of whom, for a fee, will accompany one to seats well down front and there practise upon one the same arts that are being practised upon others on the screen.[12]

We also see that in the course of time, settings, stereotypes and characters change even in pornographic cinema in order to conform to newer fashions, especially about what is considered sexy. Early pornography, for example, attempted to please its well-to-do clientele by presenting erotic scenes involving servant girls and masters, thus capturing an everyday erotic fantasy, while in more recent pornographic films these roles give way to other trades. Newer films produced for public screening and sale also differ from older ones in that they follow the letter of the law more strictly; they avoid showing certain erotic activities that *were* shown earlier, since the early films were illegal anyway. According to Curt Moreck's description of pornographic films of the 20s and earlier, individual films could be distinguished according to country of origin and target audience:

> Pornographic films reveal something about different erotic preferences in different countries. Thus French pornography presents excretory acts with striking frequency and indulges in lengthy depictions of preparatory manoeuvres, while the sex act itself often doesn't occur at all or is shifted behind the scenes. England, which produces such films mainly for South Africa and India, favours flagellation scenes and sadistic abuse of blacks... Italy, whose southern location already overlaps into the zone of 'Oriental' sexuality, cultivates the depiction of acts of sodomy as a speciality, while scenes of sexual union between humans and animals and scenes of animals mating are also popular. It has been said that Germans sin without grace. German pornographic films lend some credence to that assumption. Without exception they show well-executed, realistic scenes of coitus. On the other hand, erotic scenes with animals are totally absent. Now and again something kinky is thrown in to broaden their appeal.[13]

Apparently, early pornographic films were also divided into those with quasi-realistic settings – thus bearing some relation to the customer's everyday life – and those set in a world of fantasy or using stock settings associated with forbidden sexuality or foreign exoticism. The 'realistic' films depicted masters and servants in bourgeois surroundings – the home of an officer, for instance. The escapist ones were acted out in harems, cloisters, and so forth. This dichotomy apparently still holds true: consider, on the one hand, the 'Housewife Reports' (pornographic serials about housewife affairs with the postman, gasman, etc.) and, on the other, racist excursions into exotic domains – Thailand in *Emmanuelle*, for example.

The blue movie genre has meanwhile obviously become more professional, unintentional comic relief and unbelievable plots having given way to a routinely crafted product. Cinematography has become more skilful and the overall construction more sophisticated, with cutting for suspense and other formal procedures turning straightforward illustrations into cinematic images. Even if we assume that some ironic observations were employed by historical commentators as defence mechanisms against their own shame and excitement, we still come to the conclusion that early porn films were awkward and amateurish, made with little thought to achieving cinematic effect:

> Now came *Scenes in a Harem*. The wallpaper in the empty room, along with the carpet and curtains, suggested that the location was a red-light district, like Schlesisches Tor in Berlin. Fatima danced. The depraved girl took off her extravagant lingerie and danced – that is, she turned around casually by herself while everyone admired her. She danced in front of her sultan, who was lolling about listlessly in other harem girls' laps. He was a bon vivant. The women fanned him with large Japanese paper fans, and on a table in front of them stood a glass of *Weissbier*....
>
> *Secrets of the Cloister* and *Anna's Sideline* came on next. Two 'perverse beauties' rolled around on a carpet. One of them, I found out, was a certain Emmy Raschke, who laughed continuously, probably because she thought the whole thing a bit funny. Well, they were all there, cool and very businesslike, to act out (if the audience is any guide) the most exquisite things, while the cameraman yells directions at them....
>
> *The Captain's Wife* was playing upstairs. It was pornography come to life. While the worthy officer cheated on his wife with the lieutenant's wife, the captain's wife made good use of the time with her husband's orderly. They are caught in the act, and it leads to blows. Say what you like, the film was true to life, even though the life of French soldiers does seem a little strange: things happen so fast. In any case, there were two or three moments where the actors played their roles to the hilt.[14]

Here, Tucholsky describes the kind of porn films that abstain from so-called perversions and limit themselves to that which Curt Moreck called typical for German blue movies: 'well-executed, realistic scenes of coitus' and 'sin without grace'.[15]

Comic moments, described by Tucholsky as unintentional, occur often in the genre. We cannot assume that these comic aspects of old porn movies are merely an effect of historical distance. Even today, many sex films function as farce, dirty jokes, and witty commentary. So too, in popular older films, comic moments played a significant role:

> The comic element naturally plays an important role in pornographic films, since most people have a humorous attitude toward certain sexual practices rather than a serious or even pathetic one. Films make use of this fact by showing people in sticky situations, interrupted or embarrassed while tending to bodily needs, or getting caught in awkward positions through some droll mishap while having sexual relations.[16]

A 'humorous attitude toward certain sexual practices' probably arises out of sexual repression and anxiety; laughter and nervous giggling are often indications that a taboo has been violated. It seems as if the persistence of comedy as a pornographic form has to do with the pleasure of looking, with voyeurism itself: we laugh at the secret exposure of others. This can also be seen in the fact that TV producers and viewers concur in considering as 'comedy' shows, such as *Candid Camera*, those that involve watching people with hidden cameras.

The Knowing Look and the Pleasure of Looking: On the Autonomy of the Senses

What is new in pornographic cinema is obviously its existence as a voyeuristic amusement park. It promises nothing more or less than it advertises: the pleasure in looking, erotic activity without social contact. This new pornographic cinema is found not only in the large industrial metropolises but also in small towns and in the daily programmes of staid resorts. Those who, with good and honourable intentions, reproach blue movies for deceiving the poor consumer – instead of delivering the genuine product, 'real' sex, these films palm off on him a phony substitute – are missing the point. Such critics assume the primacy of genital pleasure over that which arises out of the 'component instincts', one of which is voyeurism, visual sensuality, *Schaulust*.

The consumer who buys his ticket at the door doesn't expect and probably doesn't even want to experience sexual gratification with another person. Like Mr Chance in Hal Ashby's film comedy *Being There* (1980), the porn movie patron is 'just looking'. Criticism of pornography thus misses the mark when it assumes that the customer has been cheated because he expects and pays for something he doesn't get. Customer fraud would hardly explain the success of pornographic movies. While having improved on their heavy-handed and awkward predecessors, the quality of today's porn films explains this success even less, since these films do not begin to come up to the formal standards of other genres. Recent attempts to have porn 'taken seriously' by enhancing the genre with stars, festivals and directors should probably be seen not so much as a gimmick to attract a wider audience as an effort by an association of craftsmen to gain credibility. Meanwhile, even apart from the hype, the porn film trend keeps on growing. The bids for credibility may help overcome the last bastions of resistance to pornographic films, but they won't do much for box office.

In my view this trend toward pornographic movies involves a more far-reaching development in society's organisation of our senses. Porn houses are not the motor but the chassis. An explanation for the growth of pornographic cinema can be found in its function within prevailing sexual organisation. Walter Serner, overwhelmed by this new invention of cinema, already proposed such an idea in *Die Schaubühne* in 1913:

All the likely reasons somehow don't add up to an explanation of the

> movies' unprecedented success everywhere one looks. The reason must lie deeper than we think. And if we look into those strange flickering eyes to find out why people spend their last penny to go to the movies, they take us way back into the history of humankind. There we find, writ large: *Schaulust*. It is not merely harmless fascination with moving images and colour, but a terrifying lust, as powerful and violent as the deepest passions. It's the kind of rush that makes the blood boil and the head spin until that baffling potent excitement, common to every passion, races through the flesh....
>
> This ghastly pleasure in seeing atrocities, violence and death lies dormant in us all. It is this kind of pleasure which brings us, hurrying, to the morgue, to the scene of the crime, to every chase, to every street fight, and makes us pay good money for a glimpse of sodomy. And this is what draws the masses into the cinemas as if they were possessed. Cinema offers the masses the kind of pleasure which, day by day, is eroded by the advance of civilisation. And neither the magic of the stage nor the tired thrills of a circus, music hall or cabaret can attempt to replace it. In cinema, the masses reclaim, in all its former glory, the sensuousness of looking: *Schaulust*.[17]

Serner prophetically anticipates that cinema's appeal lies in a Nero-like diversion: being able to participate from the bleachers in the atrocities of an epoch. Acknowledgment of this aspect of the pairing within popular culture of 'sex and violence', as the critics call it, has been suppressed. While societies have long permitted the depiction of brutal violence, hatred, war, crime, destruction and death, this has not applied to the presentation of naked bodies and sexuality. It is no wonder that, with the relaxing of sexual taboos, cinema has now seized upon sexuality as a voyeuristic object. Up to now you could see just about every possible way of killing a person. Now we can also see 99, or 150, or 'x' ways of making love. *Schaulust*, which Serner describes as a violent, volatile passion, and to which he ascribes an ultimately corruptive influence, is itself neither outcome nor origin. Rather it arose and took shape on its own out of the processes involved in the establishment of a highly rationalised and thoroughly organised society. The success of the porn house in its present form is the expression of this cultural-historical development rather than of a primal passion:

> The eye is an organ constantly under stress, working, concentrating, always unequivocally interpreting. The ear, on the other hand, is more diffuse and passive. Unlike an eye, you don't have to open it first.[18]
>
> The eye has adapted to bourgeois rationality and ultimately to a highly industrialised order by accustoming itself to interpreting reality, a priori, as a world of objects, basically as a world of commodities; the ear has achieved nothing similar.[19]
>
> Such a division of labour between the various receptive faculties of

human beings, a specialisation of the senses, was necessary for a particular stage of capitalist production, the same stage of the production process that is singled out by 'Taylorism'.[20]

In the age of Taylorism, a dramatic rise in the dissemination of pornography was observed in Victorian England. It remains to be demonstrated that this sudden interest is strictly the result of the notoriously repressive Victorian society, that is, that it was conceived as an outlet for dammed-up passions. Rather, the dissemination of pornography is connected to specific social aspects of modernisation, as well as to parallel changes in the perceptual apparatus and intrapsychic mechanisms. In a certain respect pornographic cinema is both the symptom of this development and its expression. Training the eye means adapting the sense of sight to strategies of rationalisation and modernisation. An expansion of voyeurism at the level of the organisation of the drives corresponds to this social/perceptual development, thereby bringing sexuality in line with it.

The connection between power, control and sexuality can only be made through changes in sexuality itself. Pornography may be one of those sieves through which power seeps into the inner regions of sexuality while sexuality flows out and becomes a part of this power. Michel Foucault analyses the intermeshing of power and sex in the first volume of *The History of Sexuality*, without, however, viewing the matter in terms of a simple oppressor/victim relationship of repression:

> This implantation of multiple perversions is not a mockery of sexuality taking revenge on a power that has thrust on it an excessively repressive law. Neither are we dealing with paradoxical forms of pleasure that turn back on power and invest it in the form of a 'pleasure to be endured'. The implantation of perversions is an instrument-effect: it is through the isolation, intensification, and consolidation of peripheral sexualities that the relations of power to sex and pleasure branched out and multiplied, measured the body, and penetrated modes of conduct. And accompanying this encroachment of powers, scattered sexualities rigidified, became stuck to an age, a place, a type of practice. A proliferation of sexualities through the extension of power; an optimisation of the power to which each of these local sexualities gave a surface of intervention: this concatenation, particularly since the nineteenth century, has been ensured and relayed by the countless economic interests which, with the help of medicine, psychiatry, prostitution, and pornography, have tapped into both this analytical multiplication of pleasure and this optimisation of the power that controls it. Pleasure and power do not cancel or turn back against one another; they seek out, overlap, and reinforce one another. They are linked together by complex mechanisms and devices of excitation and incitement.[21]

The history of sexuality, according to Foucault, is inscribed in the 'will to knowledge', meaning power. Pornography thus becomes nothing other than the 'will to knowledge' – the night school for sex education – where, by means of voyeurism's cognitive urge, the discourse of power is begun. In fact, some studies of the social history of pornography offer evidence that these films were only too happy to be thought of as a contribution to research on sexuality and its various forms. Then came the recent wave of porn films whose opening credits declared their intention to offer practical advice for living, to be purveyors of knowledge. Examples of these are the Oswald Kolle series, or *Helga*. The classification of formal knowledge by category still attaches to an unending series of 'Film Reports', often presenting sexual behaviour according to various occupations. Even early porn films displayed a lexicographic tendency, as an eyewitness noticed:

> A special flavour is given to obscene films through the scrupulously realistic presentation of every imaginable perversion. Although life itself very often offers the connoisseur a view of simple vice, the chance to enjoy real perversity as a spectator is much rarer; in this case, film tries to fill the void. There are some films in this genre which seem to have been staged directly from Krafft-Ebing's *Psychopathia Sexualis*, as a manual of abnormal sexual operations for civilised man.[22]

> All the vices of man flickered by on the screen. Every one of the hundred and fifty ways from the old *Treatise on the Hundred and Fifty Ways of Loving* was demonstrated, with occasional interruptions for lesbian, pederast, and masturbation jokes. All that was harmless. Sadists and masochists waved their instruments, sodomy was practised, coprophagous acts were on display. Nothing was held back, everything occurred in a banal reality, all the more infuriating for its technical crudity.[23]

The 'will to knowledge' activates the eye, which in turn casts its gaze upon sexuality – *Schaulust* as an instrument of cognition, cognition as *Schaulust*: pornography discovers its social role. Psychoanalytic theory established the notion of a relationship between curiosity, cognitive activity and voyeurism in the developmental history of the individual even before pornography revealed this connection by becoming a typical product of our society. The optical organisation of reality implies control, from the vigilant eye of the hunter to 'the great eye of the government' (Foucault). Jean-Paul Sartre notes in *Being and Nothingness*:

> In addition the idea of discovery, of revelation, includes an idea of appropriative enjoyment. What is seen is possessed; to see is to *deflower*. ... More than this, knowledge is a hunt. Bacon called it the hunt of Pan. The scientist is the hunter who surprises a white nudity and who violates by looking at it. Thus the totality of these images reveals something which we will call the *Actaeon-complex*...: a person hunts for the sake of eating. Curiosity in an animal is always either sexual or alimentary. To know is to devour with the eyes.[24]

Let us assume the correctness of Foucault's thesis that the history of sexuality is based on a will to knowledge and concede that pornography is a conduit for this transmission of sex and power. If, in addition, we consider another point made by Sartre, we might be able to explain why pornographic cinema today is a medium for conveying knowledge (in Foucault's sense) rather than a medium for aesthetic experience. Sartre assumes a difference between art and cognition that is based on their different relationships to appropriation. Works of art resist appropriation: 'The work of art is like a fixed emanation of the mind. The mind is continually creating it and yet it stands alone and indifferent in relation to that creation.'[25] Cognition, on the other hand, is constituted as an act of appropriation, thus incorporating the object of cognition and assimilating it: 'Knowledge is at one and the same time a *penetration* and a *superficial* caress, a digestion and the contemplation from afar of an object which will never lose its form.'[26]

Sartre analyses cognition as assimilation, whose end is reached when desire destroys its object, rather than preserving it through appropriation – you can't have your cake and eat it too! It seems to me that Sartre's analysis of cognition as penetration and as detached observation also characterises the appropriation process in pornographic films. If the viewer allows himself to be carried away by the desire to possess – thus relinquishing the position of a detached observer – he must sacrifice his *Schaulust* in order to take in a specific moment or image; in the meantime, subsequent images and sensations have already appeared on the screen. Thus the viewer is caught between two modes of appropriating: perception and cognition. It is like Buridan's hungry ass of old caught between two tasty piles of hay:

> When I look at a porn magazine, I don't care about the way the scene is visualised, even if the men and women are ugly or something else isn't quite right. In my fantasy they exist in a way that excites me. Besides, it's up to me which picture I choose to look at, and I can always turn the page or go back to a certain picture... The viewer of a porn film always remains alienated from the situation he's observing, because he has to keep his clothes on and can't touch, even though the pictures arouse him. He becomes confused.[27]

This description of a user experience points to the key difference between the two pornographic mediums and raises the question: why, despite such a frustrating situation, have so many people developed a distinct preference for pornographic movies? Perhaps the reaction of the regular viewer of porn films is not one of confusion at all; maybe the person like Mr Chance, who only wants to look, is quite common. It is possible that inside the porn theatre desire actually becomes transformed into the fetishism of the aficionado, who only needs to know what is available, then sits back down to watch – the ultimate triumph of the eye over the body.

This theoretical notion seems to be supported by the evidence of amateur pornographic films, like those that Robert van Ackern includes with other kinds of home movies in his scathing compilation film *Germany in Private* (1980). The films, though formally far inferior to commercial porn films, nevertheless draw on them for their fantasies. Pornographic ideas and *mise en scène* are recorded by a Super-8 camera in a totally naturalistic fashion; in fact, in contrast to more polished professional porn, one has the distinct impression that the events are taking place only for the sake of the camera. An agitated woman sprawls out on a kidney-shaped coffee table in a living room; another models sexy underwear. Pleasure in the actions themselves seems minimal; the liveliest thing about these bodies is their lascivious gaze into the camera. The recording camera creates the show. It's like Mr Chance thinking he can turn off unpleasant reality with a flick of his TV remote control. Once again the assimilation of filmed pornographic fantasies becomes alienated from erotic practice. What is assimilated is not the sexuality that is represented but the representation of sexuality. Pornographic movies beget pornographic movies.

The Realm of the Pornographic Film: Shadows, Shock, Scarcity, and Plenty

In the beginning of this essay I discussed the ways in which liberalisation through penal code reforms led, in most Western countries, to the emergence of a varied system of pornographic cinemas. This development was understood as the result of the permeation of sexuality by social power. It was also suggested that in pornographic cinema instrumental reason tailors sensuality to its own measure. The image of the human being in pornographic films is one of the body as a mechanism for experiencing and maximising pleasure, and of the person as monad – as defined by bourgeois ideology in its strictest sense – as one whose actions are guided by self-interest, specifically, in experiencing as much pleasure as possible.

The perpetual motion of desire is choreographed for us in pornographic cinema, and is constituted out of its arsenal. Everything becomes an instrument for sensual pleasure: the body, a hair brush, a dildo, a banana. Every situation leads to sex: a flat tyre, the beach, the carwash, or an office party. Bodies are linked with one another according to mathematical equations; orgies are conducted like a game of dominoes. What Horkheimer and Adorno have to say about Sade also applies to porn movies.

> What Kant grounded transcendentally, the affinity of knowledge and planning, which impressed the stamp of inescapable expediency on every aspect of a bourgeois existence that was wholly rationalised, even in every breathing-space, Sade realised empirically more than a century before sport was conceived. The teams of modern sport whose interaction is so precisely regulated that no member has any doubt about his role, and which provide a reserve for every player, have their exact

counterpart in the sexual teams of *Juliette*, which employ every moment usefully, neglect no human orifice, and carry out every function.[28]

In fact, newer pornographic films demonstrate significant advances, especially in the area of gymnastic-artistic formations. Technique has evolved from presentations of 'perverse beauties rolling around on a carpet' to orgies of group sex that demonstrate athletic control of the body along with simultaneous sexual feats. The aesthetic of the pornographic film relies on an underlying metaphor of the body as a machine: editing makes it possible to replace tired bodies with fresh ones, or with those that have been replenished in the interim. Or else in a pinch, when nothing more can be exhorted from these sexual athletes, editing can be used to create movement artificially. The performers' interchangeability and anonymity function as a material correlative to the ideology they express. There's no longer room for the old-fashioned clumsiness of a giggling Emmy Raschke. Now we have high performance professionals who, in the manner of Taylorisation, contribute specialised physical skills to the completion of the final product. Meanwhile, maintenance crews with spare parts stand ready to take care of breakdowns. These production manoeuvres are of no interest to the viewer, who pays as little notice to the rapid relay of aroused penises, wide-open mouths, spread thighs, and drawn labia as he or she does when the female performer changes wigs – from a blonde equestrienne to a red-headed lesbian.

The most sophisticated porn films are structured in such a way that the keyhole perspective of the voyeur is built right into the film. This device allows for several 'numbers' at the same time, shown through parallel editing, and helps counteract the fatigue that invariably sets in when an entire coition is presented without interruption in a single take. The latter usually gives the impression of being hard work rather than pleasure. Pornographic cinema emerges at the end of a developmental process in a society of specialisation and differentiation. Pornography itself contributes to this specialisation by promoting the autonomy of *Schaulust*. The differentiation of pornography as a product parallels developments in society, as producers speculate on the consumer's current and projected needs and taboos. Male homosexuality doesn't turn up in a heterosexual porn house and vice versa, anal eroticism only takes place between men and women, and the only way a man comes close to another man is when a woman, who lies between them, is entered both vaginally and anally. Lesbian sex does not appear either; when women caress each other, it is only because they are waiting for a man or performing for a male voyeur.

But criticism of pornography is still clearly ill at ease with its newer forms, especially its filmic forms. Despite the routine way in which the socialisation of sexuality is pursued, some quality still clings to pornographic cinema which places it into the category that Siegfried Kracauer called 'phenomena overwhelming consciousness':

Elemental catastrophes, the atrocities of war, acts of violence and terror, sexual debauchery, and death are events which tend to overwhelm consciousness. In any case they call forth excitements and agonies bound to thwart detached observation. No one witnessing such an event, let alone playing an active part in it, should therefore be expected accurately to account for what he has seen. Since these manifestations of crude nature, human or otherwise, fall into the area of physical reality, they comprise all the more cinematic subjects. Only the camera is able to represent them without distortion. ...

> The cinema, then, aims at transforming the agitated witness into a conscious observer. Nothing could be more legitimate than its lack of inhibitions in picturing spectacles which upset the mind. Thus it keeps us from shutting our eyes to the 'blind drive of things'.[29]

Kracauer suggests that only through the alienation of the image is it possible to imagine a reconciliation with objects and their recuperation from mere functionalism. The one-dimensionality of the optical appropriation of the world is mirrored in the flat screen of pornographic cinema, and somehow makes it even more scintillating and enticing than any ideological criticism – no matter how well-intentioned or well-founded – has been able to account for.

> One must learn to read between the lines of gaping flesh and labia, as if these constituted a code of prohibition and denial. ... But the whole iconography of unlived life, of anti-eroticism in capitalist systems, is only revealed to the person who remains sensitive to pornography's debasement, dirtiness, vulgarity and brutality, who has seen its leering grin.[30]

Those who, like Peter Gorsen in the above quotation, learn to read pornographic films against the grain will find not only 'a code of prohibition and denial' – in the sense that the cinema supplies what reality denies. They will also recognise the wounds that 'the code of prohibition and denial' have inflicted on desire itself – wounds that are not external to but within the iconographic system, a system that expresses rather than represses. Even with the machine-like availability and interchangeability of bodies in pornographic films, their crude naturalism harbours a wish for a realm beyond renunciation where milk and honey flow. In his study of sexuality and pornography in Victorian England, Steven Marcus traces the historical context of the era's imagery to its economy:

> The fantasies that are at work here have to do with economics; the body is regarded as a productive system with only a limited amount of material at its disposal. And the model on which this notion of semen is formed is clearly that of money. ...
>
> Furthermore, the economy envisaged in this idea is based on scarcity and has as its aim the accumulation of its own product. And the fantasy of pornography, as we shall have ample opportunity to observe, is this idea's complement, for the world of pornography is a world of plenty. In

it all men are limitlessly endowed with that universal fluid currency which can be spent without loss. Just as in the myth Zeus descends upon Danae in a shower of gold, so in pornography the world is bathed, floated, flooded, inundated in this magical produce of the body.[31]

The Victorian pornographic fantasy of abundance complemented real poverty in the external world. The wealth that pornographic cinema commands today had yet to be amassed. Thus, now, the endless flow of semen, the bodies of women doused in sperm, allude to one particular scarcity: that of the body itself. Pornographic fantasy invariably refers us back to the world of machines, of interlocking systems and cogs, in which everyone, ultimately, is caught up. But the fantasy alludes, above all, to the subjugation of the body, which suffers from want in the midst of material plenty.

Today pornographic film no longer refers to meanings lying outside its own subject matter; it refers primarily to itself by relying on what can be seen on the screen: bodies and their passions. Now we must reconsider the problem of voyeurism addressed above and pose the question: What is it that is seen? what aspects of sexuality can be visualised? I will attempt to answer this question in the next section, which deals with the iconography of the visible (the phallus) and the invisible (the vagina) in gender-specific pornographic imagery. But first I want to examine further that distance between observer and observed which, according to Kracauer, is created by the camera.

Kracauer believes distance is necessary to lessen the shock that would result from the spectator's direct confrontation with certain phenomena. Pornography obviously plays off a certain fear of crudity, coarseness, and undisguised, unsublimated sexuality. Only through the image can the observer confront that which would otherwise frighten him or her. The same process occurs within the individual in the dream-work. In the case of pornographic cinema, the camera becomes a device for creating distance and the medium of a harmless voyeurism:

Like a camera, I observe but am not involved. In a narrow place in a dark cave I look through the camera and film a scene. I see a huge scorpion, while somebody outside tries to kill it. It's four or five feet long. The guy outside uses his hands and feet to throw sand into the cave, moving it fast, back and forth – so sexual. He hurls a cold, poisoned lobster's tail as bait, so the scorpion won't bite him. Jesus, what a dream! I filmed the battle between these two jokers. It's dangerous and disturbing.[32]

This dream, as related by a patient to his psychoanalyst, provides a good description of the discharge mechanism inherent in this camera-voyeurism. The dream is interpreted by the psychoanalyst as fear of sexuality. (The camera played a role not only in the dreams of this patient, but also in his actual sexual life. He made slides from photos that he took of his girlfriend during their sex games.) Parallels with the procedures of pornographic voyeurism can thus be found at the level of individual psychology. Such everyday examples demonstrate just how deeply embedded are these organisational forms of the perceptual apparatus. Thus the idea of a bad 'influence' originating in the simple content of pornographic cinema – an idea often used by political conservatives as an argument for censorship – is not a viable one.[33]

Looking, as a form of sexual curiosity that probes an undiscovered sexuality, requires distance in order to mitigate the fear of the unknown – the Kracauerian shock. Some literary works employ shadow metaphors to create the necessary distance between observer and observed. The following example from literature demonstrates, from a different perspective, the same need for distance in sexual looking that we see in pornographic cinema:

> The shadow of the housekeeper's legs, as she lay with her back on the table, rose up with bent knees over the coachman's creeping shadow, and the shadow of the coachman, resting on his knees, rose above the shadow of the housekeeper's stomach. The shadow of the coachman's hands reached under the shadow of the housekeeper's skirts, the shadow of the skirt slipped down and the shadow of the coachman's abdomen burrowed into the shadow of the housekeeper's exposed thighs. The shadow of the coachman's arm dug into the shadow of his crotch and pulled out a polelike shadow, which in its shape and position matched his tool; he thrust this protruding shadow into the big, well-rounded shadow of the housekeeper's belly after the shadow of the housekeeper's legs had raised themselves above the shadow of the coachman's shoulders.[34]

The schematic, the stereotypical, the elaboration of persons and identities through the movements of their bodies – thus does Peter Weiss capture the voyeuristic experience in a literary form in which the action dissolves into endless genitives. As a characteristic of pornographic film, the voyeuristic experience is presented at face value and is not problematised. The transformation of persons into patterns which comport themselves according to a preconceived design refers even in pornographic cinema to the longing for a sexual life that is not predicated on the identity of 'mature personality' and 'genital sex':

> One experiences a glimpse of sexual utopia when one doesn't have to be oneself, and when one doesn't merely love one's lover for herself: it is the negation of the ego principle. It undermines that invariable aspect of bourgeois society, in its broadest sense, which defines identity as integration. …
>
> The advancing social reinforcement of genitality brings about greater repression of the component instincts, as well as their representative forms in genital relations. What remains of those instincts is cultivated

only in the socialised voyeurism of foreplay. Voyeurism exchanges union with one person for observation of all, and thus expresses sexuality's tendency to socialisation, which is itself an aspect of sexuality's deadly integration.[35]

The constant change of locations encompassed in the domain of the porn movie, the make-up and costumes that are the trappings of anonymous passion, are perhaps the last traces of a search for nonidentity in sex. The appearance in a porn movie of a proletarian captain of a steamer on the Elbe promises a two-fisted ingredient in *Firm Grip*. In *The Duchess of Porn* a black evening gown offers a touch of French decadence; and *Convent Girls* hints at sadomasochistic flagellation orgies in hair shirts. The component instincts conceal their desires in the secret code of the films' settings, desires obscured in the films themselves by the hearty gymnastic primacy of genital sex.

The Secret of the Missing Phallus and Woman's Other Place

Criticism of pornographic cinema, originally levelled by conservatives on moral grounds, is now exercised, after widespread easing of controls and liberalisation, primarily in feminist political action and analysis. But the feminist critique of pornographic film is fundamentally distinguished from that of conservative moralists in its intent. Feminists see in pornographic cinema not the erosion of existing norms but rather their expression and confirmation. Pornographic cinema reduces sexuality to the measure of a male perspective, one grounded in patriarchal myths about female sexuality and the phallus. In short, pornographic cinema is sexist. Feminists argue that sexism prevents the emancipation of sexuality, an emancipation that would liberate women's sexual fantasies and prepare the way for a well-deserved end to phallocentric primacy in the prevailing sexual order. The intent of these arguments is, therefore, not a conservative preservation of existing values but revolutionary change. The arguments arise out of the strategies of the women's sexual and political liberation movement.

The disturbing state of sexuality today makes it difficult to object to the goals of feminist criticisms of pornographic film. One can, however, object to arguments that posit a direct connection between viewing pornographic films and engaging in certain sexual acts, the argument, for example, that whoever views sadistic porn movies sees in them a possible way of behaving and an invitation to rape and sadistically torture women; or that whoever sees phallic fantasies of omnipotence endorsed on the screen will hardly be prepared to act differently in reality. It has never been proven that filmed events have a direct effect on human behaviour. It is my conviction that we can only conceive of such a connection in a broad, collective sense, not as a direct relationship as defined by behavioural psychology. In contrast to the above argument, I assume that pornography is less an expression of prevailing male sexual *practice* than an expression of its deficiency, the rehabilitation of damaged fantasies.

Although legislative and executive regulation and prosecution is no longer widespread, the subculture of pornographic movies still maintains an aura of the secret and forbidden, the sensational and the never-before-seen; it is therefore promoted not as something ordinary or potentially ordinary, but as something 'extraordinary'. A porn house in London displayed the following notice in front of the theatre: 'WARNING: This cinema is showing pornographic films depicting close-ups of sexual intercourse, oral sex, and male and female masturbation and is not for the easily shocked.'[36]

The shock, the sense of alarm used here as a promotion, recalls Kracauer's 'phenomena overwhelming consciousness'. This element of shock seems to be a constituent of voyeuristic pleasure in pornographic cinema. But what is it that is so terrible to see? Are sex organs and copulating couples really terrifying? Where does this terror that leads to fascination come from? Feminist arguments overlap with psychoanalytical ones in answering this question, because both proceed from the assumption of the primacy of male sexuality in pornographic films.

According to Freud's analysis, there is a close connection between *Schaulust* and fear of castration: a male child who sees a woman's sex organ for the first time in his life is amazed that no penis is attached. Disturbed by the fact that an object so important for him is missing from the female organ, he imagines a number of equally anxiety-laden possibilities: a) the female organ is the result of castration, or b) the woman is hiding her penis. The second possibility, 'b', is already a working through of the fears aroused by the possibility of 'a'. It is this aspect of the castration complex that gives rise to the persistent voyeuristic mania to look at the female organ, constantly and as closely as possible, in order to uncover the secret of the missing penis. The adult viewer of pornographic films seeks a confirmation of his childhood sexual theory – the phallic myth about the female organ. Because this mania is the result of the castration complex, seeing lots of penises confirms their durability and intactness; castration anxiety is also reduced by inducing the feeling of phallic omnipotence. The restless search for something that can't be found – the woman's penis – is compensated by an appeasing display of erections and potency. The endless merry-go-round of sex orgies, the reduction of a person to his or her sex organs, the mechanical, compulsive repetition in the action of pornographic films thus arise out of the male sexual organisation, rather than from a lack of imagination on the film-maker's part. A secret rite conjures up a naked body at any moment and around every corner. The fantasy world of the adult is like the magical, archaic world of the child, where time and space are freed from the constraints of physical reality. It is as if, with a magic word, an ordinary place becomes a secret site of sexuality. The world of pornographic films builds pyramids of gymnasts on an archaic foundation: on a childhood sexual theory.

John Ellis has shown that in the voyeuristic realm of pornographic films the invisible female phallus must be transformed into a visible fetish, so that pleasure can overcome the fear of castration:

> The fetish offered by these representations is no longer a fragment of clothing, or even the deceptively smooth body of the phallic woman, it is now the woman's sexual pleasure. The woman nevertheless has the phallus in sexual pleasure; the woman's lack of a phallus is disavowed in her orgasm. . . . In orgasm woman no longer is the phallus, she has the phallus. Films currently produced within the pornographic sector gain their impulsion from the repetition of instances of female sexual pleasure, and male pleasure is perfunctory in most cases. The films (and photographs) are concerned with the 'mise en scène' of the female organs; they constantly circle around it, trying to find it, to abolish the spectator's separation from it.[37]

The transformation of the empirical penis into a mythic, symbolic phallus, into a fetishistic image signifying the existence of female orgasm, also signifies the process of transformation whereby something invisible becomes visible in the fetish. It is true that many pornographic films give particular weight in their *mise en scène* to signifiers of female orgasm. But this raises another problem in the relationship of visible and invisible. For the place where the woman 'possesses' a phallus and is supposed to have the orgasm is no more visible than the phantom phallus the man seeks to find in her.

Because of the expressive poverty of its naturalistic style, pornographic film necessarily reaches its limit literally *ante portas*, before achieving its goal of seeing the secret place where woman's pleasure resides. Dennis Giles outlines this problem in a psychoanalytic essay on pornographic films:

> The interior space she encloses (identified as the woman *in essence*) is an *invisible place*... it cannot be possessed by visual knowledge. In order to emphasise its separation from the *known* space of the pornographic film, I call this central interior the Other place.[38]

The invisible, other place, affirmed by pornographic films without showing it, can be made visible through pornographic language. Steven Marcus impressively affirms it in a description of the female body as a landscape, rendered in a Max Weberian construction of an ideal-typical 'Pornotopia':

> Farther down, the scene narrows and changes in perspective. Off to the right and left just two smooth snowy ridges. Between them, at their point of juncture, is a dark wood – we are now at the middle of our journey. This dark wood – sometimes it is called a thicket – is triangular in shape. It is also like a cedar cover, and in its midst is a dark romantic chasm. In this chasm the wonders of nature abound. From its top there descends a large, pink stalactite, which changes in shape, size and colour in accord with the movement of the tides within. Within the chasm – which is roughly pearshaped – there are caverns measureless

to man, grottoes, hermits' caves, underground streams – a whole internal and subterranean landscape. The climate is warm but wet. Thunderstorms are frequent in this region, as are tremors and quakings of the earth. The walls of the cavern often heave and contract in rhythmic violence, and when they do the salty streams that run through it double their flow. The whole place is dark yet visible. This is the centre of the earth and the home of man.[39]

In film this literary, utopian other place remains invisible. Woman's pleasure is not only signified, it is also simulated by external signs; only the penis is visible in pornographic films, and it must bear the burden of proof. We hardly ever see a coition that doesn't end with a penis ejaculating on a woman. The abundance of sperm once again becomes a sign of inadequacy, an inadequacy of representation. Still, the sight of an ejaculating penis seems to be pleasurable for the straight male viewer, because to him it is a sign of intactness, an assurance that the vagina, imagined as insatiable and dangerous, has once again yielded its victim, unscathed, to see the light of day. Another reason for the choice of a naturalistic style of depiction in pornographic films is that it confers perceptual certainty on the films' guarantee of 'uncastratedness'. This convention therefore sacrifices the woman's pleasure, since the actress has to simulate orgasm after the penis is no longer inside her.

The psychic codification of sexuality can thus be seen even in the naturalistic habits of pornographic films. Films are never transparent, pure images, they are always a symbolic structuring of that which is portrayed. Thus we can now extend the definition encountered above – pornographic cinema as an instrument of the 'will to knowledge' – to the intrapsychic level: pornographic cinema is the night school of the sexual theories of children. Even though, ultimately, any such definitions remain inadequate, an analysis that measures pornographic films with the yardstick of psychopathology and concludes they involve infantile, perverse male sexual fantasies is, in a clinical diagnostic sense, entirely correct. This argument offers the feminist critique of pornographic film its strongest support.

Yet psychopathological analyses, based exclusively on a reconstruction of the male sexual perspective, cannot explain the fact that, 'with disgusted and fascinated gaze',[40] and in spite of well-founded moral and critical indignation, women are fellow travellers on the road to 'Pornotopia'.[41]

The pleasure of looking, as an exploration of a strange sex as well as one's own, is certainly a pleasure common to both sexes. Likewise, it is not only male desire that is expressed in the longing to return to the womb and in narcissistic fusion and exchange fantasies. The idea of promiscuous abundance, which saturates the images of pornographic films, is present not only at the level of symbolic abstraction – in the sense that all those visible, concrete penises and vulvas represent only a single symbolic phallus. Although always bound within a symbolic, social discourse, film images never quite free themselves from the resistance offered by the concrete world of objects, which those images transfer to the world of symbols.[42] If all these genitalia and individual bodies symbolise a single meaning, it may be because they are experienced through the abstract, generalising mania of male perception – that is, only within the systematic context of the symbolic organisation of a phallocentric world. Nevertheless, they still also exist as images of particular things whose substantiality is also real and empirical, as the naturalistic style of pornographic film never tires of reminding us. It may be that female perception is not actually integrated within a phallic discourse which can never be woman's own. It may be that women, through their own more concrete organisation, can undo the fantasy in order to move about outside the inscribed symbolic discourse.

Pornotopia would become a world of fragments, disclosing the gap between the sexes, something the phallus nervously denies. Pornotopia then becomes the empire of a phallic ruler, who is powerless against the woman's gaze at specific objects; it partitions his empire according to its own preferences. The woman's gaze at pornographic films, 'disgusted and fascinated', doesn't have to search for and find a phallus behind every penis. The fact that women react ambivalently to pornographic films, torn between fascination and disappointment, may not always be because of a prudish upbringing, which forbids an open view and leads to repulsion and a defensive attitude toward sexuality. It may still be possible for women, in spite of their criticism, to take a utopian view of Pornotopia. This may come to pass if they are able to recognise that utopian plenitude is not to be found in a phallocentric generalisation, but rather in the details of a quivering world of objects; and if, with their gaze, they manage to create, out of the shadow world, bodies of flesh and blood. Concrete criticism and reception of pornographic cinema, as demonstrated in interviews conducted with women by Marie-Françoise Hans and Gilles Lapouge,[43] indicate something more than merely women's insufficient understanding of the objective content of pornographic movies; the concrete approach also turns up a different kind of appropriation, one which is reflected in fragments. Even when women smash pornographic cinema into pieces, they bring more to light in these fragments than the whole can possibly offer: an alternative sexuality, which is as much a part of the radical feminist negative critique of pornographic movies as it is of the 'uncritical', appropriating gaze of its female patrons.

This article was initially published in *Lust und Elend: Das erotische Kino* (Munich and Lucerne: C.J. Bucher, 1981), a collection of essays on erotic film. In the period between its writing and its English-language publication, the increasingly liberal attitudes toward pornography that the essay discusses have been reversed by the coming to power of conservatives in both Germany and the US. Moreover, the changes in pornography's production, distribution and reception brought about by the advent of the home video market also occurred during this intervening period. (Ed.)

Translated by Jan-Christopher Horak and Joyce Rheuban. Reprinted from *October* 50, Fall 1989, pp. 3–29, by permission of the MIT Press, Cambridge, Massachusetts.

Notes

1. Heinrich Fraenkel, *Unsterblicher Film. Die Grosse Chronik von der Laterna Magica bis zum Tonfilm* (Munich: Kindler, 1956), p. 380.
2. Ibid., p. 382.
3. Ibid., p. 385.
4. Ibid., p. 408.
5. Curt Moreck, *Sittengeschichte des Kinos* (Dresden: Paul Aretz, 1956), p. 173.
6. Ibid., p. 175. (The adjective *sotadic* derives from Sotades [323–247 B.C.] who wrote coarse satires and travesties of mythology in a peculiar meter which bears his name. – Eds.)
7. Ibid., pp. 178–80.
8. Ibid., pp. 180–2.
9. Günter Kunert, *Ortsangaben* (Berlin [East]: 1970), pp. 123–4.
10. Moreck, p. 179.
11. Brendan Gill, 'Blue Notes', *Film Comment*, vol. 9 no. 1, 1973, p. 11.
12. Ibid.
13. Moreck, p. 183.
14. Ibid, pp. 178–9
15. Ibid., p. 183.
16. Ibid.
17. Walter Serner, 'Kino und Schaulust', *Die Schaubühne* 9, 1913. Quoted in Anton Kaes (ed.), *Kino-Debatte* (Munich: Deutscher Taschenbuch, 1978), pp. 53–4.
18. Theodor W. Adorno and Hanns Eisler, *Komposition für den Film* (Munich: Roger and Bernhard, 1969), p. 43.
19. Ibid., p. 41.
20. Oskar Negt and Alexander Kluge, *Öffentlichkeit und Erfahrung. Zur Organisationsanalyse von bürgerlicher und proletärischer Öffentlichkeit* (Frankfurt am Main: Suhrkamp, 1972), p. 237. Frederick Winslow Taylor developed a system of rationalising the work process, a conception which was widely adopted and applied to shape industrial design and management practices.
21. Michel Foucault, *The History of Sexuality*, trans. Robert Hurley (New York: Vintage Books, 1980), p. 48.
22. Moreck, p. 182.
23. Ibid., p. 181.
24. Jean-Paul Sartre, *Being and Nothingness. An Essay on Phenomenological Ontology* (New York: Philosophical Library, 1956), p. 578.
25. Ibid.
26. Ibid., p. 579–80.
27. Beate Klöckner, 'Hörst du mein heimliches Rufen? Die "gute" und die "böse" Lust', *Strandgut*, no. 26, March 1980, p. 17.
28. Max Horkheimer and Theodor W. Adorno, *Dialectic of Enlightenment* (New York: Continuum, 1987), p. 88.
29. Siegfried Kracauer, *Nature of Film* (London and New York: Oxford University Press, 1960), pp. 57–8.
30. Peter Gorsen, *Sexualästhetik. Zur bürgerlichen Rezeption von Obszönität und Pornographie* (Reinbek: Rowohlt, 1972), p. 104.
31. Steven Marcus, *The Other Victorians. A Study of Sexuality and Pornography in Mid-Nineteenth Century England* (London: Weidenfeld and Nicolson, 1966), p. 22.

32. Leon L. Altman, *Praxis der Traumdeutung* (Frankfurt am Main: Suhrkamp, 1981), p. 121.
33. In connection with these problems compare Volkmar Sigusch's summary of the *Pornography Report*, quoted in Gorsen, pp. 108–10.
34. Peter Weiss, *Der Schatten des Körpers des Kutschers* (Frankfurt am Main: Suhrkamp, 1964), pp. 98–9.
35. Theodor W. Adorno, 'Sexualtabus und Recht heute', in *Eingriffe. Neun kritische Modelle* (Frankfurt am Main: Suhrkamp, 1963), pp. 104–5.
36. John Ellis, 'On Pornography', *Screen*, vol. 21 no. 1, Spring 1980, p. 103.
37. Ibid. Ellis's analysis takes its cue from Laura Mulvey's 'Visual Pleasure and Narrative Cinema'.
38. Dennis Giles, 'Pornographic Space: The Other Place', 'Film-Historical Theoretical Speculations', *The 1977 Film Studies Annual* (Pleasantville, New York, 1977), Part II.
39. Marcus, pp. 274–5.
40. Marie-Françoise Hans and Gilles Lapouge, *Die Frauen – Pornographie und Erotik* (Neuwied: Luchterhand, 1979), p. 204.
41. If one strictly defines pornographic cinema as a medium oriented solely toward the depiction of male sexuality, then one still has to explain why women are not necessarily turned off by such depictions. They will hardly find an image of their own sexuality, unless we accept Freud's assumption of penis envy, which presupposes that the heterosexual, phallically oriented female identifies with the penis and its pleasure. The penis envy thesis, so vehemently opposed by feminist theoreticians, will not be discussed further here, although I'm inclined to accept its historical, if not its universal, anthropological validity. It might be helpful to look at Freud's assumption regarding a constitutional bisexuality, which characterises not only men but also women. In his late works Freud went so far as to state that biological bisexuality might contradict his penis envy theory. If we imagine that the strict schism between male/female, phallus/vulva is actually a relationship, whereby each sex incorporates repressed elements of the other, then we might have an explanation of why women can discover at least a portion of themselves in 'Pornotopia'. Viewing a penis would then also imply a degree of pleasure for women, and would thus not only mean subjugation by phallic power or identification with the oppressor. This would of course mean that we women would have to free ourselves from such constructs as 'evil', 'destructive', and 'misogynist' perversions, while at the same time attempting to study the utopian and anti-establishment contents of these perversions before clinically disqualifying them.
42. Compare Kracauer, pp. 57–8. Kracauer's essentialist film theory, based as it is on phenomenology, is centrally concerned with the idea of film as a redemption of physical reality, as found in the 'flow of life'. Even if one doesn't agree with Kracauer's philosophical precepts, one can hardly disregard Kracauer's having defined one of the basic tenets of film aesthetics: the preservation of the physical representation of objects, which film captures as a physical image, not an imaginary image as, for example, painting might. According to Kracauer, film is – and this definition seems to me to hold true for pornography – 'the shimmering sky reflected in a dirty puddle'.
43. See note 40. Compare Gertrud Koch, 'Von der weiblichen Sinnlichkeit und ihrer Lust und Unlust am Kino. Mutmassungen über vergangene Freuden und neue Hoffnungen', in Gabriele Dietze (ed.), *Die Überwindung der Sprachlosigkeit* (Neuwied: Luchterhand, 1979), pp. 116–38. (Koch's theoretical essays on women's reponses to film have been published in English in *Jump Cut*. See 'Why Women Go to the Movies' [no. 27] and 'Female Sensuality: Past Joys and Future Hopes' [no. 30].)

LINDA WILLIAMS

Second Thoughts on *Hard Core*

American Obscenity Law and the Scapegoating of Deviance

When the editors of this volume asked me to contribute an essay that would collect my thoughts about hard-core film pornography a few years after writing a book on the subject, they jokingly listed my contribution as 'The Afterglow of *Hard Core*'. Having long ago learned that *any* sexual pun or innuendo was to be vehemently eschewed in the attempt to write as neutrally as possible about the volatile genre of hard-core pornography, I changed the title. Afterglow, with its suggestion of smug satisfaction, I do not have; afterthoughts, even second thoughts, I have in abundance and some will be developed in what follows.

First, however, I would like to address the overarching issue that lurks beneath and motivates many of the jokes and innuendoes – including afterglow – that arise so frequently around discussions of sexual representations. When Paul Reubens (*aka* Pee Wee Herman) was arrested in a Florida Adult Theatre for exposing himself, he was publicly embarrassed for doing in a public place what many viewers of pornography do in private. Pee Wee's sad fate of banishment from children's television suggests just how explosive is the question of a genre-induced arousal and satisfaction, especially when linked to an effeminate public personality with an influence on children.

Pornography is a volatile issue not simply because it represents sexual acts and fantasies, but because in that representation it frankly seeks to arouse viewers. Perhaps more than any other genre its pleasures are aimed at the body. Indeed, pornography fails as a genre if it does not arouse the body. *Hustler* magazine's 'peter meters', which measure the quality of a porn film or video in terms of degrees of erection of the male organ, are just one, blatantly phallic, example of this expectation. Arousal, which is not always controlled by proper aesthetic or moral constraints, can be publicly embarrassing. Hence one reason for the sometimes defensive, sometimes aggressive humour around it; hence my own reason for resisting the implication that I had enjoyed the progression from arousal to satisfaction in the title 'afterglow'.

For example, attorneys involved in prosecuting obscenity cases report that jury members who see the works in question are sometimes unexpectedly sexually aroused, especially if permitted to see works in their entirety. Prosecutors oppose the showing of the contested works in their entirety because once jurors have so responded it becomes harder for them to declare a work obscene (Downs, p. 21). In other words, when jurors find a piece of pornography arousing *to them*, the old division – it if turns the other person on it's obscenity, if it turns me on it's erotic – doesn't hold.

An older era of American jurisprudence could more simply dismiss a range of sexual representations that were presumably only 'for sex's sake' – that is, just for purposes of arousal. 'Pure lust' was once the very definition of obscenity, and that, so it seemed, was that. But this definition has gradually changed as 'sex' has become an increasingly important motive force, so entwined with all aspects of human desire and endeavour as to be difficult to isolate in an absolutely pure state of obscenity. Thus, while the very word obscenity has been interpreted by many to mean that which is or should be off (*ob*) the stage (*scene*) of representation, and while confused concern about obscenity has been mounting steadily in the wake of the Meese Commission Report, National Endowment for the Arts defunding of artists, Senator Jesse Helms's legislation forbidding the spending of federal funds on 'obscene' art, and the Robert Mapplethorpe and 2 Live Crew trials, sexual representations are now so much *on the scene*, even in the arguments about these representations, that they cannot be easily dismissed as *ob scene*.[1]

In this essay I would like to explore the repercussions of what I am calling this historically unprecedented on/scenity in the context of current attempts to define and prosecute an elusive 'hard core' of obscenity. My main argument is that Americans are experiencing a remarkable on/scenity of sexuality which, in pornography no less than in all the arts, has become an important means of representing a wide range of sexual identities once labelled deviant – gay, lesbian, bisexual, sadomasochist, not to mention the female sexuality which has functioned throughout Western civilisation, and certainly in much pornography, as the basic deviation from a male 'norm'. Paradoxically, however, this new on/scenity, which has been remarkably liberating for previously closeted and repressed sexualities, has also been the means to a new form of scapegoating of which the tendency to blame pornography for a wide range of crimes is the most insistent example. For in the wake of the greater presence on/scene of diverse sexualities as a motive force in all human endeavour and identity, there has also been a tendency to blame 'sex' and especially sexual 'deviants' for such diverse societal ills as AIDS, child molestation, rape, and sexual harassment. My goal in what follows, then, is to trace a major change taking place in American obscenity law and the prosecution of sex crimes as they have moved away from the notion of explicit sex and towards the targeting of scapegoatable 'deviants'.

Since we are no longer able to claim, as sexual libertarians could once claim, that sex is a private matter, since sex has, in effect, become so very public a matter, even to those who would argue to keep it private, we have not attained the 'end of obscenity' predicted in the late 1960s by Charles Rembar.[2] Rather, we have seen an increasing politicisation of represented sexualities in a context of proliferating sexual discourses, and an intensified 'speaking sex'. Anti-pornography feminists have vociferously engaged in this intensified speaking sex. Not only do the novels and the critiques of pornography written by Andrea Dworkin themselves qualify as pornography, but the critique of pornography offered by Catharine MacKinnon is not, as has sometimes been assumed, that pornography *causes* harm to women, but that pornography *is* in its very representation of (heterosexual) sex harmful to women.[3] What MacKinnon and Dworkin, and the legal attacks on obscenity they have fostered, object to is not the bad influence of pornography on susceptible 'others', but what they see as the essence of pornographic speech: 'Pornography is exactly that speech of men that silences the speech of women' (MacKinnon, p. 209). To MacKinnon, pornography is the essence of the power exercised by men over women through sexuality. That pornography could be a form of the sexual speech of heterosexual women, gays, lesbians and others who have been suppressed by male heterosexuality is to MacKinnon unthinkable. I hope to show the cost of this unthinkability in the context of the changing meaning of obscenity.

The Miller Test

The event in American jurisprudence which marks the most important shift towards the new awareness that sex cannot easily be relegated to a place off-scene is paradoxically a 1973 case tried before the American Supreme Court. In *Miller* v. *California*, the court arrived at a three-pronged legal test designed to clarify, once and for all, what was and what wasn't obscene. The Miller Test, as it has come to be called, asks whether a work, taken as a whole, appeals to *prurient interest*, whether it depicts or describes sexual conduct in a *patently offensive* way, and whether it lacks *'serious literary, artistic, political or scientific value'* (emphases mine).[4] If lacking all these qualities a work may, according to *prevailing community standards*, be judged obscene (Downs, p. 17).

In recording the 1973 decision that presented the Miller Test, Justice Warren Burger asserted the concept of a non-socially redeemable prurience, a 'hard core' of mere 'sex for sex's sake', defined as explicit or graphic representations that went 'substantially beyond customary limits of candour'. Burger attempted to offer some 'plain examples' of hard-core depictions. These were 'patently offensive representations or descriptions of ultimate sexual acts, normal or perverted, actual or simulated, including patently offensive representations or descriptions of masturbation, excretory functions, and lewd exhibition of the genitals' (de Grazia, p. 567). The case was designed to reassure the public that the law could define – and thus keep 'offscene' – the obscene, but in practice the very vagueness of the Miller Test, coupled with the undeniably growing importance of sexuality as an overt and 'on/scene', not a hidden, force in contemporary society, meant that unprecedentedly wide varieties of sexual representation increasingly found their way on to the scene of representation. Even X-rated film pornography, which aims to be prurient, was acknowledged to be more than mere prurience.

Another difficulty was how to determine what these words – prurient interest, patently offensive – really meant. In a 1985 case that attempted to clarify the definition of prurient as that which 'incites lasciviousness or lust' the Supreme Court decided that 'lust' referred to 'normal' while 'lascivious' referred to 'abnormal' sexual responses (Downs, p. 29). Thus prurience was supposedly 'clarified' as containing both abnormal and normal sexual response. In other words, some level of prurience was admitted on/scene and the line was now drawn at a lasciviousness considered abnormal.

From Justice Burger's original attempt to clarify the definition of obscenity in the Miller Test, we can see a shift in attitude: in 1973 the censorable hard core included, at least in theory, depictions of 'ultimate sexual acts, normal and perverted'; by 1985, in the ruling mentioned above, the line between acceptable and censorable was drawn between a normal lust and an abnormal lasciviousness. 'Hard core' depictions of ultimate sexual acts, by which Burger seemed to mean 'normal' heterosexual acts, were no longer perceived by the court as the place where the line would be drawn. Gradually, in the wake of proliferating sexual representations, a new line was being formulated. We can see the emergence of this line in a later ruling which noted, for example, that while some depictions of heterosexual intercourse may be obscene, 'most hard core pornography emphasises various *other sexual practices*, such as homosexuality, bestiality, flagellation, sadomasochism, fellatio, cunnilingus, and the like.'[5]

Once it was no longer mere sexual explicitness that could be used to define an unacceptable obscenity, American courts were often compelled to specify which sexual acts were obscene. The Miller Test itself did not so specify. This lack of specificity has been its value in establishing freedom of speech in sexual expression. And it is important to remember, as Carol Vance points out, that the Miller Test still stands as the predominant legal definition of obscenity. Yet I would point out that the ruling that justified it, as well as many subsequent rulings, have frequently tried to provide some 'plain examples' of what constitutes obscenity. And not surprisingly, when these 'plain examples' are invoked they turn out to be 'other sexual practices'. Thus in the definition of obscenity, explicitness has given way to the deviant sexuality of the 'other', defined in relation to a presumed heterosexual, non-sadomasochistic norm that excludes both fellatio and cunnilingus. Presumably these specified 'other sexual practices' would turn the 'normal' juror off. Burger's specification thus shifted obscenity from mere explicitness in the representation of 'ultimate sexual acts' – for example, heterosexual intercourse (Downs, p. 17) – to a paradoxical lack of the 'ultimate' – an absence of an end goal or direct gratification – that is often the hallmark, and the literal meaning, of perversion.

What Burger was grappling with in his original attempt to define the elusive 'hard core' was the paradox of the existence of some sexual acts that epitomised (to *his* heterosexual male norm) an alien perversion, and the fact that such acts do not necessarily depict the sexual organs and genital actions whose simple visibility had previously sufficed to define obscenity. Because they are not 'direct' or 'ultimate sexual acts' they are difficult, under the earlier standard of 'pure lust', to define as obscene. In what precise sense, for example, is flagellation obscene?

Burger's definition, as opposed to the Miller Test itself, thus already left open the possibility that obscenity is not limited to explicit sexual acts (typically but not exclusively male and female genitals in coitus), but actually leans toward more 'deviant' sexualities – those sexual acts and fantasies that 'prevailing community standards' do not want to admit to be arousing. In the intervening years *these* perverse sexual acts have been targeted as the most important obscenities. We may note, for example, as both Carol Vance (1990) and Judith Butler (1990) have done, the wording of Jesse Helms's NEA bill forbidding the spending of Federal funds in the arts if the works proposed for funding 'promote, disseminate or produce obscene materials, including but not limited to depictions of sadomasochism, homoeroticism, the exploitation of children, or individuals engaged in sex acts' (Vance, p. 51).

Helms's bill (Public Law 101–121, passed in the Senate in September 1989 but subsequently softened in a House-Senate compromise bill that reverted to the Miller definition of obscenity) has been seen by Carol Vance as a contradiction and betrayal of the Miller Test which did not specify which sexual acts could be considered obscene. I agree with Vance's point that the Miller Test, which has paradoxically functioned to admit diverse sexual representations, was undercut by Helms's attempt to attach a 'sexual laundry list' to the word obscenity. Interpreters of the bill could all too easily understand it to mean that any depiction of sadomasochism or homoeroticism is obscene (Vance, p. 51).

However, if we compare Helms's amendment to the language with which Burger tried to explain, and specify, the 1973 Miller Test (as opposed to the Miller Test itself), then we can see that Helms's bill was not so much a contradiction of Burger's original intent as an attempt to reorder the list of the censorable. Burger's original 'sexual laundry list' included at the top heterosexual genital acts and then mentioned various 'perversions'. In contrast, Helms places the 'perverts' at the top and 'individuals [presumably heterosexual] engaged in sex acts' at the bottom, almost as an afterthought. The difference between 1973 and 1989 is striking. A wholesale reversal of the hierarchy of obscene sexual acts has taken place with the installation of sexual perversion, especially sadomasochism, at the top of the list. Despite the failure of Helms's amendment, its text remains significant for its indication of how variants of sadomasochism or homosexuality have gradually grown to become the most prominent of the obscenities in popular consciousness.

Jesse Helms says, in effect, look at how disgusting these deviant sexual acts and fantasies are. Yet in pointing the finger to condemn, he brings the representation on/scene just as surely as any pornographer.[6] He gambles that readers and viewers will share his disgust. But the risk he runs is that they won't. Like the risk to the prosecutors who must show contested works in, rather than out of, context, the danger is that the more sexual representations of all sorts are on scene, the more they contribute to the recognition, by jurors and casual viewers alike, that it is possible to be turned on by very irrational things, indeed by some very 'patently offensive', 'obscene' things that are exciting precisely because they are transgressions of reason and 'normality' and a 'properly' aesthetic, heterosexual, non-sadomasochistic erotics.

We have seen that debates over eroticism and pornography tend to prove only that one person's erotica can be another's porn and, somewhat similarly, that one person's perversion can be another person's norm. Though we can point in general to pornography's tendency toward the explicit depiction of 'ultimate sexual acts' and the existence of a more aestheticised, less explicit erotic, there simply isn't any hard and fast line to be drawn between the two. In fact, if we look closely at Helms's language we see that he has tossed 'depictions of homoeroticism' which could be entirely non-explicit into his list of obscene materials. What does emerge, however, is the way the line has tended increasingly to be drawn between a normal and a perverse rather than a nonexplicit and an explicit representation, and how these two poles depend on one another for definition. Pornographers, just as surely as Jesse Helms, need the idea that there is a line. The history of pornography, like the history of censorship, shows how variable that line has been and how paradoxically on/scene the various obscenities of pornography have been.

The McMartin Preschool Trial

My second example of the 'on/scenity' of obscenity only indirectly concerns pornography. Yet it probably would not have occurred without the public hysteria over the putative harms of pornography that came to a head in the convergence of 'moral majoritist' activism against sexual representations with anti-pornography feminists in the 1986 Meese Commission hearings. In 1983 Raymond Buckey, an employee at the McMartin preschool in Manhattan Beach, California, was accused by a mother of molesting her two-and-a-half year-old son at the school. Buckey was arrested, then released for lack of evidence. But during their investigation police sent letters to 200 parents naming Buckey as a suspect in child molestation. Nearly 400 children were subsequently interviewed by Children's Institute International, a Los Angeles agency that cares for abused children. The interviews were videotaped by an unlicensed therapist and eventually introduced as evidence in the trial of Buckey and his mother, Peggy McMartin Buckey, administrator of the preschool. Both were accused of sexually molesting forty-one children and of making 'kiddie porn' with them (*New York Times*, 19 January 1990).

The trial began in April 1987, after Buckey and his mother had already spent five years in jail before being able to raise the $1.5 million bond. It ended in January 1990 with the Buckeys' acquittal on fifty-two counts and a mistrial on all thirteen others. At two and a half years, the trial was the longest and costliest criminal proceeding in American history. Though no one will ever know for sure what actually transpired between the Buckeys and the children, in the end jurors could not separate fact from fantasy in the controversial videotaped interviews with the children admitted as testimony in the trial. If the Buckeys did the deeds they were accused of doing, they certainly committed not only obscene speech but, much more importantly, illegal, abusive and harmful acts. The jury could not determine, however, whether these illegal, abusive sexual acts occurred or whether they were transmitted to children via the videotaped interviews.

Sexual crimes of the most fantastic sort were recounted by the child witnesses in these interviews. But since the only way the children could be made to describe acts for which they had no words was for adults to give them the words, there was no guarantee that the children were not contaminated by adult sexual fears and fantasies. In these interviews the children were given anatomical dolls and urged to show how they were molested. As one juror put it, 'The children were never allowed to say in their own words what happened to them' (*Los Angeles Daily Journal*, 19 January 1990). Another juror said it appeared the children were coaxed into charging that the Buckeys had raped and sodomised them and touched their genitals (*New York Times*, 19 January 1990). The entire trial could thus be a remarkable demonstration of what Foucault has called our modern compulsion to 'speak sex' and to incite sex – to bring sexuality on the scene even where we most fear it: in the lives of children.[7]

For example, in an interview with one seven-year-old boy, Kee MacFarlane, the social worker who conducted the videotaped interviews, asked what the 'stuff' from Buckey's penis tasted like, explaining to the child, in an attempt to speak the child's language, that they were 'trying to figure out if it tastes good'. The boy replied, 'He never did that to [me], I don't think.' MacFarlane then asked a puppet – one of the anatomical dolls used by CII – if it knew what the 'stuff' tastes like, 'if it tastes good like candy?' The boy then replied, 'I think it would taste like yucky ants.' MacFarlane: 'Oh. You think it would be sort of – you think that would be sticky, like sticky, yucky ants?' A clinical psychologist who was a witness for the defence commented that prior to MacFarlane's introduction of the idea of ejaculation no mention of it had been made by any of the children. But once the acts were brought on/scene in the interviews with the children, as one clinical psychologist witness for the defence put it, it did not take 'a great leap to identify [Buckey] as the potential person who was involved in all those other things that have already been placed on stage.'

We can note, of course, just who had done this placing 'on stage'. It was the adult social worker, responding to what may have been the delusions of the original accuser (this mother died of alcohol-related illness before the case was brought to trial), who provided the explicit word, 'sticky'. Jurors who were originally inclined to believe that some of the children may have been molested, if not by the Buckeys then 'in some sense, by someone', finally objected to the 'no holds barred' fantasies incited by a publicity-hungry prosecution (*New York Times*, 19 January 1990). In the end, probably the most tangible evidence of molestation in this case was that of the prosecuting parents and social workers who brought sexual obscenities so dramatically on/scene.

MacFarlane and the mother who instigated charges that a sadistic, devil-worshipping Raymond Buckey had anal intercourse with the children of the preschool offer a prime example of the new importance of certain obscene fantasies in which, as with Jesse Helms, 'homoeroticism' functions as a key transgressive content. In order to prosecute the case MacFarlane had, in effect, to become the very kiddie pornographer she suspected Buckey to be. If Buckey and his mother are innocent, then it was MacFarlane who corrupted the children with her incitement to discourse via videos and dolls.

Trials such as the McMartin molestation case have been increasing in the wake of public hysteria about the harms of pornography ever since the Meese Commission hearings – hearings which were themselves a dramatic display of the 'on/scenity' of pornography.[8] These sex panics are a remarkable demonstration of the fact that the more we look for obscenity in order to ban it, the more we do not so much find it – as if it were an objectively existing cause of harm – as produce it in our own, and in this case in our children's, subjective fantasies. No evidence was ever found that the Buckeys were making kiddie porn, though the FBI, the US Customs Service and Interpol all sought it and the parents in the case offered a reward of $25,000 for photos that would prove pornography had been made. Nothing was found (*Playboy*, June 1990). Yet the attempt to link alleged sexual crimes of child molestation with pornography continued. For pornography is public in a way that the elusive crimes of sex offenders (most of which take place not in schools and not in pornography but privately in the home) are not. Because of this public, exhibitionist quality it is often pornography, and those who can be vilified through its use or production, rather than real sexual harassers, who end up being blamed and punished.

I do not want to minimise the existence of sexual harassment and molestation; indeed, my point is that these actual crimes are too often minimised while on/scene displays of sexual representations take their place as convenient objects of blame. This is undoubtedly why in the McMartin case police and FBI looked so long and hard for pornography. The familiar image of a perverse, obscene deviant forcing a powerless victim to satisfy his sexual whims needs to be recognised for what it is: a sex-negative fantasy which blames bad sex on the perversions of a villainous other. Perhaps the most fantastic thing about this fantasy is the melodramatic idea that bad, obscene, perverse sex can be so conveniently identified in the persona of a conventional villain – that is, someone 'other' than 'us'. We saw above how that villain has increasingly been defined as a homosexual sadomasochist stalking defenceless children. This villain is convenient, Judith Butler has noted, because he can be located outside the home (Butler, 1990, p. 116). We do well to remember, however, that not too long ago the villain was a heterosexual man in a raincoat whose enjoyment of pornography was considered harmful to the civil rights of women.

I have traced the elusive concept of obscenity in American law in order to suggest the mixed blessings of the loss of mere explicitness as a measure of obscenity. On the one hand, this loss of explicitness as a criterion has meant the arrival on/scene of many different kinds of sexual representation. On the other hand, it has meant the increasing politicisation of those representations. While this politicisation has in many ways been beneficial to feminism and to sexual minorities, it has also led to the finger-pointing condemnations of the bad sexualities of 'others' and to a mood of sexual hysteria that can erupt into witch-hunts and trials such as the McMartin case. Feminist anti-pornographers have participated in this process even though their goal has not been to attack either obscenity or deviancy. Their attack is on male power. While they have not directly intended to blame deviancy, the result of their efforts has been to aid the work of Jesse Helms. I will cite a very recent, and to me very disturbing, example of how anti-pornography feminists collude with this blame-the-deviant method of opposing pornography.

A recent ruling by the Canadian Supreme Court has been hailed as a victory of 'world historic importance' for feminism by Catharine MacKinnon,[8] who with Andrea Dworkin devised the city ordinances formulating a 'harms' approach to pornography defined as the sexual subordination of women by men. In this ruling, the court decided that obscenity is to be defined by the harm it does to women's pursuit of equality. Canadian Justice John Sopinka wrote: 'If true equality between male and female persons is to be achieved, we cannot ignore the threat to equality resulting from exposure to audiences of certain types of violent and degrading material' (Landsberg, 1992, p. 14).

The court rejected a free-speech appeal by a Winnipeg porn video dealer who had been convicted in 1987 for violating Canada's obscenity law. Obscenity had been previously defined in Canada, which has a weaker tradition of free speech than the US, as 'undue exploitation of sex' violating (undefined) 'community standards'. The court's 'clarification' of obscenity no longer includes issues of morality and taste, but it relies heavily on the idea that violence and degradation can be the determination of obscenity. A threat to women's equality is thus now an acceptable ground for placing limits on freedom of speech in Canada. The court decided that pornography does harm to the self-respect and safety of women. It was not even necessary to prove a direct cause between pornographic representations and harms, since there is a 'reasoned apprehension' that pornography's 'gross misrepresentations' may lead to 'abject and servile victimization'. In other words, as *Ms Magazine* triumphantly summarised: 'Porn lies, and it hurts' (Landsberg, p. 14).

But what is this pornography that lies and hurts and so clearly reveals harm to the self-respect and safety of women? It turns out to be the scapegoatable deviant sexuality of the 'other' and not at all an example of masculine power over women. Kathleen F. Mahoney, professor of law at the University of Calgary, who represented the women's Legal Education and Action Fund which successfully argued the case, told *Ms Magazine* that their group won because 'We showed them the porn – and among the seized videos were some horrifically violent and degrading gay movies.' Mahoney claims that the reason these films worked to convince the court was that the 'abused men in these films were being treated like women – and the judges got it. Otherwise, men can't put themselves in our shoes' (Landsberg, 1992, p. 14). Although Mahoney argues that showing gay porn allowed the male justices to identify with the position of 'victim' – as if identification in sexual fantasy were a simple matter of identifying with one's sexual like[9] – I think she really won the case for the same reason Jesse Helms first succeeded in passing his version of the NEA amendment: the ability to point the finger at that same homosexual sadomasochist 'other', rather than to offer any real challenge to male power and authority in sexual representations.

This Canadian decision is of special interest to Americans since it may be a harbinger of a new harms-oriented American approach to obscenity, as proposed in a bill that is before the Senate as I write. Senate Bill 1521, called the Pornography Victims Compensation Act and now under debate by the Senate Judiciary Committee, would allow civil damage suits against publishers, producers and distributors of pornography under the assumption that these representations can cause sex crimes. The author of the bill, Senator Mitch McConnell, maintains that hard-core pornography is a 'form of group libel, principally aimed at women and children. Its techniques echo the propaganda that others have used to cultivate hatred toward specific groups: it is typically degrading, distorted, dehumanizing and brimming with misogynist malice.'[10]

This new 'harms' approach to pornography would permit plaintiffs in civil suits to collect damages if they can show that obscene materials 'caused' the crimes committed against them by third parties. As Henry Louis Gates Jr has argued, 'Criminals, like the rest of us, are happy to attribute their bad behaviour to an external agency (mother, Hostess Twinkies, demon rum, *Playboy*), thus diminishing, in some measure, their own culpability' (*The Nation*, 29 June 1992, p. 902). If the bill is passed, we can expect a whole new level of blame to be placed on those obscenities most easily prosecuted in courts of law. As I have argued above, and as the pattern of prosecution by the Justice Department over the last few years reveals, it is not pornography depicting rape and violence against women that has been most consistently prosecuted. Indeed, as I have argued elsewhere, there is today comparatively little pornography depicting rape when one considers the amount of rape and abuse depicted in many more mainstream forms of mass-market representations, and sadomasochistic consensual violence can be very tricky to analyse as straightforward abuse.[11] Rather, it is the scapegoatable sexualities of sexual deviants that are prosecuted. In a recent Oklahoma case, for example, a video produced by the Pink Ladies, a support group for women in the adult video industry, was charged with obscenity. In this video, entitled *Sorority Pink*, there was no violence, rape or degradation of women. There was, however, a lesbian orgy (Lilly, p. 2).

Afterthoughts/Second Thoughts

The above is a roundabout way of getting to my most pressing 'afterthought' regarding my 1989 book, *Hard Core: Power, Pleasure and 'the Frenzy of the Visible'*: the unfortunate result of my concentration on heterosexual hard-core pornography. At the time of writing, the Meese Commission and anti-pornography feminists had themselves concentrated on the aggressive nature of the heterosexual masculine 'norm'. It seemed natural, therefore, to address this notion of pornography even if that meant ignoring other pornographies that were also on/scene – the vast market of gay pornography; the emerging, tentative markets of lesbian and bisexual porn. I did make a gesture towards the more diverse forms of pornography in a chapter on sadomasochistic pornography and in another on new forms of heterosexual pornography by women. But I now recognise that my focus on the 'mainstream' as constructed by the then dominant discourse on pornography was too reactive, and too prone to the main error of all condemners of pornography who view it as a monolithic example of whatever seems 'bad' to them in sexuality. The reaction led, unfortunately, to my own 'containment' of deviancy in a single chapter on sadomasochism, when the more useful political move would have been to map the remarkable decentring effects of proliferating sexual representations.[12]

Another reason for my failure to address the diversity of sexual desires was that, as a heterosexual, I felt I had no right or authority to analyse gay and lesbian porn. Speaking from what I now recognise to be a false sense of fixed sexual identity – an identity theoretically wedded to a sexual binary divided neatly into masculine and feminine heterosexual desire – I was unable to see then that what I was learning from the book was actually how easy it was to identify with diverse subject positions and to desire diverse objects, indeed how polymorphously perverse the genre of pornography could be. One did not necessarily have to be lesbian or gay to enjoy these 'other' pornographies. Nor did one have to be heterosexual to enjoy the more 'normal' ones. I had far too rigid a sense of the proper audience for each sub-genre.

Another problem related to the diversity of desires articulated by pornography was pornography's challenge to the feminist film theory dictum that the 'gaze is male'. I had already suggested this challenge with respect to heterosexual porn in *Hard Core*, but gay, lesbian and bisexual pornographies presented an even greater challenge to this oversimplified Lacanian formula. For gay porn could not be reduced, as it would seem the Canadian feminists did try to reduce it, to an aggressive male gaze at a feminised object. Nor did new lesbian porn with its butch/femme dichotomies and s/m orientation fit expectations of the 'kinder, gentler', more nurturing sexual pleasures of women. And bisexual porn, which makes a point of articulating a female gaze at male couples, is even more confounding of heterosexual presumptions of the workings of desire. With the best of intentions, then, my book's focus on the heterosexual mainstream may have actually strengthened the idea of a monolithic pornography that I wanted to challenge. I regret this now, especially in the context of the above shift in line-drawing from explicit to deviant.

Yet another 'second thought' has to do with the question of the researcher's gendered relation to his or her object of study, in particular: *what is a 'proper' female relation to the classically bad object of pornography?* Feminist engagement with pornography arose from a critique of the most masculine and misogynist of genres. Yet the more I looked at the genre, the more it seemed that previous discussions of pornography had been tainted by descriptions of films and videos supercharged with the emotions of the critic's own reactions. Looking at the short tradition of critical writing about pornography of all sorts, I knew I did not want to emulate any of the already established reactions to pornography. These included: Steven Marcus writing the whole of *The Other Victorians* while seemingly holding his nose; Susan Sontag in a more celebratory mode giving the avant-garde literary, high-serious French treatment to the Sadien-Bataille tradition; Andrea Dworkin offering the most meticulous descriptions of pornographic writing or images in tones of monumental outrage yet still complicit with the word's and the image's power to arouse.

Neutrality of tone seemed the obvious solution to these condemnations or overly defensive appreciations. I therefore resolved to skip the nervous jokes and the easy condemnation of aesthetic or moral shortcomings and to avoid condemnation of defensiveness. I would ask instead what the genre does, how it does it, and I would remove myself from pro or con arguments as much as possible. Yet this objective, distanced stance of the reasoned observer, neither partisan nor condemner, placed me in a position of indifference, as if above the genre. Was it right, or even useful to analysis, to assume to be indifferent to, or unmoved by, these texts? Or, if I was moved, as I was sometimes to either arousal or offence, what was the proper place of this reaction in criticism? While I attempted, ever so neutrally, to simply describe, wasn't something of my personal reaction already embedded, in a coded way, in the attention I gave to certain texts and subgenres and not to others? Donna Haraway once said in passing that one should not 'do' cultural studies of objects to which one is not vulnerable. In my case I had begun with what I thought to be an invulnerability, even a disdain for the texts of pornography, but was then surprised to find myself 'moved' by some works. What was the place of this vulnerability in writing about the genre? I don't know the answer to this question, but I grow increasingly convinced that there must be some place for this in writings about mass culture.[13]

There is a related problem in that, as a woman writing about a traditionally male genre, my interest in the genre is, at this historical conjuncture, more acceptable to many readers than a man's might be. For example, I was once asked if my contribution to the understanding of pornography would have been as well received if it had been written by a Larry instead of a Linda. The question was somewhat hostile, implying that men, who are too readily condemned by a politically correct feminism for enjoying porn, must condemn it or be condemned in turn, while I could 'get away' with having a scholarly interest in pornography. There is a certain justice to the criticism: masculine sexuality has been under siege by feminism for its very real abuses, and has often been forced into a rather cringing and unproductive *mea culpa* for its aggressive fantasies.[14] Yet if, as I have tried to argue both here and elsewhere, pornography is not the monolithic expression of phallic misogyny that it has been stigmatised as being, then there is good reason even for heterosexual men to explore the pleasures of the genre without having to admit too many *mea culpas*.

My final 'second thought' concerns the methodology of the study of pornography, in particular the question of *what theories best explain the genre*. Freud and Lacan are indispensable theorists of sexuality, fantasy and desire, yet to adopt them is on some level to ignore both history and the social, to accept a hermetically sealed explanatory system based on the woman's 'lack' of a penis and the hegemony of heterosexual desire. Foucault and new historians of sexuality are indispensable theorists of the historical contingencies of material bodies caught up in competing discourses of knowledge, power and pleasure, yet to adopt them is to lose an ability to account for the driving force of desire and fantasy so important in pornography. In addition, both theories are remarkably silent about women's sexuality, fantasies, desires and experience.

My solution to this problem is an admittedly makeshift and sometimes inconsistent oscillation between psychoanalytic and Foucauldian theories tempered and corrected by feminist critique. The key area of difficulty in the application of both psychoanalysis and Foucault is the status of perversion within their notions of sexuality. On one level both theories see all sexuality as inherently perverse. Freud theoretically accounts for this inherent perversion, but there is still a sense in which adult sexual perversion remains for Freud... well, perverse (that is, Freud's use of the term often exists in contrast to a proper heterosexual and heterogenital norm). Foucault, on the other hand, sees the history of sexuality as the 'implantation' of one perversion after another. Perversions are, for him, in a sense the norm. This is a more progressive attitude but it does not adequately account for the apparent dynamic between norm and perversion in the texts of pornography, where the excitement of the genre lies, at least partly, in the transgression of whatever sexual norms happen to be in effect.

Conclusion

The question that now faces both feminists and sexual minorities is the political one of whose sexual desires and pleasures will be permitted on/scene now that we no longer conceive of sex as containing a 'hard core' of obscenity. For our current sexual politics can no longer be that begun by Kate Millett and continued by anti-pornography feminists. This politics of condemning the evil masculine 'other' feeds all too easily into the condemnation of the deviant sexualities of 'perverse others'. Now that these perverse others take their place, not simply as freak contrasts to a dominant norm, but as authoritative subjectivities, both explicit *and* erotic, on the scene of sexual representation, the anti-pornography feminist vilification of a reified masculine lust backfires as a strategy for the furtherance of feminist goals.

In *Hard Core,* I described what seemed to me to be the uneasy bargain struck between the 1986 Meese Commission on Pornography and the anti-pornography feminists who joined forces with the Commission to condemn pornography. It seemed to me then that the Meese Commissioners gained the radical feminist critique of phallic pleasure as a violent form of male power, but at the cost of curbing their own desire for an equally strong critique of gay or lesbian pornography or sexual practice. The rhetoric of violence against helpless victims could not be mobilised against this pornography because women were not its victims. In this tacit bargain, the Meese Commission gained new leverage against some forms of obscenity but not the gay and lesbian deviancy it also targeted. In turn, anti-pornography feminists got to assert the abnormality of a graphically depicted phallic power that had once been considered a natural aspect of (hetero)sexual pleasure. However, unless these representations could be construed as violent they could not be condemned.

Thus, although the two interests had very different notions of what the norms of sexual behaviour should be, in the end they condemned only those they could agree to hate. Today, as we have seen in both the changing notion of obscenity and the new pattern of blaming deviant sexuality for sexual abuses that are deeply embedded in patriarchal culture, there is greater agreement to hate homosexuals. If we do not want to be in the business of condemning the sexuality of villainous others, we need a better sexual politics. This sexual politics must be aware of the diversity of sexual fantasies which cannot be simplified into an easily scapegoatable aggression, perversion or evil. One way to explore this diversity would be to become aware that pornography is no monolith, that it has a history, and that in that history it has appealed to many more 'bodies and pleasures' than are dreamt of in any feminist anti-pornography philosophy.

Notes

1. One possible etymology of the word obscene is the literal Latin meaning of 'off scene' – those things which are, or should be, kept off (ob) the scene (scena) or stage of public representation. Andrea Dworkin (1979, p. 9) has noted this etymology along with the alternative Latin meaning of filth or excrement.
2. See Charles Rembar's influential 1968 work, *The End of Obscenity*.
3. See Dworkin's *Pornography: Men Possessing Women* and *Intercourse*; and MacKinnon's *Feminism Unmodified*.

4. I take the text of the Miller Test, as well as much of the following discussion of the vagaries of the attempt to define obscenity, from Alexander Downs's very helpful *The New Politics of Pornography*. This book offers a meticulous assessment of the changes taking place in the politics of pornography since the rise of anti-pornography feminism. Downs is a liberal who defends free speech and objects to the intolerance of pornography's attackers and defenders. While I do not always agree with his liberal stance, his book, along with Walter Kendrick's *The Secret Museum*, offer the two best surveys of the legal battles over the definitions of obscene sexual speech. Another recent book is Edward de Grazia's *Girls Lean Back Everywhere: The Law of Obscenity and the Assault on Genius*.
5. Frederick Schauer, *Law of Obscenity*.
6. While running for re-election in 1990, Helms quite literally performed a prurient finger-pointing that was reminiscent of a men-only stag smoker. At a barbecue in Burlington, North Carolina, Helms invited, as he had already done on the floor of the Senate, only the men in the audience to examine three portfolios of Robert Mapplethorpe nudes, guarded by his assistants. The photos were from the 'Perfect Moment' exhibit whose National Endowment for the Arts funding Helms opposed (*Time*, 10 September 1990, p. 17). His point was to outrage voters that taxpayers' money funded the exhibit. His method – to bring the offending photos to the barbecue but only to let the men see them – participates in the very titillation he opposes. (On the Senate floor Helms asked 'all the pages, all the ladies, and maybe all the staff' to leave the Chamber so that the male Senators 'can see exactly what they're voting on' (de Grazia, p. 637).
7. I owe thanks to Elizabeth Losch, whose unpublished essay on videotaped testimony of children in sexual abuse cases alerted me to the question of adult incitement of children to sexual discourse, and to Kee MacFarlane and Jill Waterman's 1986 book about the techniques of coaxing child witnesses.
8. I have learned of this recent ruling just as this essay goes to press and have therefore not had time to research the details of what would appear to be a quite dangerous precedent.
9. Since it has taken feminist film theory a long time to break from the assumption that desire as articulated by the various 'looks' of cinema can be anything but heterosexual and male, it is perhaps not surprising that the operating assumptions of anti-pornography feminists have, in so far as they have theorised desire at all, also deployed a masculine heterosexual model of desire.
10. Mitchell's statement is quoted in the newsletter written by Bobby Lilly, *Californians ACT Against Censorship Together* (14 May 1992).
11. Both these points are discussed at length in *Hard Core*, pp. 164–6, 184–228.
12. I map these proliferating forms of gay, lesbian, bisexual and sadomasochistic pornographies in a recent essay (Williams, 1992).
13. Constance Penley (1992) has recently spoken to this problem in a fascinating account of her own involvement as student and fan of amateur fan magazines that offer explicit sexual relations between the two main male characters of the *Star Trek* series. Since the fans of these 'zines' tend to be women, and since women's desires are articulated through these apparently gay representations, Penley, unlike the Canadian feminists who used such representations to stigmatise a deviant other, asks about her own implication as a fan, a feminist, a critic and a voyeur of such texts (p. 484).
14. See, for example, Michael Kimmel's interesting but guilt-ridden, even self-pitying, *Men Confront Pornography*.

Works Cited

Butler, Judith. *Gender Trouble: Feminism and the Subversion of Identity* (New York: Routledge, 1990), pp. 105–25.
de Grazia, Edward. *Girls Lean Back Everywhere: The Law of Obscenity and the Assault on Genius* (New York: Random House, 1992).
Downs, Donald Alexander. *The New Politics of Pornography* (Chicago: University of Chicago Press, 1989).
Dworkin, Andrea. *Pornography: Men Possessing Women* (New York: Perigee Books, 1979).
Gates, Henry Louis Jr. 'To "Deprave and Corrupt"', *The Nation*, 29 June 1992, pp. 898–903.
Kendrick, Walter. *The Secret Museum: Pornography in Modern Culture* (New York: Viking Press, 1987).
Kimmel, Michael S. (ed.). *Men Confront Pornography* (New York: Crown, 1990).
Landsberg, Michele. 'Canada: Antipornography Breakthrough in the Law', *Ms. Magazine*, May–June 1992, pp. 14–15.
Lilly, Bobby. *Californians ACT Against Censorship Together* (14 May 1992).
MacFarlane, Kee and Waterman, Jill. *Sexual Abuse of Young Children* (New York: The Guilford Press, 1986).
MacKinnon, Catharine. *Feminism Unmodified: Discourses on Life and Law* (Cambridge, Mass.: Harvard University Press, 1987).
Marcus, Steven. 1974. *The Other Victorians: A Study of Sexuality and Pornography in Mid-Nineteenth Century England*. (London: Weidenfeld and Nicolson, 1966).
Millett, Kate. *Sexual Politics* (New York: Doubleday, 1969).
Mulvey, Laura. 'Visual Pleasure and Narrative Cinema', *Screen*, vol. 16 no. 3, 1975, pp. 6–18.
Penley, Constance. 'Feminism, Psychoanalysis, and the Study of Popular Culture', in Lawrence Grossberg, Cary Nelson and Paula Treichler (eds.), *Cultural Studies* (New York: Routledge, 1992).
Rembar, Charles. *The End of Obscenity: The Trials of Lady Chatterley, Tropic of Cancer, and Fanny Hill* (New York: Random House, 1968).
Sontag, Susan. 'The Pornographic Imagination', in *Styles of Radical Will* (New York: Dell, 1969), pp. 35–73.
Vance, Carol. 'Misunderstanding Obscenity'. *Art in America*, February 1990, pp. 49–55.
Williams, Linda. *Hard Core: Power, Pleasure and the 'Frenzy of the Visible'*. (Berkeley: University of California Press, 1989).
Williams, Linda. 'Pornographies on/scene, or "diff'rent strokes for diff'rent folks"', in Lynne Segal and Mary McIntosh (eds.), *Sex Exposed: Sexuality and the Pornography Debate* (London: Virago, 1992).

JENNIFER WICKE

Through a Gaze Darkly

Pornography's Academic Market

Adventuring in the skin trade: pornography is one of the most salient new critical domains of interest, compelling an orgy of publication and commentary that maps and mimics the equally unstoppable flood of pornographic materials into all cultural interstices. While this second tier of pornographic exploration is not represented in the racks at the 7-Eleven, say, along with the discourse which it feeds on, there is a discernible increase in the academic pornography market. Casual browsing through the programme bulletin of the yearly MLA meeting – to take just one academic barometer as an index – yields a sudden profusion of 'Pornography and...' topics, the generic noun usually being linked to rather unwonted proper nouns, like 'Milton', a yoking actually to be found in the 1990 bulletin. Courses are being offered, seminars suggested, books emerging apace, and even the instinctive feel one acquires for what will radiate as hot and imperative in a book or essay title is shifting to 'pornography', having supplanted the early 80s thrill of 'power' and the delights later in the decade of 'sexuality', perhaps because pornography so neatly conflates the two.

The dimensions of pornography are much larger than the parochial corner of academic discourse I am going to patrol, but the very immensity, and the intensity, of the social discourse on pornography precludes its consideration; better the tip of the iceberg one can actually see. Moreover, the extreme interest in pornography on academic fronts at the moment – and I include not only strictly institutional venues but the intellectual journals, magazines, journalistic debates, television opinion shows and independent film-making efforts – has created a metapornography well worth investigating for its symptomatic meanings. Such an investigation does not imply that all these takes on pornography are somehow equally deluded, or contaminated, or beside the point; rather, it asks what use value pornography has in our current academic exchanges, and how it plays its role in the academic market-place.

Pornography plays a major, if sometimes invisible, role in academic discussion because it represents the flip side of the argument about what texts or representations can hope to accomplish in general. Pornography is the dark side of this particular moon, the segment of social discourse whose effects are almost entirely agreed to be negative. I propose that the focus on pornography in academic circles often stems from a corresponding and more taboo fear – that 'good' or 'serious' works in fact will not save us. Stripped to barest premises, it is thought that pornography is a form of representation whose perusal will cause people, read men, to devalue women even more than they already do, and encourage them to express this in violent ways; the strongest statement of this position is that perusing the pornographic image or words already constitutes such violence, that the act of reading or looking is intrinsically demeaning and violent in its 'objectification' of the women, or, less likely, the men represented. Pair this with its partner in social discourse, the fate of representation in general. Normally, pornography is not linked to the debates on the worth of studying particular texts, except in those rare instances where crossover texts emerge, and Joyce's *Ulysses*, for example, has to pass a legal challenge to disabuse itself of the pornographic label before qualifying as a work of serious merit, a classic. Because these realms are then usually so disjunct, it may seem peculiar to claim that an animating impulse for the debate on pornography is the seemingly much more rarefied, or even incontrovertible, status of great books and/or great works of art.

There is a hinge connecting these two realms of discourse, however. Pornography is a secret sharer in the canon debate, and a hidden partner of the high art/mass culture conflict that rages beyond the perimeters of the canon. Ultimately, pedagogy in general is involved, or 'paideia', to give it its Greek etymology and correspondingly enlarged social sense: pornography peeps out from its brown paper wrappers and asks how a culture reproduces itself, in and through the images and texts it disseminates, in a paideia at large. Pornography confutes and scandalises and banalises the intensely held beliefs of a text-based culture that people are what they read. The politics of this belief do not break down neatly into right and left camps, and this is perhaps why pornography is so insidiously stimulating as an academic subject – behind the complexities of the arguments about pornography often lies a philosophical discourse about representation and education, seeing and knowing. It is more than possible to want to guard against any censorship of pornography, and nonetheless to feel that good books make people good along the same lines of reasoning that help to buttress pornography's enemies. As a consequence, pornography strikes very deep into the sociocultural formation of education, knowledge and cultural awareness, arousing a profound need to write about pornography, almost as an act of exorcism. This is the largest of the embedded circles of my argument, and one to which I will return.

The current profusion of works about pornography also stems from the unique interdisciplinary and intratheoretical role pornography as a subject is capable of playing at the moment. Pornography is 'hot' now, or at least galvanising in academic circles, because it serves a variety of discursive and political purposes no other subject area can quite encompass at this juncture. These arenas are several, and can only be mapped rather fuzzily, since they have ways of blending into one another quite promiscuously. The primary amalgam, though, is the meshing of an ahistoricist, apolitical American feminist criticism with certain discrete and selectively chosen pieces of (psycho-analytic and Althusserian) feminist film theory, giving it enough theory to posit an 'objectifying gaze', in collision with the deep social conservatism of so-called 'radical' feminism; this mixture operates in tandem with or sometimes parallel to an unexamined attitude toward the complexity of mass-cultural formations, or the perpetuation of a Frankfurt School culture-industry disapprobation. This is a heady stew, and, moreover, not every text on the topic shares these features. Some diverge strikingly and profoundly, but my point in assaying the mixture in the first place is to account for the hectic frenzy surrounding the topic and the marketability of responses to pornography.

For feminist critics who are women, the article or the book on pornography has taken on a *de rigeur* status, since pornography is the latest inflection of feminist discourse and appears to have a genuinely extra-academic reality – giving such messages on pornography a political piquancy, activist overtones that are played with the solemnity of organ chords by some (here one would list all the radical feminist texts of Andrea Dworkin, Catharine MacKinnon, Robin Morgan, *et al.*, and works like Joan Huff and Susan Gubar's *For Adult Users Only* and Susanne Kappeler's *The Pornography of Representation*), and in a more playful and tolerant tenor by those opposing censorship of pornography, particularly in the name of feminism (like the *Caught Looking* collective, gay male feminist theorists such as Scott Tucker and Jeffrey Weeks, and literary and social theorists like Andrew Ross and Walter Kendrick, for example). In the back of any feminist's head the little ditty 'pornography is the theory, rape is the practice' is always sounding, whether as mental inspiration or annoyingly reductive muzak. Answering to the real, incontrovertible facts of the rape and battering and murdering of women (the ever-rising statistics that comprise women's actual social lives) more and more has needed to be done by taking a stand on pornography, in part because feminism and pornography have come to be intertwined in the public and political realms. At the risk of simplifying, there is a laudable desire to write about arenas that seem to have genuine political impact, and pornography, as a primarily visual and textual manifestation, can be 'read' by those best trained in critical reading, to the benefit of concrete social policy. That bottom line position also is mirrored in professional terms by the turf wars over feminist theory and the desire to stake out domains for the exercising of feminist critique. Sexism and misogyny having been thoroughly uncovered in the major works of the male authors and painters and so on, it remains to go back over them to find specifically pornographic modes of expression and representation.

It is imperative to deal one's hand early on in any essay on pornography, because positions are always being crystallised in such works, despite the ironically limited number of positions available, in a field whose metier is proliferating positionality. That being the case, it should be said that this article rests on the bedrock foundations, or the missionary position, that pornography is not, perforce and *tout court*, violence to women, that pornography should not be censored or prohibited, except quite obviously in the case of child pornography, where what is being regulated is the abuse of children by adults, and that pornography is not what is wrong with everything, especially not the cause of the hierarchical social relations of domination that obtain between men as a group and women as a group. The social reality of the ongoing domination of women by men can be so frustrating that it is tempting to isolate pornography as the sole basis for its perpetuation, and in some feminist circles it even defies common sense to say that pornography is not violence toward women, so ritualistic has that equation become. Nonetheless, to deny this is to step outside a circle drawn claustrophobically close by mistaken theoretical assumptions and accidents of intellectual and academic history, into a more ambiguous, historical and indeed social understanding of pornography.

My assumptions are general and unwieldy and could be superimposed on theoretical and political premises very different from those I will try to develop here, but in the climate of Jesse Helms and the Reverend Wildmon words cannot be minced. What is intriguing is how often the second proposition against censorship is, albeit reluctantly, conceded, and how rarely the other two claims, that pornography is not simply violence against women and that it is not the root of all gender hierarchy, are stated with vigour, at least in writing about pornography by women. The feminist historian Christine Stansell, for example, has given talks based on her brilliant research into the history of pornography and in particular its ambivalent and even vital relation to American social and sexual change, only to be met with some hostility because the sacrosanct position about 'violence' cannot, in her analyses, be preserved; for perhaps obvious reasons of gender, reactions to Andrew Ross's proposal that pornography has a complicated and important place in social life have been even more severe. In other words, it costs real feminist points to deny that 'pornography' is the appropriate appellation for the social pathology of gender hierarchy and violence; even where the climate is not as frosty to considerations of female desire and sexual fantasy as it is in radical feminist areas of the academy, it is still hard to be unadulteratedly 'for' pornography. The grid of certain feminist theoretical and critical vectors has discovered pornography at the centre of its discursive concerns. It is difficult, but necessary as well, to agree that pornography is important while disagreeing with the constraints on the discussion of it. To displace pornography from the centre by (self-)reflecting on the reasons for its centrality may also dislodge the received ideas about pornography and how it should play in academic/feminist/theoretical/political inquiry.

One leaves those precincts upon entering a book like the off-puttingly named *For Adult Users Only*, edited by Susan Gubar and Joan Huff, with an introduction by the former. To report my own feelings honestly, this book makes almost any seedy tabloid indecency look like a refreshing excursion into normal, carnivalesque perversity, not because all of its contributed essays are so bad, although a number of them are, but because the book smacks of crass bad faith and unbearable academic pretension. The opening essay situates us in this queasy territory, by explaining how the book came to exist, which we are meant to take as a more serious and urgent matter than the publication of, say, another collection of essays on Renaissance literature or a philosophical festschrift. After a paean to the bucolic and middle-class joys of Bloomington, Indiana, where no one had apparently any worries, even during the Reagan era, and academic complacency proceeded without a qualm, Gubar narrates the intrusion of two horrific murders of women upon the peace of the town. The first murder involves a son killing his mother, with whom he has long resided in a trailer home, while the second is described with even more detail because, sadly enough, the victim was a former graduate student in the English department who after apparently suffering a breakdown had begun an eccentric life with numerous cats in a depressed area of town, where she was ultimately violently killed.

These tales are very grim, under any circumstances; what defies belief is that they are adduced as the reason a 'task-force' discussion group on pornography was eventually formed on campus, leading to the publication of the book. This gives the text a self-important 'white paper' or Kerner Commission overtone that comports ludicrously with the contents. An essay by Gubar on Magritte as, basically, surrealist pornography and an essay by Mary Jo Weaver on religion and sexuality are so rhetorically academic and specialised that the notion that a reader is meant to be continually reading with the image of poor dismembered Mrs Adams or the tragically violated graduate student haunting the pages comes to be very disturbing. The frisson of terror and pity elicited by the introductory recital of these murders is then used to segue seamlessly into the 'realm' of pornography, as if the murders had any connection, obvious or abstruse, with the topic. One wonders whether psychopathology, or economic decline, or alcohol or drug-related violence, or any number of other social problem areas might not have suggested themselves first for study, but no, pornography it is, and any balking at this connection implies a lack of concern for the victims hovering before us.

What pornography might be meant, then – (extremely rare) snuff material? Mother/son bondage duos? Not at all. Pornography, it turns out, is the David Lynch film *Blue Velvet*. The segue is dizzyingly fast: from a pair of distressingly familiar murders a diagnostic case is made.

> In *Blue Velvet* (1986), a crazed man tortures a woman whose child he has kidnapped and whom he calls 'mommy' when he repeatedly batters and rapes her. Pumping himself up by breathing through a sinister oxygen mask, the character portrayed by Dennis Hopper reduces his 'mommy' to a fleshy thing presumably because he is still traumatised by the otherness of the first woman in his life, his mother.

And lest *Blue Velvet* account only for the murder of the mother, Mabel Adams, it has gruesome relevance to the killing of Ellen Marks.

> Both *Blue Velvet* and *Angel Heart* evince a fascination with bloody parts that permeates the letter written by the man who may have spent three years planning to dismember Ellen Marks: in the first case, the ears that the psychopath slices off his victims as well as the mouths which he stuffs with pieces of blue velvet...

Gubar follows this assessment with a carefully nuanced treatment of the aesthetic features of the film(s) in question, even including the point made by many that such films can be read as critiques of masculine socialisation. But Gubar can't finally buy that: 'How different, then, are these comparatively ambitious films from *Deep Throat* or *Debbie Does Dallas*?' And later, 'All of the essays in this volume necessarily engage the problem of defining pornography to determine its relationship to violence against women.' The circularity of the argument means that only violence will be found, or that only violence will be found to be the common denominator that allows *Blue Velvet* to be the equivalent of *Debbie Does Dallas*. Of course, it is just as wrong to suppose that the latter film is responsible for the two murders Gubar cites; her manoeuvre goes in two directions and each is equally factitious.

Pornography jumps many disciplinary boundaries and critical barriers in its translation into metapornography, a discourse for all seasons. Many of the implicit assumptions about pornography in feminist theory and criticism have affinities with debates further afield, especially with considerations of consumption and mass culture often unacknowledged in what seem to be much more pressing matters of sexual politics. The subterranean connections are there, however, in myriad guises, especially when pornography is set up as an objectifying and commodifying form of patriarchal expression, and when more subtle differences between pornography and artistic practices are probed.

At the bottom of the so-called pornography debate lies a mystified relation to the conditions of mass culture, and this problem infects the very interpretation of what is pornographic. The visceral energies directed 'at' pornography by social forces concentrate on its visual aspects, on the film, video and photographic incarnations of pornography, largely to the exclusion of its literary modalities, which don't seem to exercise people as thoroughly, except in the academic debates, which often privilege the textual and find 'pornography' in texts many others would consider too dreary to read. While pornographic books and magazines are also mass-produced and consumed, they are less visible as targets of critique or analysis because the prevailing figure for pornographic consumption lies so squarely in the arresting of the visual, in the enthralled spectatorship of the eye, where pornographic images seem to fuse themselves directly to the eye, rather than taking the more circuitous route of the mediation of print. To many commentators, the ease and rapidity of mass cultural consumptive visual strategies is appallingly emblematised by pornography itself, where the languor and voluptuousness of consumption in general gets raised to its apotheosis. As a consequence, visual pornography seems not only worse, but more typical, especially because new visual technologies are rapidly enlisted for pornography production along with the entire range of mass cultural forms and representations.

The model of consumption most often culturally proffered is that of simple assimilation, of the taking in of the consumed object in a mindless or insensate state, the engorgement of pleasure. When this construction or understanding of consumption is simply mapped onto the pornographic scenario of consumption, the metaphorical understanding appears to become doubled and thereby literalised by what pornography actually does – arouse. In other words, if all acts of consumption bear some relation to a mindless infusion of hedonic frenzy, then pornographic consumption adds the quotient of physiological arousal to the intoxicated state of consumer possession in general, which already mimes sexual abandon, at least in these descriptions of it. All the valences of affect used to discuss consumer states of mind come into play with redoubled fervour and seeming relevance when translated into the arena of pornography consumption – satiety, passivity, absorption. Thus part of what is suspect about pornography stems from its ubiquitous availability, and from the proliferation of its visual and verbal forms.

Pornography needs to be understood as a genre, indeed a genre of consumption, with many branches, in order to break down the monolith of 'pornography' that can only serve to turn it into an allegory. To view pornography as a genre would immediately make suspect (in my view, rightly) the tendency to assimilate Milton's *Paradise Lost* or Dante Gabriel Rossetti's poems or Magritte's surrealism to pornography. Pornography might be said to be a quintessentially mixed genre, but not mixed in the sense that it can easily assimilate works like those just cited – instead, mixed in that while a genre of pornography exists, defined in large part by its production and distribution and consumption strategies, which are all sui generis, it has internal divisions and distinctions that follow their own laws of genre over time. For example, the mildly pornographic magazines concentrating on enormous breast size to be found at many newsstands are caught up primarily in extending the genre of the sexual pun. Yes, breasts and their photographic representation are involved, but the magazines exist to establish erotic connections between language and image in the form of somewhat tedious puns – 'Yvonne pours her jugs for you', and so on. This is a far generic cry from the intricate confessional/medical mode of a publication like *Forum*, and both are at a great remove from the genre constraints of *The Police Gazette*. The genre distinctions within pornography are drawn on aesthetic and social grounds; the punning of 'jugs' is related to a working-class British tradition of pun and rhyme melded to sexual content, while *Forum* builds verbal fantasy worlds out of middle-class managerial and professional milieux, interlaced with a vocabulary of the aesthetically upscale, or 'beautiful'. Some genres of pornography have vast historical lineages and equally complex codes; others spring up when a commercial space is suddenly made available in the plenum of capitalised opportunities, like miniature pornographic pictures sold in condom machines newly placed in truck stops.

An objection can be made to this array of genres, of course, by saying that in heterosexual pornography, at least, they all depend on the woman's body, on the objectification of that body for the male subject of desire. It is precisely at that spot that the discourse of objectification – what John Berger memorably calls 'the woman as the to-be-looked-at' – crosses over into the discourse of the object or the commodity, and the result, in discussions of pornography, is to embed objectification, itself conceived of as an either/or, entirely negative phenomenon, in the thickets of consumption, as these objects are invariably seen as something to then be consumed by a subject. The critical geometry is drawn tight, and q.e.d., in pornography the woman is an object to be consumed by the man.

In a sophisticated and trenchant essay, 'The Antidialectic of Pornography', in *Men Confront Pornography*, Joel Kovel takes on this difficulty with mass culture from a Frankfurt School, left-wing perspective that leads him to differentiate pornography and eroticism on the grounds that the former is contaminated by mass culture – in short, that it is mass culture. Eroticism, on the other hand, typified by works by de Sade and Bataille, engages the metaphysical aspects of sexuality untainted by the culture industry, whose adventures into eroticism inevitably produce pornography. Kovel is very careful not to base the pornography/eroticism distinction on moralism, as is so often done; he wants instead to provide an ontological difference between them that will not rest on whether eroticism is 'nicer' to women or more 'reciprocal'. Nonetheless, a moralism of another sort creeps in through the Horkheimer and Adorno back door of culture industry analysis. What is wrong with pornography is that it is a ruthless, totalising system of mass cultural entrapment, freezing its consumers in postures of reification rather than the sportive sexual positions it ostensibly favours. 'From another angle, pornography is the captivity of the erotic within mass culture. It is the erotic less its negativity, less its ambivalence, its association of sexuality with death, and, finally, its truthfulness.' Eroticism makes people think, it offers the autonomy of negative critique, whereas pornographic material is such a slippery consumer slope it can give no purchase to critical thought. As Wittgenstein wrote, 'We need friction. Away from the smooth ground!' Pornography is thus on a par with the depredations of advertising or the induced delusions of television narrative; what it gives proof of is the penetration of capital into yet another legitimate conduit of desire – the desire for sexuality, here trammelled by, made less serious by, its usurpation by mass cultural forms.

This notion of the fallenness of pornography, mass culture's stranglehold on sexuality, requires the avant-gardism of Adorno's theses about the work of art in the modern age, a defiant object of negative critique. If one assumes a less programmatic 'culture industry' capable of brainwashing its consumer victims, and looks instead at mass cultural forms as produced also by their consumers, used and transformed and redeployed, the image of consumption alters considerably. I'm not proposing anything utopian about this transfigured pornographic consumption, nor making the familiar claim that sexuality is always and everywhere transgressive and consequently liberatory. Rather, I want to direct attention to what is usually left out of the equation in discussing consumption, let alone pornographic consumption, which is the work of consumption. Pierre Bourdieu and Michel de Certeau have each helped to theorise this aspect of consumption, Bourdieu by referring to 'that production which is consumption', and de Certeau in his emphasis on the 'tactics of the weak', examining popular culture for its infinite capacity to reorder dominant social hierarchies. John Fiske's *Using Popular Culture* makes explicit this shift, drawing on these two theorists as well as others to sketch out the domain of popular, as opposed to mass, culture – popular culture being what it becomes at the user's end.

Without romanticising the pornographic per se, a similar shift needs to be undertaken in gauging its cultural scenario. In other words, it needs to be accepted that pornography is not 'just' consumed, but is used, worked on, elaborated, remembered, fantasised about by its subjects. To stop the analysis at the artefact, as virtually all the current books and articles do, imagining that the representation is the pornography in quite simple terms, is to truncate the consumption process radically, and thereby to leave unconsidered the human making involved in completing the act of pornographic consumption. Because of the overwhelming focus on the artefacts or representations of pornography, such 'making' has been obscured in favour of simply asserting that these artefacts have a specific or even an indelible meaning, the one read off the representation by the critic. That act of interpretation is at a far remove from what happens in pornographic consumption itself, where the premium is on incorporating or acquiring material for a range of phantasmic transformations. When the pornographic image or text is acquired, the work of pornographic consumption has just begun. Some may feel that by labelling such activity 'work' an overly valorising appraisal is set up; without investing that act of fabrication with any special grandeur, I want to insist that some real consuming 'labour' transpires here too.

What is the nature of this work? Without being facetious, it is not the undoubted minor physical labour needed to complete the arousal, but instead the shuffling and collating and transcription of images or words so that they have effectivity within one's own fantasy universe – an act of accommodation, as it were. This will often entail wholesale elimination of elements of the representation, or changing salient features within it; the representation needs to blur into or become charged with historical and/or private fantasy meanings. To insist on this for pornography flies in the face of one's interest in seeing the mechanical, repetitive or even the alienating qualities of pornography, which are manifest. People in many, if not most, cases do not get the pornography they deserve, or the pornography one might imagine. Still, the pornography debate must move beyond the supposed transparency or univocity of the pornographic artefact to ask highly specific questions about the consumption of pornography by actual persons in radically different situations. One wing of the pornography discussion does, of course, already move beyond the artefact, by assuming that the consumption of pornography injects men with violence toward women, which they then act out, if only in the very fantasy entailed by looking at the pornography. So much historical and social analysis renders this dubious that it may not need to be rehearsed here; a particularly incisive rejoinder is to ask why then pornography does not have the same effect on everyone who reads it or sees it, or how to account for violence against women in its relative absence. Moving beyond that impasse, the crucial issue is to explore how what we now call 'sexuality' is imbricated with pornography's work of consumption, how integrally and intricately and unpredictably pornography figures in the *phantasmic* sexual constructions men and women both engage.

Linda Williams's recent study of pornography, *Hard Core: Power, Pleasure, and the 'Frenzy of the Visible'*, is distinguished by its meticulous focus on genre, and by its dispassionate intertextual untangling of the history of the hard-core film. By zeroing in on a generic realm of pornography, she avoids entirely the impulse to totalise the pornographic that is so endemic to feminist analyses; by taking seriously the conventions, constraints and historical specificity of hard-core film, Williams can show its internal development and its sensitivity to cultural changes and consumer markets. Free-floating 'misogyny' or historically omnipresent 'violence toward women' drop away as explanatory vehicles as the book speculates that pornography intersects with the technologically induced 'frenzy of the visible', mass culture's need to bring to sight what technology can allow to become visible. A key crux of this analysis involves the hard-core film as an instrument for forcing the 'confession' of female sexuality, a demonstration which, ever since Diderot's *Les bijoux indiscrets* as cited by Williams, is doomed to founder on the invisibility and the unknowability of female sexual pleasure. The visual elaboration of this lack runs up against the paradox of invisibility, even in the hardest-core scenario. Williams makes deft use of her thesis, which also happens to mesh with a desire to see pornography as structured around the presiding absence or invisibility of female pleasure.

Williams's adherence to the tenets of feminist film theory produces a fascinating result when set up against the strictures of film pornography. Her thesis overcomes the paralysing limits of Laura Mulvey's original formulations of the objectifying nature of the male gaze as transferred to the film camera, because Williams breaks down that paradigm through finely tuned historical and generic investigation; what remains is the mass cultural/avant-garde binary so deeply embedded in the theoretical practice of film theory. As played out in much of film theory, including Mulvey's seminal essay, narrative is the ideological villain, and the politically progressive film text must be anti-narrative, resisting visual closure at every turn, so that the alienation effects of anti-narrative can do their revelatory work of demystification.

Williams finds her version of this Brechtian cinema within hard core in the sadomasochistic genre, because it is here that sexual identities appear to be less fixed, more labile and mobile. By her own premises Williams is forced to privilege one particular sector of pornographic production over the others, in a sense painted into this corner by the belief that 'unfixed' sexual identities may provide the epiphany such consumers need – the moment of negative critique that will strip away the illusions of sexual hierarchy. What is intriguing is that labile sexual identities are not assumed to inhere in any and all of these representations; this could only be realised by Williams and other prescriptive avant-gardists if the work that consumption pornography, and other mass cultural forms, entails were also recognised. At this moment in her analysis, Williams takes a position of distance from the presumed viewers of such hard-core films, the same rather precious stance of political enlightenment that tends to mar the avant-gardist aesthetic strain of film theory (and its affiliated discourses).

Williams will wait patiently in the audience for this group of pornography consumers to encounter the rupturing moment of gender disidentification and receive their revelation, an epiphany about gender Williams already knows, and which she has not needed pornography to allow her to experience. The problem with this is not that Williams or others have hopes for a utopian overcoming of politically rigid gender identities, but that the hopes rest on a fairly hidden assumption that mass culture is a degraded form within which embryonic avant-garde progressive texts are struggling to get out. Because sadomasochism is performative and theatrical, because it is a mode of 'play', it segues neatly into theories that need to stress the performative and the constructed. This is far, far preferable to the literalist reading so prevalent in the pornography-obsessed world of Andrea Dworkin *et al.*, where sadomasochism is anathema, impossible to view even as representation. If anything, one would wish to have it valorised if only to circumvent such misunderstandings. Still, the uncanny fit between film theory's favourite 'perversion' and the practice of hard core too readily makes for an evolutionary narrative, and then the contingency and the historicity drop out. The pornographic film becomes an exercise in estrangement for its presumably naive viewers, who can build on the revelatory shock of recognition that gender identities are mutable. Julia Kristeva hopes people will read *Finnegan's Wake* to find out the same thing; *chacun à son goût*.

If one problem with theories of pornography is that they in fact disdain consumption, or presume that the real work is done somewhere else, then attention should be paid to the practices of consuming pornography and its nature as an activity. The collection of pornographic images and accompanying essays gathered under the title *Caught Looking* is meant to offer actual pornography to consume, but it turns out to be exemplary of the role of historicity and sheer accident in desire, and can serve as a cautionary document in the forgetting of, the repression of, the work of fantasy entailed by the consumption of pornography. This very delightful and cogent compilation, interlaced with acute brief essays and on-target polemics against censorship, testifies not only to the embeddedness of desire in time, but also, in the modern era, to its embeddedness in fashion, style and image, in patterns of consumption.

A riveting picture of a man rather desultorily having intercourse with a woman on what looks like a cafeteria table before some slightly bemused onlookers is riveting not for the act in progress, the flashes of buttock and pubic hair, but for the incredible sideburns he is sporting, as well as the insouciance of the ribbed poor-boy turtleneck he hasn't had the energy to doff. The turn-of-the-century photo of a woman easing down on a man's penis is remarkable not for its hearty, graphic genital frankness but for the accoutrements of these organs – the outmoded lingerie styles, the moustache, the grainy texture of the photographic technique and the assessment of how long the participants must have had to hold their poses in obedient tumescence. The entire book is alluring not as a pornographic volume, although one or another of these pictures might possibly 'speak' to someone in that voice, but instead as a gloss on the imbrication of mass cultural styles in the pornographic response of modernity. Hair, body language, body morphology, bedroom props only have to be a shade off to sunder any sexual response to the pictures and to instead open up a reverie on the *punctum* of any particular image, a *punctum* which is more mass-cultural than Barthes's rather ahistorical nostalgia for a past, frozen time. An image of two men getting it on on a beach somewhere is difficult to date except for the jeans pulled down to halfmast – those jeans occasion almost infinitely proliferating meditations on James Dean, California, an age of grace.

Caught Looking is an empowering book in that it dares to offer these images under the rubric of feminism itself, a bold move in the Meese Commission climate of its publication (and even bolder under current conditions). What it suggests, too, is the difficulty of intervening in the pornography debates with anything like 'real' pornography, pornography produced out of the academic discourse itself, since the album version of *Caught Looking* is extremely compelling but immediately self-cancelling as pornography. What it violates is the mass cultural contextuality so essential to contemporary pornography. In other words, the reassemblage of 'pornographic' photographic images under the imprimatur of critical consciousness empties out the pornographic moment, a moment that is experienced on the continuum of such pornographic exposures. The pornographic artefact lodges in the meshes of a mass-cultural pornographic discourse, and it does not 'mean' or 'read' as pornographic outside those necessary nets. By singling out images garnered over relatively vast historical and sexual expanses, and then making an inventive bricolage of the resulting singularities, pornography is vitiated.

This is not to preclude someone's finding one of these images such a treasure that they felt compelled to scissor it out and put it to pornographic (masturbatory) use; what it does mean, though, is that the collection isn't pornography and never will be. Pornography registers *in relation*; each pornographic 'item' speaks the name of its fellows, distinguished along lines of genre, activity, character, or medium. When that relation is violated by creating a pornographic miscellany, a type of art is formed or posited – each piece of the collection is given singular, auratic status by virtue of how we look at it. This is not how mass culture functions, and as a consequence, pornography withers in its absence.

The academic surfeit of texts on pornography does not arise uncontextually itself; it has been fostered by or is reactive to the intense cultural concern with pornography, which it echoes. This context is not always explicitly about pornography, and requires another term to locate it on the social spectrum. Social pornography is the best phrase I can muster for the substitutive collective pornographies our culture produces; social pornography is the name for the pornographic fantasies the society collectively engenders and then mass-culturally disseminates, usually in the cause of anti-pornography. The past decade's fascination with explicit and imaginary child sexual abuse is the best example, although there are many others, not the least of which is the public discussion of pornography, which allows for pornographic enactment in the most explicit if mediated forms. (The Wildmon attacks on what it calls 'gay pornography' are stunning creations of gay pornography; Wildmon et fils ignore legal and explicit gay pornography, i.e. magazines, to rant about a gay pornography they discern in various art works or films, necessitating their arcanely hermeneutic explanations, social pornography to perfection.) The graphic replication in the media of the acts alleged to have been committed in the McMartin preschool trial, for example, allowed an astonishing social fixation on sexual acts and sexualised children's bodies to flow into public discourse unimpeded, in the guise of a repudiation of these acts.

A most unintentionally amusing contribution to the social pornography discourse is offered by David Mura in *A Male Grief*. These latter-day confessions of a pornography eater are remarkable for the way they consolidate the incipient discourses that flutter about pornography and suck from its stem, to wit, addiction, sexual abuse, male feminism and confessional mania. While Mura has written a very interesting book on his visit to Japan as a Japanese American, has contributed to the Greywolf multicultural annual, and so on, *A Male Grief* is highly problematic, and can help to demonstrate the uneasy place of mass culture in the profusion of discussion on pornography, because it is lodged so tightly within various mass cultural forms and yet considers itself a *cri de coeur*, a departure from the pornographic. Pornography is shown to be a disease; like heart attacks or alcoholism it is a disease that strikes the already vulnerable, those made vulnerable by the perversion of family bonds through alcohol abuse.

This criticism is not meant to minimise the devastating impact of the sexual abuse of children, nor to question the importance of its exposure; what must be addressed is the slippage of an addiction theory into a singular explanation for interest in pornography. The etiology of pornography 'addiction' is traced directly to several rather murkily presented acts of abuse by an uncle figure; ironically, these sections are the most 'poetic' in form and, in this text filled with solecism and ungainly writing, are the best-written and most evocative interludes, presumably because they reflect the fact that Mura, a poet, is on shaky ground in more sustained modes of exposition. The notion that other men might read, look at or be otherwise absorbed in pornography for different reasons, or with less haunted and urgent sensations than those he reports, seems never to strike him; the 'secret' of pornography is revealed, and its Rosetta Stone is child sexual abuse. Mura embraces woman-against-pornography attitudes with wholehearted approval – yes, he is one of those men who have done violence to women in their thoughts by the very act of rushing home from the convenience store and burying themselves in *Hustler*.

No doubt an actual addiction to pornography can exist, and can be infinitely painful and poignant. The answer to such addictions is not to define all pornography as such an addiction, nor to claim that what was unfortunate about the addiction in this case was 'violence toward women'. Mura portrays himself in the piece as out of touch with women altogether, and instead incredibly eager to have some time to read his magazines. There are few male commentators more eager to embrace the views of Andrea Dworkin and Catharine MacKinnon, *et al.*, with a disconcerting, enthusiastically hysterical cry of 'mea culpa, mea maxima culpa!'

> In this particular case, the argument that pornography is 'natural' ignores the fact that there are men who have given up their obsession with pornography and who have not died... Even if men's desire for pornography is natural (i.e., genetically determined), this does not mean we must recognize it as good or inevitable. We do not turn to the diabetic and say, there is nothing you can do, you must enjoy your disease.

It's true what they say, Mura concurs, and, moreover, it can't be helped – men have a tragic addiction to pornography arising out of the dysfunctional family, and the solution will require its own version of a twelve-step programme and abstention from pornography for life. Would this last were even possible: alcohol can be avoided, with some difficulty, by staying away from bars and package stores and ordering alternative beverages; pornography will wink out at you from every billboard and husting, from matchbook covers and *Life* magazine covers and mainstream TV. Women, of course, have nothing to do with pornography; they are uninterested in it, and even if abused they express their victimage in less damaging, or more victimlike, ways. One wonders if Mura's wife was buying romance novels at the supermarket to counter his men's magazines; what Ann Snitow refers to as 'pornography for women' might give Mura a turn if he read some of it. The judicious exclusion of women from the torments of pornographic addiction is partially due to Mura's notion that they do not possess an 'objectifying' sexual desire, or maybe any desire, but also springs from his certainty that women are not as connected to this form of consumption.

The disease model of pornography denies phantasmic necessity for pornographic representation at all; there is no safe 'level' of consumption, helpfully linking pornography with the new American view of drug use, where even that one puff of marijuana inhaled at a party in 1973 has left discernible scars on the internal moral soul. However, men are not to blame – they are victims, compensating for the scourge of sexual abuse with the elixir of pornography. An ecstatic round-robin is set up, a sort of circle jerk of social pornography, which helps to show how deeply implicated pornography is at all levels of mass culture, even those levels that would fervently deny such complicity. It is more typical to assume that these discursive forces are conflictually engaged; for example, that the upsurge in trials of daycare operators for child sexual abuse is a counter-swing of the pendulum that has pornography at its nether end, so to speak. The phenomena seem more intimately tied than that; the enlarging and eager audience for the recital of child sex abuse details has more to do with making the everyday pornographic in its familiar sites, those of the home, the school, the day-care centre. In any such discussion one has to take enormous pains to acknowledge that the silence that formerly prevailed on the prevalence of sex abuse, especially within the home, and the silencing of its many victims, preponderantly but not exclusively female, was of course an atrocious wrong. To imagine that the audience for all the hyperbolically embellished sexual descriptions in the Hilary Foretich case had as its primary interest the salvaging of the child's life, though, is quite absurd. 'Hilary', as a media construct, was a deliciously harrowing Alice in Wonderland of social pornography.

The nadir of arguments about pornography could be said to be reached with Susanne Kappeler's book, *The Pornography of Representation*. This excruciatingly reductive work fills the slot allocated to a seemingly 'Marxist' feminist critique of pornography, since Kappeler throws out words like 'commodity' and 'capitalism' at strategic junctures, a critique which by extension includes all of representation. Simplistic arguments and poor reasoning aside, *The Pornography of Representation* bears scrutiny because it fascinatingly demonstrates the farther, wilder shores of the feminist pornography battle; ultimately, all representation becomes, or is, suspect. Whatever this text may think it is doing, it is really a book about the perils and dangers of representation, which of course includes not only art in every form, but the very representational nature of human language and psychic structure. Pornography is imbricated in every representation, because representation is 'the reification of the message'. Kappeler wishes to sweep this away with one broom, so that in place of complicitous representation of any and all stripes, women could set 'communication'.

If anything is to be done about pornography, if a cultural shift in consciousness (revolution, not coup d'état) will eventually move away from pornographic structures of perception and thought, then the arts themselves will necessarily also have to change, Art will have to go.

That final admission is the one Kappeler has been avoiding throughout the book, while its *sotto voce* muttering has been implicit under the text's breath. Somehow, women will produce new forms of communication practices, not what we now know is suspect – Art. How is it that women will be exempt from or immune to the omnipresent regime of pornographic representation? A touching and befuddled Marxism provides the answer: women – all women, even Margaret Thatcher – are outside the hegemonic power structure, and they are just waiting for the chance to escape its nets and begin the perceptual millennium.

> If women, black people, workers, listeners were allowed to contribute to the culture's description of 'its' condition, Hegel might be challenged, the dominant versions of the partial collectivities of the family, of the brotherhood, of the mafia, of the nation, of the first world, might be rejected as unacceptable models of groups that are based on self-interest rather than solidarity.

All oppression is homologous in Kappeler's analysis, and all dominations run together: capitalists are pornographers are wife-beaters are slave-owners who keep pets. (Kappeler devotes a chapter to a delirious historical free-for-all that links the bourgeois keeping of pets to the commodification of women as sexual 'pets', seemingly unaware that in that case she has failed to consider the vast proportion of women not so favoured by class or whose gender oppression is poorly modelled on the paradigm of the family pet or even the imprisoned zoo animal, Kappeler's other indictment of the nineteenth-century male.) Aesthetic endeavours of any kind are simply part of this large conspiracy, men's demonic attempts to use women as sex objects or 'speech' objects (men do all the talking in Kappeler's universe). 'Pornography' is really Kappeler's name for the conspiracy of patriarchy; it is the quintessence of domination, hegemony's substrate, the reified, metaphysical form of power itself.

Kappeler's argument has the virtue of being deeply symptomatic, a ground-zero representation of the pornographic. Ironically, what Kappeler wants to deny, to expunge, to vilify and to overthrow is representation; to achieve this end, within analysis at least, women become the purest victims of a pornographic regime, the very name for gender hierarchy. *The Pornography of Representation* has a goofy dignity achieved through its haphazard amalgam of quasi-Marxist analysis and aesthetic *ressentiment*. What it ignores is that there is nothing outside representation, including language, the eminently representational. Kappeler's book is deeply symptomatic of the intimate tie between pornography and the representations of culture in general, especially those of literature and the plastic arts. Her slash-and-burn thesis cannot sustain its own logic, but one remembers how tenuous maintaining the differences between cultural objects proves to be. Allan Bloom locates the downfall of American civilisation in the ravishments of Mick Jagger's pelvic gyrations, sufficient to thrust aside the greater merits of Plato and Nietzsche. His position is simply ludicrous, predicated as it is on his own fantasy of and desire for the cultural power of those protean hips, and his certitude that without mass culture the young would be safely ensconced in the library; still, it points to an undercurrent in the academic pornography market. Pornography is sexy, and so is writing about it; pornography can't and won't replace political philosophy, but it does bring to the fore all the worries our culture has about representation and its lack of guarantees.

A central difficulty in adjudicating this debate, or even in participating in it, is the essentialisation of 'sexuality' that is the often invariable accompaniment. Sexuality in this reified form gets parcelled out over the population, atomised as individuals with 'a sexuality'. At times this refers to the broad division hegemonically made by society in characterising heterosexual and homosexual behaviour, in order to legally proscribe the latter and to police the forms of the former. At other moments, sexuality refers to the supposed essence of one's sexual being, one's sexual feelings or orientation or particular slot on the spectrum of speciality tastes. These macroscopic definitions are necessary and inevitable, but they also serve to skew discussions of the place of the pornographic and its role in sexuality. A more supple and elastic conception of sexualities – not, however, the forfeiting of sexual identities or discrete practices linked to those identities – such as is suggested in the dispersal of sexuality across several ambiguous 'types' of its practice in our everyday lives, could help to dislodge the essentialised sexuality of contemporary discourse, which gives rise to, among other noxious things, the Dworkin view of male sexuality, where intercourse is, simply, rape.

Sexuality might better, or more richly, be conceived as discontinuous or adjacent practices, many or most of which are not enacted, multiple formations with loose, instead of rigid, psychosocial affiliation. A possible metaphor for the interaction of these sexualities might be sedimentation, or, more conceptually put, overdetermination again, although one could also, in order to preserve a singular sexuality, describe this as a sexual economy with numerous simultaneous circuits. Among these layers, there is a sexuality emanating from family relations, a family romance that never disappears and is not simply absorbed into 'adult' sexuality. Childhood sexuality remains as more than a residue or a sublimated resource; it is not 'outgrown' or transformed only, but continues to exist as a rich social dimension of sexual practice, even where it is seemingly forgotten. A vector of sexuality is concerned with animals and the natural world; here I'm not speaking of bestiality or of anything considered perverse, but of the utterly familiar and undeniably sexual relations people exhibit with their pets and their sexual attraction to other animals. A specific sexuality belongs to the realm of images and phantasmic representations; these highly charged relations are a practice unto themselves. A considerable amount of the sexual economy can be given over to this circuit, which tends then to seem to be 'sexuality' emerging in some straightforward preference for particular images. Here is where pornography enters in, showing why it is too simple to annex pornography to one invariant sexual mode of being, or to one invariant attitude toward women. Pornography consumption is or can be one quite distinct realm of sexual behaviour as transcribed onto images, words, memories, repetitions. It is only a part of an ensemble or a constellation of sexual possibilities and realities, and its isolation in most current discussions is formidably at odds with its highly particular, material, and contingent places in the spectrum of individually constructed sexualities.

Scott Tucker's recent essay, 'Gender, Fucking and Utopia' (*Social Text* 27), makes a beautiful and idiosyncratic argument for the necessity of representation and the multiple iconographies of pornography, and offers a powerful statement against sexuality as a pure 'social fiction'. Tucker is not willing to dispense with nature quite so easily, not in the form of a 'natural' sexuality, but as a determinant of and a limitation on all human existence. Gay pornography is the most telling revision of the thesis that pornography is violence against women; certain theorists have had to turn cartwheels to assimilate gay male pornography to the dire objectification thought to run rampant in heterosexual pornography. Tucker's stance on this – himself a gay male pornography star, among other professional accomplishments – reverberates with the truth: 'I don't doubt our current identities are too restrictive; I also don't doubt that definable identities will emerge even in utopia.'

To conclude is to mediate on the perilous nature of the object. The academic market is hot for pornography because pornography is both the object and the subject of desire, the representation and the reader, the consumer and the consumed, in one inextricable package. We need to resist the reification of pornography into one singular phenomenon or social form, to acknowledge its multiplicity, to accept that people transform the mass-cultural objects that come before them in a variety of ways, to admit that men and women develop their own pornographic lexicons, whether through entirely home-made images or in purchased form, and to see that 'objectification' need not be in itself a violent act. Objectification in the liminal form of images or words encountered in private may in fact be a *sine qua non* of desire; how this is translated into social relations of equality and justice is a pressing issue, if not *the* pressing issue, but about pornography it can fairly be said 'you can't get there from here.' The charge of 'pornography' has again become a potent cultural weapon, and at this moment it is more crucial to support the potential for transgression and critique still inherent in pornography as an outlaw discourse, than obsessionally to pursue the hidden inner secret of the pornographic as violent or objectifying. In our lust to pronounce on pornography, we measure our envy of the truly consumable, and consuming, text.

Reprinted from *Transition*, issue 54, pp. 68-89, by kind permission of Oxford University Press, Inc.

Works Cited

Ellis, Kate, *et al.* (eds.). *Caught Looking: Feminism, Pornography and Censorship* (Seattle, WA: Real Comet Press, 1988).

Gubar, Susan and Huff, Joan (eds.). *For Adult Users Only: The Dilemma of Violent Pornography* (Bloomington: Indiana University Press, 1989).

Kappeler, Susanne. *The Pornography of Representation* (Cambridge: Polity Press, 1986).

Kimmel, Michael S. (ed.). *Men Confront Pornography* (New York: Crown Publishers, 1989).

Mura, David. *A Male Grief* (Minneapolis: Milkweed Editions).

Williams, Linda. *Hard Core: Power, Pleasure, and the 'Frenzy of the Visible'* (Berkeley: University of California Press, 1989).

MAUREEN TURIM

The Erotic in Asian Cinema

Since the mid-60s, various Asian cinemas have embraced erotic imagery as central to their production; this tendency has developed historically at slightly different times and in different ways in specific countries, depending on individual governments' and industries' regulation of sexual imagery and on the larger social milieu. It often came as a shattering of codes of restraint in the depiction of sexuality and desire that had foreclosed any depiction of intimacy or touching, and had even forbidden the Western symbol of such intimacy, the kiss. If I choose to address this issue of the development of erotic imagery comparatively across East Asia, it is because recent events have brought aspects of pornographic and sexual imagery in East Asia into the news; new laws, which I will discuss later, have been adopted in India and Japan and China, while Hong Kong has been the site of film industry protests that are linked to its role as a leading exporter of Asian pornography. Furthermore, as I will also discuss later, the domination of pornographic film production has contributed to edging out other genres in several countries, threatening the ability to finance other types of film. Still, the issue of explicitly erotic imagery is a complex, contextual one, seen often, particularly in Asia, as a progressive outlet for political expression; this essay does not ignore the multiplicity of meanings coinhabiting this genre. It does not, even implicitly, call for censorship. Yet it is not simply an argument appreciating all pornography. Rather, it re-examines the representation of power and the force of attraction of Asian erotic imagery in the present context of East Asian distribution, hoping for analytical understandings of the forces at work in the production and reception of such images.

Let me begin then with a quote I came across which forcefully posed for me the question of the social context of East Asian eroticism. In his *Cool Memories*, Jean Baudrillard provides a revealing hint of the danger of ignoring political context in addressing this issue, when through his cynical and ironic voice the most sexist and exploitative thoughts echo when discussing the sexual tourism that has made Thailand (as well as

Singapore and the Philippines) sites of widespread prostitution for foreign as well as local consumers of sexual commerce:

> The Women of Thailand are so beautiful that they have become the hostesses of the Western world, sought after and desired everywhere for their grace, which is that of a submissive and affectionate femininity of nubile slaves – now dressed by Dior – an astounding sexual come on in a gaze which looks you straight in the eye and a potential acquiescence to your every whim. In short, the fulfilment of Western man's dreams. Thai women seem spontaneously to embody the sexuality of the Arabian Nights, like the Nubian slaves in ancient Rome. Thai men, on the other hand, seem sad and forlorn; their physiques are not in tune with world chic, while their women's are privileged to be the currently fashionable form of ethnic beauty. What is left for these men but to assist in the universal promotion of their women for high-class prostitution? (p. 168)

We might simply conclude after reading these thoughts that orientalism survives all pretence at the postmodern, or simply dismiss the more recent Baudrillard as the rambling reflexive gestures of a man whose self-consciousness pathetically lacks any awareness or insight on the very issues he addresses. For to frame Thai prostitution in this manner, to the exclusion of considerations of poverty, child labour, indentured servitude and coercion, sexism, AIDS and other sexually associated diseases, or an authoritarian government seeking a balance of payments surplus and a tourist trade at any price to its own people, is to ignore what is at stake in the interdependent economies of sex, power and finance in Southeast Asia. It is to act as an 'innocent' tourist at an erotic show in which others' suffering does not matter as long as one's own pleasure (or detachment) is guaranteed by the next boat or plane out, permitting one's memories to remain cool.

These are the kinds of questions I have been confronting as an outgrowth of my research on the films of Nagisa Oshima, films in which eroticism is coupled with both innovative filmic expression and ideological critique. I wish now to examine the broader theoretical frame necessary to understand the erotic in an Asian context, particularly in connection with issues of mass-market pornography and gendered representations of power. Before I can simply address the Oshima films as attempts at liberating sexuality and linking it to rebellion, I feel I must see even the involvement of such radical voices as Oshima's in the framework of Asian sex industries. The commerce in the imagery of sexualised bodies specifically in East Asia must be seen in the larger history and current patterns of sexual commerce and oppression in these countries, problematising a singularly liberating reading of sexual display, pornography and prostitution in the area.

Recent events in Hong Kong suggest the need to rethink the frame, to take into account the sociological implications of the culture industry as manipulating Asian sexual desires for international profit. On 15 January 1992, actors, actresses and other production personnel marched under banners proclaiming 'show business against violence', to protest against the domination and intimidation of sectors of the Hong Kong film industry by Triads (Hung Men, organised crime syndicates) such as the Sun Yee On and the Big Circle. Stars talked in the Chinese-language *Oriental Daily*, Hong Kong's largest-circulation newspaper, of being forced, sometimes at gunpoint or under threat of repeated rape, to shoot scenes against their will, or of being coerced into participating in productions they opposed. In other words, the violence and sexuality depicted on screen apparently depended on similar tactics used to force performers to lend their bodies to the representation being produced. The *Far Eastern Economic Review* analyses the current situation as an outgrowth of the triads' involvement in local, small-budget pornography that has grown into a mass-consumption pornography market. Hong Kong has become a major producer of both hardcore and softcore pornography, though it is joined by Taiwan, Korea and Japan, particularly in the softcore markets. As others have remarked, limitations on representing genitalia, for example in Japan, have been a factor in pushing much of East Asian pornography towards sadomasochistic representations and to the exclusion of non-violent depictions of sexuality. However, this explanation seems to me only partial; if it assumes a moment in which, if allowed, the unrepressed depiction of genitalia would have decreased sadomasochism, it is hard to believe that any such alternative would have eliminated it. Sadomasochism has other appeals, and the explanation of its dominance in certain pornographic imagery should be coupled with other factors, such as the exploitation of misogyny and the appeal to desires to contain women socially, economically and sexually.

Already in the 60s, Japanese pornography was taking the direction of emphasising narratives and scenes of brutality, rape and bondage. We can recall how Wakamatsu was celebrated by Noël Burch as a 'primitive' and as an auteur of pornography primarily for his *The Embryo Hunts in Secret* (Taiiji ga mitsuryo suru toki, 1966). The film is a *huis clos* examination of a sadist submitting a female captor to increasingly escalating violence in his apartment. Wakamatsu's is a disturbingly intense film that through its unrelenting, repetitious fixation on attacks and forced submissions sustains a compulsion that does not allow the viewer a comedic response to its excesses, except as a rejection of its premises. In other words, its aesthetic impulses force a complicity with its lust for violence, which is precisely what makes it such an extreme and unsettling example of the way pornography, rather than other forms of sexuality, became an outlet for desires for overpowering the Other. If in the end the victim escapes and then returns to kill her torturer, this ending is a weak, but intriguing, guilt reaction to the pleasure the film has suggested can be found in a fantasy of unrestrained violent negation of the will of the Other. As a gesture of repressive retribution of a desire relentlessly evoked and celebrated, it hovers over the closure of the film as an ironic justification of all that came before, permitting the fantasy in a way that a simple ending with the woman's corpse would not.

What ghostly traces of women haunt this film and others like it? What memories evoke a guilt that solicits this pleasure in violence towards women? One way to answer this question is to extend the obvious psychological cue offered by this film itself, which locates the violence in the Oedipal fascination with the mother of the film's embryonic hunter, as depicted in the flashback sequences to the sadist's childhood, his primal scenes of paternal violence and his desire to be once again inside his mother as adored and peaceful foetus. We might simply extend this psychology of character to a psychoanalytic reading of male Japanese lust and ambivalence toward the maternal, but I think it is also necessary to seek additional historical answers by looking at past events in Japanese history. For example, the forcible establishment of brothels by the imperialist Japanese military during the Pacific War, finally acknowledged by the Japanese government in its recent apology to Korea, reveals a link between nationalist conquest, violence and assumptions of the sexual servitude of others to the Japanese male population. In the postwar period, such events were mostly denied. With the general denial and refusal to investigate this past comes the desire to repeat this experience (Japanese businessmen comprise a substantial part of the sexual tourism to brothels in Singapore, the Philippines, Thailand and elsewhere) and to give it renewed, but indirect and imaginary, life in pornographic fantasy representations. If the pornographic scene is the site of a displaced lust and a nostalgia for power over the Other, its appropriation to an expression of rebellion against the state seems more problematic than ever.

We might also compare the issues raised by Southeast Asian brothels in the present and the earlier brothels, called *karayuki*, in which Japanese peasant women were procured into overseas prostitution in China and India. Historian Tomoko Yamizaki has traced the imperialist purposes of such brothels (first set up in the 1920s), both in providing foreign currency at a point when Japan needed such currency to balance its trade, and in allowing for economic penetration of foreign countries through the merchants and, eventually, communities that surrounded the brothels. Shohei Imamura's documentary film *Karayukisan: The Making of a Prostitute* (1975) traces this history, and Kumio Kei's *Sandakin 8* (1974) is a fictional adaptation of Yamazaki's work and one of the most directly feminist and anti-imperialist films ever produced in Japan, as it traces the efforts of a female anthropologist to uncover the history of the *karayukisan* through field work in Borneo. Prostitution and pornography have different statuses, one a service industry in which individuals perform acts, the other a culture industry of representation and artistic expression. Yet from another perspective, the obvious differences blur when both are considered within a sector of the entertainment industry in world commerce, which we might call sexual entertainment. In East Asia in the nineteenth and twentieth centuries, the historical fluctuation of patterns of supply and consumption of both prostitution and pornography are linked to larger patterns of East Asian trade and the ascendancy of certain nations as economic and political powers. Furthermore, since both institutions are marginal and in disrepute, though sometimes sanctioned and exploited by governments, they are subject to the domination of the most criminal and corrupt of capitalists. When Yamizaki points out the legitimation of these industries in government policy planning, she is speaking to the willingness of the Japanese government to embrace its illegal sectors.

Some of these quandaries are taken up in a film by Imamura, *The Pornographers* (Jinruigaku nyumon), also from 1966. The narrative follows the work and personal life, as well as the memories and fantasy life, of an independent pornographer, Ogata, who makes short sex films in Super 8. Prefiguring the situation in Hong Kong, his artisanal pornographic production is usurped by Yakusa, a gang called the 'crow organisation'. The film's comedic treatment is coupled with a systematic framing within the image, in which grids, bars and multiple windows construct not only the boundaries of a voyeuristic pleasure but the imprisonment of desire. While often seen as self-conscious, the film raises complex questions as a fiction and a spectacle which the label 'self-conscious' does not completely address. What are we to make of the depiction of pornography as artisanal production at a time when half the films made in Japan are in the pornographic genre and in which major studios, such as Nikkatsu, which had earlier made its fortunes in youth and gangster films, began to specialise in pornography? Is this a form of denial of the actual industrial dimensions of Japan's pornographic production? Or is it simply irrelevant, as the conflicts of an individual about the means and meaning of his pornographic preoccupation are explored? Or are we to take metaphorically the difficulty of finding stars for these small-scale productions, so that, when Ogata's last film in *The Pornographers* depends on the exploitation of a young mentally retarded girl, this becomes a generalised commentary on extremes of coercion? The use of metaphor and allegory here might be necessitated by fear of Yakusa retaliation, as demonstrated by the recent beating of film director Juzo Itami by the Yakusa for his film depicting their brutality and their penetration of the Japanese economy.

What I find most interesting about *The Pornographers* is that its very multiplicity, coupled with its lengthy, reiterative form, displays the ambiguity in the relationship of artistic meta-commentary and the pornographic enterprise. Coexisting in the same culture industry, feeding off each other as they do in 1960s Japan, they allow perhaps no ideology of aesthetics to enable us finally to distinguish the two-bit pornographer of *The Pornographers* from the artist using the erotic or pornographic genre, or from the industrial giants trading in pornographic distribution. Certainly legal rubrics, for example those proposed in the US as 'socially redeeming values', only imply an intentionality, a content analysis and a dominant aesthetic and morality from the outset, rather than a study of visual representation and the complexity of ethics in images and narration. Further, much pornography is meta-critical and self-conscious at some level, so the argument that degrees of meta-commentary distinguish different regimes of erotic functioning can get surprisingly circular, and imply that there is something 'lower' about the art of direct arousal of sexual feelings.

These are precisely the issues surrounding the name Oshima, issues that were largely evaded since his forays into the pornographic came after his political and artistic reputation was established. His highly articulate interviews and writings present both his personal fixation on pornography and violence and his conception of his films as political allegories about sexual desire. Yet from the outset the marketing of his films depended on an appeal to youth and pornography markets; *The Sun's Burial*, for example, was promoted in English-language press materials aimed at the Asian market as softcore porn. Coinciding with the biographical, intellectual and personal expression came a resourceful tapping of the desires of a preconstituted market with an admittedly transformed product, one that had many more textual implications and interweavings of problems posed by the erotic text in a political context.

By the mid-60s, at the moment when Oshima returned to feature production after a two-year hiatus, his films such as *Pleasures of the Flesh* (Etsuraku, 1965) and *Violence at Noon* (Hakuchu no torima, literally 'Ghost at Midnight', 1966) are studies in sadism, obsession and torture not unlike the themes and visual motifs favoured by the pornographic genre. Yet what is significant in each of these films is the juxtaposition of erotic violence with its context and consequences. Still, as the comparison between Noburu Tanaka's *The True Story of Abe Sada* (1975) and Oshima's *In the Realm of the Senses* (1976) shows, though the first film may appear more conventional in its codifications, more predictable and less rich in innovation than Oshima's, there is never any clear line between generic pornography and the sophisticated erotic text. Ironically, not even certain distinctions made by some feminists regarding eroticism will hold, as the Tanaka film seems to grant Abe Sada more subjectivity, more development as a character, than does Oshima's film, which, as part of his overall strategy of undercutting the unity and fullness of character, maintains a much more opaque and contradictory representation of this character.

Oshima's *In the Realm of the Senses* plays a crucial role in the history of Asian eroticism for another reason. It forced the question of visual representation of genitalia and coitus in Japan and in other Asian countries where such images were still against the law. The trial which Oshima's film engendered couldn't save the film from the masking of genitalia in its Japanese release; Oshima then published his speculations on the political significance of this trial in a move quite similar to Brecht's article on the *Threepenny Opera* copyright infringement trial, using the decisions as an opportunity to argue a critical cultural theory. It is ironic, then, that Japan's recent reconsideration of hardcore representation was instigated by Jacques Rivette's film, *La Belle Noiseuse* (1991), in which a nude model is shown posing for a painter, not for a short scene but for so much of the narrative that distributors argued that masking the pubic area would destroy the film. The artist and model theme, which is one of the images that began filmic eroticism in the nickelodeon period, might be considered 'art' enough to obtain the first exclusion to the law ever granted a film in Japan (photographic exhibition has received earlier exceptions). If this nervousness towards pubic representation seems particularly anachronistic and convoluted in contemporary Japan, it does indicate how an arbitrary prohibition on a given representation can quickly become absurd and why pornography often gets a radical charge simply because the state becomes its enemy. The statistics on hardcore pornography confiscated in luggage checks at Narita airport indicate that the maintenance of such prohibitions in the age of video simply means that the government gets no economic returns by forcing its citizens to become cultural smugglers.

The situation in Japan makes an intriguing comparison with that of the People's Republic of China. In the PRC, underground pornography merits first and foremost being considered as a form of political resistance. In his article 'Hand-Copied Entertainment Fiction', historian Perry Link looks at texts that circulated during the Cultural Revolution, including pornographic ones. The sample pornographic text he summarises was not only widely read in China but was published in Hong Kong under a different name; it celebrates sexual encounters between a young student and her cousin, which end when he is sent to study in the Soviet Union. The heroine later marries another man, enjoys similar pleasure with him and never suffers any detrimental consequences from her actions. Female pleasure without negative consequence may stay within the confines of male fantasies of adoration and female accessibility, but the whole tone of the story challenges the ethics of discipline, sacrifice and control that characterised the Cultural Revolution. Further, this text seems so light and joyous compared to the brutality and the obsessive qualities of some Japanese pornography that one imagines that these underground texts might supply East Asia with alternative models of eroticism if made more available. One sees the relationship between this narrative and Zhang Yimou's *Ju dou*, a film significantly subject to internal censorship that forbids its screening in the PRC. The current government has seen the eroticism of its young directors in economic terms. It promotes their production to ensure a balance of trade through a double mechanism, gaining both through the investment by foreigners who co-produce these films (Hong Kong, Taiwan, Britain and France) and also from revenues earned from foreign distribution.

In the case of Korea, Hyeonseok Seo argues that restraints on production and the popularity of foreign products made it 'a common industry strategy to produce sexual images in order to reach the largest audience possible'. The inclusion of erotic scenes becomes a market strategy for a national industry seeking to maintain its viability and leads to a 'double exploitation of the female body' in Seo's terms, meaning that even as sexual exploitation is depicted in the films, it is being simultaneously marketed by the films.

Pornographic imports now come under new laws in India. Since 1984, Indians living overseas can finance the importation of foreign pornography, which the government taxes. India is in many senses a worst case, as all legal pornography is foreign, produced in the US, Europe and Hong Kong. Meanwhile, restrictions on sexual depictions in Indian-made films remain severe. If industry sources report how soft-porn movies are edging out the Bombay-made musical melodramas that for years packed theatres in cities and villages, as noted by Sheila Tefft, such statements need to be seen in the context of struggles for domination of the national film market. While foreign pornography is considered by some a threat to the Indian film industry and may be affecting the number of films that can be made in India's different languages other than the official Hindi, Paul Willemen usefully points out that disparate groups are now attacking pornography (and videotape in general) on 'moral' and political grounds, as well as for being a threat to commercial Indian cinema. 'Softcore pornography' is therefore a highly politicised term, even a code-word, according to Willemen, one which has various meanings when used by separate groups. Sexual representation in Indian cinema thus interacts with complex issues of cultural domination tied to colonialisation and issues of ethnic diversity in India.

There are diverse economic incentives for Asian countries, especially those with large numbers of displaced males in their labour forces, increasingly to seek to regulate and profit from pornographic enterprise. It does seem that traditions of banning pornography are being transformed, but unevenly, in response to market forces and through loopholes in import laws. That this comes at a time when issues of national and regional identity and female equality have a renewed urgency means that the analysis of these images has much to reveal about how these cultures are responding to these challenges in the realm of sexuality.

Some Asian feminists have organised against pornography in Japan and India. It is certainly possible to understand their anger and depression as they confront scenes of symbolic subjugation. Pornography is only fantasy, but in many instances its fantasies emanate from historically and psychoanalytically masculine perspectives, confirming a cycle of guilty lust in which images of female degradation seem to play a necessary and fundamental role.

What I have attempted to do here is to set the complex stage for an alternative to censorship that still responds to the way in which pornography and eroticism are the troubled shadows of gender and national power histories, the troubled shadows whose most unresolved shades are exploited both by gangsters and by states. Yet this very problematic terrain is inevitably that to which contemporary art and culture must return, for similar historical, psychoanalytical and even economic reasons.

Works Consulted

Anderson, Joseph, and Richie, Donald. *The Japanese Film: Art and Industry* (Princeton, NJ: Princeton University Press, 1982).
Baudrillard, Jean. *Cool Memories*, trans. Chris Turner (London and New York: Verso, 1990).
Brecht, Bertolt. 'Der Dreigroschenprozess', *Gesammelte Werke in 20 Banden* (Frankfurt: Suhrkamp, 1967), p. 18, trans. in *The Three Penny Opera* (New York: Ungar, 1984).
Burch, Noël. *To the Distant Observer: Form and Meaning in the Japanese Cinema* (Berkeley and Los Angeles: University of California Press, 1979).
Cooke, Kieran. 'Survey of Singapore', *Financial Times*, 1 June 1992, p. 1.
Desser, David. *Eros plus Massacre* (Bloomington and Indianapolis: Indiana University Press, 1988), pp. 82–6.
Handley, Paul. 'The Lust for Frontier: Sex Trade is So Entrenched that Neither Aids nor Embarrassment Threatens It', (Thailand) *Far Eastern Economic Review*, 2 November 1989, p. 4.
'Japan Apologizes on Korea Sex Issue; Miyazawa, In Seoul, Regretful over Women Forced Into Prostitution in War', *New York Times*, 18 January 1992, p. 2.
Lau, Emily, 'Hand in Glove: Triad Boss Alleges Police Collusion', *Far Eastern Economic Review*, 31 May 1990, p. 11.
Lent, John A. *The Asian Film Industry* (Austin: University of Texas Press, 1990).
Link, Perry. 'Hand-Copied Entertainment Fiction', in Perry Link, Richard Madsen and Paul G. Pickowicz (eds.), *Unofficial China* (Boulder, San Francisco and London: Westview Press, 1989).
McCarthy, Terry. 'A Hairy Time for Japanese Censors', *Independent*, 19 May 1992, p. 11.
Mosher, Stacy. 'Shot by the mob: Stars of the Silver Screen Protest Triad's Hold on the Film Industry', *Far Eastern Economic Review*, 30 January 1992, pp. 28–9.
Oshima, Nagisa. 'Texte du Plaidoyer', *Ecrits 1956–1978: Dissolution et Jaillissement* (Paris: Gallimard, 1980), pp. 325–58.
Seabrook, Jeremy. 'Cheap Thrills (Sex Tourism in Thailand and the Philippines)', *New Statesman and Society*, 31 May 1991, p. 12.
Seo, Hyeonseok. 'Sexual Representation and Female Positions in Korean Cinema: Double-Exploitation of the Female Body in Oudong'. Unpublished manuscript of paper given at the Society for Cinema Studies conference, 1991.
Stanbrook, Alan. 'The Arts: Peking's Nice Little Earner: Why Do the Chinese Make Films and then Ban Them?' *Daily Telegraph*, 27 April 1992, p. 15.
Swain, Jon. 'Triads Step Up Reign of Terror on Back Lot', *Sunday Times*, 17 May 1992. 'Triads go into Films with a Vengeance', *Sunday Times*, 19 January 1992.
Tefft, Sheila. 'Lust for Foreign Exchange Arouses Eager Moviegoers', *Chicago Tribune*, 2 December 1987, section C, p. 5.
Willemen, Paul. Correspondence, 1 September 1992.
Yamizaki, Tomoko. 'Sandakan no 8 Brothel', trans. Tomoko Moore and Steffen Richards, excerpt from *Sandakan Hachiban Shokan: Teihan Joseishi Josho* (Tokyo: Chikuma Shobo, 1972).

BETTE GORDON and KARYN KAY

Look Back/Talk Back

Introduction

The following conversation occurred over two meetings in the spring of 1992. Initially, we felt that pornography was no longer of major relevance to us. It seemed that in these conservative times, there were other, more pressing issues which needed to be addressed: censorship, abortion rights, AIDS, to name but a few. However, through this conversation, we realise that we are still interested in pornography as an expression of women's sexual representation. We realise that, for us, pornography remains a compelling issue when used as intervention and as a challenge to a cultural system that has become anti-sex. Pornographic investigation is a radical act in and of itself. Essentially, we've returned to the positions we held when we made *Variety* and *Call Me*. We are saying that issues remain regardless of the discussion – AIDS, abortion rights, harassment, the family, pornography. The fundamental issue always remains the same: sexuality and its representation.

The Conversation

Bette Gordon: Why is pornography less of a crucial issue than it was when you wrote *Call Me* and I made *Variety*? Maybe it's this simple – once you deal with something in a work of art, it's finished for you. You felt you've said what you have to, and you can go on to something else.

Karyn Kay: Certainly, there are other issues that interest me, and they are also about women's sexuality. For example, obsession – women obsessed – usually with men.

BG: Is obsession something that traditionally has been seen from a man's point of view? It seems like the only people I know who are obsessed are women.

KK: Yes, but what about *Obsession*, *Magnificent Obsession*, *Rear Window*, *Marnie* and *Vertigo*? Then there's *Fatal Attraction* and the view of the ulti-

Variety

Variety

mately lethal female obsession. What's interesting about obsession is that it allows you to lose yourself. You become a reactive object in relation to other people. Their stories are more important than yours. It is the denial of self; the death of you for the sake of the other. You live only in relation to the other. Carried to its furthest extreme, I think it's an incredibly pornographic idea. We don't necessarily think of it as pornographic because no one strips to do it. But it's the 'stripping of the individual'.

BG: You give yourself over to another so that you don't exist any more.

KK: Yes. It's like the *Story of O*.

BG: Usually the object of your obsession is less important than the fact of being obsessed. You think you want the object, but then it becomes more than that – the object becomes almost irrelevant. It's being obsessed that takes over. Seduction works in the same way. You sometimes forget about who you want to seduce; it's just the act itself.

KK: It's because of the pleasure of seduction or obsession, it takes you away from yourself and all the things that are uncomfortable or difficult for you.

BG: To get back to pornography; it is something that I was involved with from 1982 till 1984 when I began *Variety*. My interest in pornography came

Call Me

out of film theory as opposed to feminist social issues. I'm less interested in theoretical pursuits now. I don't know if that's something personal or if the theory itself has become less engaging. I only became interested in pornography because it was such an extreme example of the way all cinema works. It seemed such a classic way of looking at film, taking the idea of voyeurism and pushing it to the extreme. It was also during the 70s, at a time in my life when film theory was vibrant.

KK: Porn is obviously concerned with issues of voyeurism, sexuality and spectatorship, but it was also taboo, which made it obviously exciting. I wanted to ally myself with the forbidden – make sacred the unsacred. My inclination – 'This must be fun because it's a no-no.'

BG: I do think pornography offered itself up as a perfect study vehicle when looking at the cinema, as did Hollywood films of the 40s. With *Variety,* I thought: what about a woman who sells tickets in a porno theatre? It took the classic case of Hollywood cinema and allowed the woman to be a voyeur and a spectator. If, as Laura Mulvey's first essay on Visual Pleasure implied, there was no place for the female spectator and mainstream Hollywood cinema set up a situation whereby the spectator was male, then the idea, the meaning, of a female spectator of pornography was exciting to me. If she was a female voyeur, she would be a character seldom seen in cinema.

Fantasy interested me as well, female fantasies, and how they may involve things women don't even talk about among themselves. I think I'm still interested in that. When women fantasise about being held down and made to fuck, it's about not wanting to take responsibility for desire. In a society where sexual desire is so repressed, it makes sense. For men, it's easier to find an outlet for sexual desire – through prostitution, sex or strip clubs. It's more accessible and acceptable. But ultimately, of course, nothing ever satisfies desire.

KK: I'm interested in the way female fantasy becomes submerged. Sometimes I feel uncomfortable watching men watch pornography. I am aware that it's usually for the man. It's not about my sexuality, fantasy or desire. I am distanced from that image.

BG: But remember when I told you stories about going to porn magazine stores and peep shows. I'd go into a store, walk down an aisle where there were a lot of magazines and only male customers. The minute that I physically inhabited the same space as them in the porn store, the guys moved away from me. They couldn't deal with a woman except as an object on the page. It was interesting because I felt a kind of bizarre power. That my presence made these guys uncomfortable gave me satisfaction. I like to use that.

KK: That's the power of the taboo itself and a breaking of that taboo.

BG: Pornography works because the viewer imagines him/herself overlooked in the act of looking. Caught looking. Interesting that my real pleasure in the porn shops broke such a fantasy. I'm not saying I had actual power, but to make somebody uncomfortable is good. It goes back to the idea that you and I have always had about intervention. We thought it was important to disrupt, to challenge, to change, and were always more interested in making interventions into existing structures rather than making new ones.

KK: It's about trying to compel someone to see differently, ask a different question. I was looking for that in the writing of *Call Me*, which explores the role of danger and violence in sexual fantasy and its implications for women's independence. The obscene caller is able to maintain control and manipulate desire by his anonymity and, significantly, by his absence – just as my heroine's real lover can do by simply never being available, always being out of town. I wanted to know what would happen when she picked up the phone and started talking back, actively manipulating his pleasure. I'm not sure *Call Me* worked out the way I initially intended. The irony is that some aspects of the film actually look like soft-core porn to me. The sexuality was played in such a way that her on-screen masturbation became a kind of lure for people to see the film instead of confront the viewer with a sexual spectacle – masturbation.

BG: But when you wrote the screenplay it wasn't about masturbation on screen.

KK: No. Actually it was about story-telling and desire. But a woman masturbating on screen is certainly a rare image in mainstream cinema. When I wrote the script, I wanted to take possession of that image. The shock: a woman masturbates for her own pleasure, not that of the male spectator. She's not, so to speak, on call for him. In my original screenplay, we don't know for sure what she's doing. Like Anna with her caller, we can only hear her until the camera pan's completed and we see she's eating an orange, not masturbating with it. She's manipulating his fantasy, with the added edge of being caught at it by her own lover who has been secretly watching her.

BG: Speaking of on-screen masturbation, one of my students at Columbia, Tabitha Allen, just made a short film about desire in older women. A seventy-year-old woman, the actress Jane Smith, is shown masturbating. At the end, she smiles in satisfaction, and the audience just lets out this great sigh. It's a wonderful film.

KK: Of course, *Call Me* is very different. As we've said, it's not about masturbation. It's about talking back – in this case to an obscene phone-caller. It is disruptive – of his fantasy and control – and therefore very powerful.

BG: Talking back and looking back become startling. In *Variety,* I never had any intention of redefining what pornography could be for a woman or from a woman's point of view. I still have the same position. I'm not interested in making porn that would be sexy for women. That doesn't really interest me.

KK: It all comes back to women's position within the structure of pornography and creating the moment that can shift its and our unconscious structures.

BG: Exactly. I'm interested in twisting around what exists, playing with those structures.

KK: I believe that something that acts on you invisibly, for some notion of erotic pleasure, at least in this culture, has to emerge from patriarchy. I don't think it matters much if the makers of pornography are called Sam or Gilda or Candida or Deborah – it is still an overwhelmingly male view.

BG: Right. Which is not to say that you can't have a rupture in the male industry. Remember *Dance, Girl, Dance* when the Maureen O'Hara character comes forward to challenge the burlesque audience. She says, 'You're all looking at me. Well, you know what we're doing up here? We're laughing at you.' She turns the look around. And it's really just a moment in a conventional, mainstream Hollywood narrative, yet it turns the gaze back onto the audience. It's a very powerful moment. Why is that more powerful than creating a whole new language?

KK: Because you can't just create a whole new language. That would be creating a false solution. The breaks, the interventions are more compelling, and the resistance they create more powerful.

BG: Even though I say pornography is not so much of an issue for me any more, I recognise that indirectly it is. There is a need to be subversive in this culture that is becoming increasingly conservative. A culture that is becoming asexual demands sexuality.

KK: To be sexual at all – particularly outside what we know as the nuclear family – seems to be a subversive act. Asexuality has become the response to AIDS. But it's tied to the Republican Party's new cult of the family, inspired, I believe, by a desire to divert Americans from the real issues that begin with the failing economy, unemployment, homelessness and the AIDS epidemic.

BG: It's also about fear of women. An active, intelligent, sexually aware woman is a piranha. Look at what the Republicans did to Anita Hill and Hilary Clinton. In a movie like *Fatal Attraction*, a woman's sexual aggressivity represents a threat to the family. It represses the issue of man's fear by positing it as a threat to society.

KK: The Far Right is opposed to difference and autonomy in the name of 'the family'; the fundamental institution of American life – socially, culturally and even economically.

BG: I saw an ad for *Family Circle* magazine. It said, 'The family is back . . . but we never knew it was out.' And it was never out, just a new emphasis.

KK: 'The family' is in trouble, not because of sexual difference or choice, but because of a failing economy. A real concern for so-called family values would mean attention to economic growth and stability: food on the table; affordable health care and health insurance; no one sleeping on the streets; money for public education; AIDS and cancer research and abortion on demand.

BG: What I'm trying to understand here is what we both found so compelling when we did our respective works. In the case of *Call Me*, we're talking about the screenplay, not the movie. In the early 80s, we were both engaged in these projects that were about sex, pornography. Are these issues still a part of our work, and how do they relate to the present social climate? It seems that if pornography was so important then, today we don't have the luxury of sexual exploration because there are some basic sexual rights that we are about to lose. Abortion rights are so much in the foreground. The level of conservatism and censorship in the US is so extreme that we need to refocus on some of the more basic things we used to take for granted when we were investigating pornography.

KK: Yes, it's true. The immediate social climate has changed. Look at the Republican Convention and you see the Right in its most frightening manifestation. But the issues that brought us to explore pornography, or rather the processes of women's representation, are fundamental, have not changed and are part of the core of right-wing hysteria – the very movement towards censorship and a disavowal of difference. As if you could disavow difference. Whether it's Anita Hill challenging Clarence Thomas or Hilary Clinton talking about children's rights and refusing to bake cookies – the danger remains one of a woman speaking out about her own sexuality and identity. In *Fatal Attraction*, the fear is that she will come to kill your family. In real terms that killing of the family becomes a metaphor for the destruction of society. It's not a new idea. In *Double Indemnity* the murder plot is hatched in a supermarket under a baby food display. The force of danger is the sexualised female. The male is her dupe.

BG: There are issues today that make it difficult to get so involved in pornography – the problem of reproductive rights, censorship, AIDS. Yet, here I am, five years after *Variety*, with an option on *Love Me Tender*, a novel about a woman who works as a stripper. I am still interested in the life of the sex worker. It still intrigues me – I guess because of what it has to say about other things – about the body, the power of the body, using the body for pleasure, and then, whose pleasure? In an industry such as the sex trade, which is generally considered to be for male pleasure, how can women find pleasure? And where do women and economics, or lack of economic power, fit in? Do you think that a film that deals with sexuality today has to deal with AIDS? How do you show a sexually active woman boldly exploring her sexual pleasure without having it be all about AIDS?

KK: It's a hard question. I don't think every movie has to mention AIDS, although some would argue that avoiding it is irresponsible.

BG: But AIDS is obviously a real threat to the continued investigation and exploration of our sexuality.

KK: Should it be?

Double Indemnity (Billy Wilder, 1944)

BG: No. We need more AIDS education.

KK: AIDS is being used as an excuse for other fears. It's a disease which is fearsome in and of itself, and is not just about sex. But once again, difference – sexual and racial – is being used to avoid dealing with the real issues which AIDS brings to the forefront.

BG: Yes – I find the hysteria most annoying. A hysteria which avoids the real issue of finding a cure.

KK: Funding for New York high school AIDS education projects was put on hold recently unless such programmes preached sexual abstinence. I wonder to what extent that puts the burden of responsibility once again on the woman: her power to say no; her wisdom to carry condoms. There are those cartoons in the subway: a man walks out on a woman who insists he wear a condom. No less, right? But I wonder if the burden of abstinence is on the female – to repress and deny her sexual pleasure.

BG: The message people are receiving is that having sex is bad and will kill you. We need responsible ways of encouraging safe sex. Young people particularly need information and education so that they are able to explore their sexuality safely.

KK: We grew up with the message that having sex was bad because you might get pregnant. Sex wouldn't necessarily kill, although you could get syphilis. Of course, we never worried about that. We had penicillin.

BG: Nobody ever talked about death, so it's more frightening today. But that goes along with the whole conservative cultural environment.

KK: We've turned back the clock. Before, being pro-sex and pro-drugs was rebellious. Now you'll get sick and die. So be good. That's the message. It's like that Reebok commercial. 'Life is short. Play hard.' Athletics instead of sex. The cold shower syndrome. On TV, people have sex, couples are in bed together all the time – but marriage is the ultimate goal. Our culture deifies romantic love.

BG: But sex is all over the place. Like the sex telephone lines – the 900 numbers [in the US] and it's constantly on mainstream TV and movies. People are in bed together in prime-time programmes like *LA Law*. How can we be living in a repressive time when such programmes and so many commercials, are using overtly sexual images?

KK: The conservatives like Bork and Quayle and Helms worry about those images. They like to point out the dangers of that type of programming, blame the destruction of family values on prime-time. But in fact those sexualised images on TV are appropriated; they become part of the television tapestry, wallpaper. We don't even see them any more or notice the impact, if there is one. It all goes by so quickly. *LA Law* is supposed to be quite daring, but it's pretty conservative. There is a major character, a lawyer, who created quite a stir by coming out. But in the last episode, she's ready to go to bed with her blind male legal opponent. They don't take it all the way. She's not a lesbian after all. Nothing too unsettling.

BG: The problem is that those sexualised images are never really analysed or put into a critical context. Their meaning is never explored.

KK: I think it's also to do with the invisible narrative structure of television. The drama goes on week by week, in a kind of dramatic realism, nothing penetrates the structure, so even somewhat radical ideas are subsumed into the traditional form. The only TV show that currently butts against the structure is *Northern Exposure*. But that show, with its diversions into fantasy and its nod to sexual differences, is actually somewhat asexual.

BG: What about Madonna? Isn't she the emblem of sex in the 90s?

KK: She's sex in your face. In a way, that's great. You are forced to deal with sex and her sexuality.

BG: But in another way, it's media overkill. The more you see her, the more what she represents slips into what's acceptable. Her sexuality loses its punch because it's all over the place.

KK: Do you think she's become so much of a joke you don't have to take her seriously? Maybe the reason people love her is that she knows how to package her sexuality, i.e. she's a good businesswoman. A yuppie.

BG: She fits right in.

KK: Are we saying you can't explore sex – only sell it? Perhaps that's why Madonna is so successful.

BG: You *can* explore sex. You just don't make any money off it. Is Madonna transgressive?

KK: She sells sex. That's not what businesswomen usually sell – well, not overtly.

BG: I think that in our work we have both been struggling to tell the story of sexuality. How you use language and images in a confrontational way.

KK: Our work isn't about pornography *per se*. It's about transgression. We're interested in transgressive behaviour, breaking the rules – following someone, talking dirty on the phone, murdering people. Pornographic fantasies are all part of representing female characters who don't play by the rules.

BG: Yes, think of *Thelma and Louise*.

KK: You can compare it to *Bonnie and Clyde* or *Gun Crazy*. They're all outsider films – two women who die because of their gender/sexuality. A

Thelma and Louise (Ridley Scott, 1991)

man can shoot another man for raping his girlfriend, but a woman cannot. *Thelma and Louise* and *Fatal Attraction* are both important films of their decade. In *Fatal Attraction*, Glen Close seems unconscious of what she's doing. She's killing for the man. *Thelma and Louise* are doing it for themselves. Killing the guy is a moment of clarity. Rage and madness may be the most clear moment. Haven't you ever wanted to kill anyone?

BG: Yes, but I didn't want to go to jail.

KK: Neither did they; so they didn't!

LIZ KOTZ

Complicity

Women Artists Investigating Masculinity[1]

Introduction

Some of the most powerful work being done today around sexuality and the body inhabits a messy, ambiguous space where pathology meets pleasure, where what we most fear is what we most desire. Such a strategy is not about the critique of 'misrepresentation' – from the presumed plain of greater enlightenment – but about a cautious entry into the discourses of entrapment and subjugation as fields of fantasy or sites of exploration.

This space of potentially complicitous fascination offers a provocative, and provocatively dangerous, site for contemporary feminist art-making. Recent work by media artists Lutz Bacher and Abigail Child probes what it means for women artists to appropriate and obsessively explore specific discourses, representations and stances conventionally regarded as 'masculine' – particularly those involving misogynist or pornographic representations. Though pornography, with its highly charged narratives of subjugation and entrapment, constitutes a key site in their investigations, the strategies they employ could not be more different from those of anti-porn feminists. For while Bacher and Child acknowledge that these registers of fantasy and desire are indeed troubling, they dive headlong into this moral morass in all its grotesque hilarity, seduction, and horror, insisting that this terrain should be obsessively explored rather than proscribed.

Working at the edges of feminist theories of sexual representation, these artists challenge a kind of 'first stage' feminism often predicated on constructing an identification with female characters and subject positions and a critique of male or 'masculinist' ones. Instead, they investigate the kinds of *instabilities* and *ambivalences* elicited when female artists invite female spectators to identify with conventionally male subject positions – enacting and exploiting instabilities and ambivalences which recent feminist theoretical models suggest are already structured into the very project of gender identities.

Echoing the radical readings of Freudian and Lacanian psychoanalysis undertaken by North American theorists such as Judith Butler and Kaja Silverman, Bacher's and Child's interests in moments of fractured psychic identification point to the very transversality and instability of gender categories. In questioning rigid categories of 'sexual difference' established in more traditional psychoanalytic feminist theory, both Butler and Silverman have emphasised the intense ambivalence at the heart of mimetic incorporations, and the complex interpenetrations of desire and identification which make fixed, stable or unified gender positions difficult at best. Investigating psychic mechanisms of obsession and repetition, these writers suggest how the very 'compulsion to repeat' that seemingly structures and consolidates gender identities can perhaps be made to subvert and disperse them as well.

Taken seriously, these radically reconfigured theoretical projects mark a critical shift in practices and assumptions, one which revolves around the articulation of feminist strategies which do not rely on the fiction of an authentic female subject. Indeed, the very questioning of what counts as 'feminist', once categories of gender are envisioned as neither stable nor self-evident, is central to this shift. Since both Silverman's and Butler's theoretical projects have important consequences for understanding Bacher's and Child's appropriation and repetition of problematic images and materials to shift and disperse gender positions, I will outline some of these theorists' key insights before returning to a discussion of the two artists' work.

In her book *The Acoustic Mirror,* film theorist Kaja Silverman has probed the relationship of women film-makers to their 'masculine' characters and materials, proposing the idea that women artists must first assume masculine identities in order to dismantle or disperse them. Silverman has written on the films of Liliana Cavani which, in her analysis, work to erase some of the boundaries separating male from female subjectivity, positing highly transversal and unstable heterosexual relationships.[2] Probing this project of what she terms 'phallic divestiture', Silverman identifies 'the psychic transfer at the center of Cavani's cinema: the transfer from female to male and back again',[3] positing a preoccupation with femininity and with masochism paradoxically mediated through male representations. Just as, for male artists, intense identification with female characters or personas may challenge culturally enforced regimes of gender and sexuality (although not unproblematically, Silverman is quick to note), the female exploration of male subjectivity offers a potentially productive, if easily misunderstood, site for feminist art-making.

Tracing female authorial desire and subjectivity in a a number of avant-garde texts, Silverman articulates an implicitly performative theory of authorial gender, one which locates authorship in the 'libidinal coherence' of a body of films, in a reading of 'the desire that circulates there' as organised around a primal fantasmatic scene or scenario. In order to challenge reductive readings of authorial gender (which presume authorial identification along stable gender lines, or rely on normative readings of authorial intention), Silverman focuses on texts by female authors which operate precisely along series of problematic or deviant identifications, texts in which authorial gender 'within' and 'outside' the text must often be read against each other, relationally, rather than assuming their straightforward correspondence.[4]

Butler's own project, articulated in her book *Gender Trouble* and more recent critical essays, has focused on strategies of 'parodic imitation' and 'gender insubordination' evident in many lesbian and gay cultural practices. Butler's emphasis in fact is precisely on the destabilising and denaturalising effects of such problematic identifications, effects which, she argues, serve to destabilise the very naturalness or self-evidence of the more normative psychic processes (for example, male identification with male figures) they ostensibly mimic or imitate.[5] Her key insight that 'the copy of the origin *displaces the origin as origin*'[6] offers a compelling account of why female artists might choose to copy or re-enact male representations rather than romantically attempt to create their 'own'.

Such strategies of gender insubordination are not incompatible with Silverman's insight into the potential transgressivity of female imitations of male models, so aggressive as to verge on impersonation, which potentially challenge the stability of both 'male' and 'female' terms. Yet by insisting that all gender is structured on mechanisms of repetition and imitation, Butler's performative theory of gender implicitly extends this notion of 'impersonation' to include diverse cross-gender and intra-gender imitations as well.[7] Countering the feminist epithet that some women are 'male-identified', Butler's work contends that in this symbolic system we are all to some extent 'male-identified', and that the feminist pursuit of some mythic state of authentically female identification is illusory at best and often rigidly exclusionary and regulatory in effect.[8]

By emphasising the possibility of multiple identifications, and putting the kinds of 'subversive and parodic convergences that characterise gay and lesbian cultures' at the centre of her analysis, Butler questions the stability of any form of gender identity constructed on a strict binary framework.[9] An understanding of radically dispersed and disorganised gender identities, and of the body as the surface upon which gender is inscribed, leads Butler to a consideration of a possibly radical *disjuncture* between body and identity, and the possible confusion and redistribution of the various attributes upon which gender identification constructs itself. Noting that 'transexuals often claim a radical discontinuity between sexual pleasures and bodily parts', Butler suggests such disjunctures between 'real' and 'imagined' bodies are hardly limited to clear-cut instances of gender dysphoria. Pleasures and desires are always imaginary, representing fantasmatic processes with complex relations to the real. Rejecting a heterosexual matrix which would naturalise illusions of continuity and causality between sex, gender and desire, Butler insists on the many possible disjunctures, excesses and confusions operating among these terms, including the very role desire plays in fantasmatically constructing the body: 'the phantasmatic nature of desire reveals the body not as its ground or cause but as its *occasion* and its *object*. ... This imaginary condition of desire always exceeds the physical body through or on which it works.'[10]

Such rigorous interrogations of the relations between gender, identification and desire are indeed critical to a more complex understanding of pornographic representations, since they serve to question, for instance, the pervasive tendency to conflate fantasy and the real which produces all-too-familiar readings of porn. Even progressive analyses of heterosexual porn, such as Andrew Ross's[11] (and, arguably, Linda Williams's [but see pp. 00-00 of this volume]), which argue in favour of 'pornography from a woman's point of view' – varying sexual scenarios and offering more 'equality' of representation, such as portraying the woman on top – rest on a completely naturalised reading of gender relations, in which it is assumed that readers or viewers identify along predictable male/female lines – a binary model of gender which, as Butler demonstrates, naturalises and restabilises gender within a heterosexual matrix. A very different reading, primarily derived from lesbian and gay cultural practices, would emphasise the possibility for multiple and contradictory gender identifications which shift and disperse within the scene, so that the woman viewer, in effect, can be anywhere. Challenging more normative feminist readings of female authorial desire and spectatorial identification, both Butler and Silverman help us to tease out the consequences of these fractured psychic identifications, and to embrace the proliferation of possible gender identities. Thus they offer ways of theorising the diverse strategies of resignification, imitation and repetition at play in the work of artists such as Lutz Bacher and Abigail Child.

The Compulsion to Repeat: Minimalism and Pornography

Lutz Bacher is a Berkeley-based conceptual artist who has worked in photography, video and installation formats since the mid-1970s, when she formed part of the Bay area group 'Photography and Language'.[12] Her work is critical in its excavation of masculinity, from her early photo projects such as *Men at War* (1975) to her current installation projects and feminist reappropriations of canonical male art works.[13] Throughout her career, Bacher has investigated the twisted representations of sexuality and desire found in pornographic books, pulp sociology, medical texts, televised trials and the art-historical canon, among other sources, enacting the warped relationship of a female viewer to such perverse historical documents.

These interests link Bacher's work with that of Abigail Child, a New York-based experimental film and video-maker.[14] In recent years, Child's work has been exhibited internationally, including screenings at the 1989 Whitney Biennial and the New York Film Festival. Her seven-part series *Is This What You Were Born For?* (1981–1989) combines found footage and recreated elements of film noir, pornography, soap opera, early cinema and home movies relentlessly to probe gesture and the body. While her work, as film, employs very different means to engage and disturb its viewer, Child, like Bacher, delves into this obsessive interrogation of gender and sexuality as sites of pleasure and unease. In her short, dense and highly poetic films, Child teases out the moments of rupture and excess in cinematic melodrama and popular cultural forms.

Ambivalent, obsessive, and focused on materials which are somehow 'not okay', Bacher's and Child's works are controversial within traditional feminist contexts. This controversy may in part reflect their interest in the excavation of masculinity, particularly normative male heterosexuality, as a site of female analysis and obsession. Yet while their use of pornographic texts is clearly a key issue, the difficulties their works pose may have less to do with the *kinds* of found materials they work with than the *ambiguity* with which they approach them. There's a kind of camp axiom that 'you have to love the materials you're working with'[15] which suggests something of the ambivalence, the inseparability of horror and fascination, built into the relationship of women artists toward their borrowed images and materials – and to the borrowed artistic and formal traditions within which they work.

Animating both artists' work is the use of serial structure (or in Child's work, the sequencing possibilities of film) to undo the stability of gender positions, and of repetition to produce and proliferate these unstable identifications: by relentlessly denaturalising the content of representations and constantly shifting the subject position of the viewer.[16] Indeed, despite its often aggressively pop content, almost all of Bacher's work is structured along devices derived from classic minimalism: duration, repetition, serial structure, sequencing, attention to scale, etc. These strategies also inform earlier works by Child, such as her 1985 film *Covert Action*, which selectively fractures and repeats sequences from found 1950s home movie footage of two men and two women on vacation; as with Bacher, the repetition functions to put the viewer in a constantly shifting and ambivalent relation to the material, and to shift attention from the incidentally topical material to the basic structures of gender, gesture and the corporeal theatrics of the body.

As the centrality of these formal strategies of repetition and proliferation suggests, Bacher's work constructs a relation to minimalist art analogous to Child's relation to structural film-making.[17] Both represent feminist projects located partially within the legacies of historically male artistic practices, which adapt their rigorous attention to structure and materiality and reinscribe these from a conviction that the cultural meanings of images and materials *do* matter.[18] Working in a visual vocabulary that references minimalist forms and strategies (typified by the serial presentation of large, often industrial, objects), Bacher has a strategic interest in pushing art towards the everyday, in exploring the charge which art can produce as a bearer of the real.[19] Her obsession with the serial presentation of messy pop cultural materials suggests an intersection between pop and minimalist concerns. In a series of projects which, over the past sixteen years, have focused variously on found photographs, porn images and texts, self-help narratives, medical devices and other everyday materials, Bacher seems to suggest that all these things are minimalist objects now.

As this curious conjuncture of sexually-charged scavenged materials and minimal strategies attests, both Bacher's and Child's projects suggest a joining of the tropes of pornography and minimalism. As oddly matched as these two spheres appear to be – one canonical and art-historical, the other everyday and sexual – their intersection is critical to understanding how both artists work these formal strategies of repetition and accumulation to unsettle the kinds of stable subject positions that would produce predictable, predetermined responses to these materials.[20] For just as both minimalism and pornography undeniably offer sites for the female investigation of masculinity, both also tend to be structured around repetition, one psychically and the other materially.

As the critic Hal Foster has argued, minimalist art practices historically operated to 'push art toward the quotidian, the utilitarian, the non- or anti-artistic.'[21] Rejecting a traditional art-historical account of 1960s art movements of minimalism and Pop as *opposing* practices, Foster sees them as united through their common embrace of serial structure and their response to a new order of serial production and consumer culture. This embrace of seriality serves to sever art not only from the subjectivity of the artist but also from the very representational paradigm that has structured post-Enlightenment art production. While conventional histories have focused on the challenge to representation posed by the negation of content in abstract art, Foster suggests that the simulacral nature of seriality and repetition, derived from the commodity structures of late capitalist society, may be far more significant. Indeed, he argues, 'in any serious social history of paradigms, repetition, not abstraction, may well supersede representation.'[22]

Rather than contesting representation in terms of content – as criteria of 'truthfulness' or 'positive representation' in effect do – strategies of repetition and proliferation offer means of subverting the referential logic that underpins representation, of emptying the referent of its meaning, of its status *as* representation. Such a strategy animates both Bacher's and Child's use of mass cultural materials, one which operates by repeating certain highly charged images or sequences until they effectively implode, rather than attempting to judge their veracity in relation to some original truth. This strategy, derived from a conjuncture of pop and minimalist practices, is perhaps most visible and most powerful in their redeployment of pornographic materials, since it allows them to exploit instabilities of fantasy and identification that are always already embedded in pornographic representations.

In his revisionist, psychoanalytically informed readings of minimalism and surrealism, Foster privileges the simulacral effects of both repetition and fantasy as modes which, debased within high modernism's perpetual 'search for origins', now offer potentially useful post-modernist mechanisms for superseding a representational paradigm. Citing Gilles Deleuze on *Difference and Repetition* (a key text for Butler as well), Foster suggests that in a commodity-saturated culture it is largely difference, artificially produced, that we consume, and claims this structure as what unites pop and minimalism. Arguing for the structuring role of this logic of 'difference and repetition', in all aspects of modern culture, Foster considers its potentially contradictory effects:

> More than any other mass cultural content in pop, or industrial technique in minimalism, it is this logic, now general to both high art and popular culture, that redefines the lines between high and low culture. Though involvement with this logic must ultimately qualify the transgressivity of minimalism and pop, it is important to stress that they do not merely reflect it: they exploit this logic, which is to say that, at least potentially, they release difference and repetition as subversive forces.[23]

This effect, of releasing difference and repetition as potentially subversive forces, can be seen as what links Bacher's and Child's engagements with minimalism with their relentless interrogations of gender. Their tendency to combine tropes of pornography and minimalism stands in for what is an overarching strategy: the obsessive repetition and proliferation of problematic images in order effectively to undo their referential logic – a project in which, to reprise Butler's key formulation, 'the copy of the origin *displaces the origin as origin*'.

Yet, among all the possible forms of pop and mass cultural representation, certain instabilities inherent to pornography as a genre make it particularly susceptible to such mechanisms of repetition and recontextualisation. As Abigail Solomon-Godeau has argued, pornography tends to offer a set of 'limit texts' for the study of sexuality and representation, embodying certain functions at their most extreme and most visible. 'The very nature of the subject,' she asserts, 'functions to elicit the investigator's own stake in an explicitly sexual visual field.'[24] As such, pornography represents a place where distance breaks down, where subjectivity is insistently engaged, even uncomfortably so. Even its incorporation into a project of critique is notoriously unstable, since even the most determined efforts to reframe pornographic representations as objects of a politically motivated examination can go deeply awry, subverting authorial intention in fascinating if problematic ways.[25]

As Judith Butler has written, pornographic representations, as a register of fantasy, have a notoriously complex relation to the real.[26] Butler is responding to the realist and mimetic readings of porn offered by North American feminists such as Andrea Dworkin and Catharine MacKinnon (and right-wing American politicians like Jesse Helms), which conflate the fantasmatic and the real, and rely on the kinds of straightforward, unproblematised gender identifications that both Butler and Silverman, along with others, have relentlessly questioned. Butler uses psychoanalytic theory to emphasise the displacement and multiplicity of the very 'I' that fantasises, already split inside and outside the fantasmatic scene. Citing Laplanche and Pontalis's contention that 'fantasy is not the object of desire, but its setting', Butler notes that fantasy entails a proliferation of identifications distributed among the various elements of the scene, its dispersal including setting, all characters, and all actions.[27]

While I agree with Butler's assertion that fantasy disperses identification throughout the scene (and with the anti-censorship politics with which she aligns her analysis), her framework appears to neglect precisely what Dworkin and MacKinnon cling to all too single-mindedly: the notion that while one may identify with the scene as a whole, one may well also experience a particularly compelling identification with a certain specific position, figure or role (an identification that need not, as Silverman's work clearly demonstrates, always align itself along fixed gender lines, although the weight of compulsory heterosexuality indeed forcefully acts to compel such identifications). The very elegance of Butler's rebuttal of Dworkin and MacKinnon seems to rest on a politically motivated systematicity that appears to disavow these very kinds of contradiction (a theoretical consistency and rhetorical elegance for which MacKinnon's writing is well known, disavowing as she does any contradictory information or experience). For if identifications can be dispersed in fantasy, they can also be consolidated and reconfigured.

Both Bacher and Child enact a more complex and ambiguous strategy, one which acknowledges the power of both analyses, and the instability of a practice that cannot be elegant because it must work from these implicitly messy contradictions and discontinuities. Neither conflating nor severing fantasy and 'real life', they seem to work from a position that acknowledges the undeniable *tension* between the fantasmatic and the real embodied in pornography, a tension which plays on both the oscillation between the subject 'inside' and 'outside' the scene, and between a diffuse identification with the 'scene' as a whole and a particularly compelling identification with a specific position or figure – an identification that need not rest on the gender or 'actual' physical body of the viewer.

This tension seems located precisely in the very filmic and photographic media with which these artists work. As Solomon-Godeau notes, in her inquiry into the history of pornographic photography (a history which appears to be co-extensive with that of photography as a technology), photography imparts to visual representation, however problematically, an undeniable 'aura' of the real. In her examination of the shift from pre-photographic practices (erotic paintings, engravings, drawings, and so forth) to the introduction of erotic photography, Solomon-Godeau suggests that, far from involving a mere change in media or materials, this particular conjuncture – pornographic representations and photographic technologies – initiates some kind of paradigm shift, one which invokes a very different, more indexical relation to the real. The effects of such a shift, it seems, cannot fully be accounted for by relying on analogies between intra-psychic mechanisms of visual fantasy and actual visual representations.

Both Bacher and Child effectively exploit this inherent instability and tension in filmic and photographic pornographic representations, and use techniques derived from minimalism to push it to greater extremes: to fragment further and shift viewer identifications, to engage and displace the fears and desires such representations provoke, and to heighten the potential diffusion of attention, not only between male and female subject positions, but more formally, from act to frame, or sequence to sequence. Proliferating instances of repetition, fragmentation and excess within these borrowed materials, their interventions exploit the very kinds of distraction and disruption that pornographic conventions attempt, however unsuccessfully, to contain, and produce very different kinds of pleasure in the process.

In a key project, *Sex with Strangers (Obscenity, Misogyny, Desire)* (1986), Bacher presented a series of large photographic images with accompanying captions, taken from a 1970s porn book thinly disguised as a sociological text. The black and white images, of 'rape' and fellatio, are disturbing and eerie, awkward and explicit. Shot in very high contrast, the images take on an edge of abstraction. Yet their effect is made all the odder by the captions, which veer between registers of parody, porn narrative, and the faux-scientific in their lurid accounts of female nymphomania and wayward hitchhikers. One reads, 'In countless oral adventures some girls are overreacting to a restrictive lifestyle that was imposed on them by parents.' By crossing disciplinary languages, such texts bring out the perverse voyeurism embedded in porn narratives and sociological discourses alike. Whereas in much 80s text/image art the verbiage effectively repressed the visual, in *Sex with Strangers* the preposterous, high-blown captions fail to 'anchor' the images: graphic, repetitive and obsessive, they spin hopelessly out of control.

With its predilection for such 'limit texts' embodying relations of power and sexuality at their most densely congealed, disturbing and humorous, Bacher's work asserts the necessity for women to explore these messy spaces of culture and desire. *Sex with Strangers* is about power *and* the erotic, about their very inseparability. By blowing the images up on a gallery wall (the mural-like prints are 72" × 40"), but refusing to alter, reframe or comment on them in any other way, Bacher forces the viewer to confront a potential instability of responses: a constant slippage between positions of 'looking on' and identification, between psychic dispersal and fixity, and between feelings of pleasure and unease, attraction and repulsion. While the scenes depicted are heterosexual, the subject positions they construct need not be – particularly since the abstraction and scale of the images elicits identification with the scene or with actions more than with specifically gendered participants. The image/texts are offered up not only as objects of analysis (a by now familiar trope, one that would attempt to stabilise a univocal reading), but as objects of an aesthetic, indeed an aestheticising, gaze. As Bacher has suggested, in her statements about the project, her use of these debased materials is as much about reconfiguring the sublime as addressing questions of sexuality and gender; indeed, her engagement with these deeply visceral images suggests the very inseparability of the two projects:

> I don't think about whether something is pornographic or obscene. This is just not the approach I take. I mean I don't look for the most

inflammatory or controversial approach to any subject either. Rather I look for images and texts that embody a certain complex of ideas in the most visceral and direct way. Now the image/texts from *Sex with Strangers* are representative of that complex nexus where gender, sex, and language meet – which seems like something preposterous to say about a bunch of pictures of sucking. ... I always return to the enormous feeling of desire and subjugation in the images.

My use of [the images from *Sex with Strangers*] has as much to do with reconfiguring the territory both of what images can be looked at as art, and what a woman as an artist would need to look at if she's seriously concerned with questions about the sublime and about sex and gender and language and that nexus.[28]

Bacher has continued to elaborate this project in her most recent work, some of which returns to explicitly sexual materials.

Evincing a continued preoccupation with male subjectivity, Bacher's work engages Silverman's suggestion that women artists usurp masculine identities in order to dismantle or disperse them. Both her early installation *Men at War* (1975) and her more recent project *Men in Love* (1990) involve Bacher as the female author re-enacting, and implicitly watching, male group rituals of submerged aggression – a repeated trope that echoes Cavani's repeated filmic re-enactments of male divestiture and masochism, which Silverman reads through the Freudian 'beating fantasy'.[29] What is at stake when a female artist stages scenes of threatened or impaired masculinity? What is her relation to this 'scene', and, more importantly, what positions does she construct for the viewer? Or, as Silverman poses the question, 'What desire finds expression through this constant return to and preoccupation with male subjectivity?' and 'why [does] that preoccupation require the support of a male representation?[30]

In *Men in Love*,[31] a collection of confessional narratives taken from a quasi-instructional, quasi-pornographic male masturbation manual, Bacher assembles an idiosyncratic collection of impaired or pathetic masculine subjectivities.[32] Alternately funny and grotesque, and sometimes arousing, the installation offers a mini-catalogue of perversions, in which such familiar topics as exhibitionism, voyeurism and paedophilia are joined by far more obscure and unnamed practices – which range from getting off on the warm vibrations of a washing machine to the pleasures of jerking off onto the mirrors in fancy men's rooms. By presenting the thirty-one texts on 12" mirrors, the installation foregrounds both the baroque qualities of the first-person stories – the incredible variation within the sameness – and the intense self-consciousness they both display and provoke. There's an unavoidable element of narcissism in reading them, with your face staring back at you, which draws the reader into some kind of identification, however awkward, with the men whose names provide the titles of each piece.[33]

The paradox Bacher works with is that these documents are both deeply twisted *and* deeply conventional. By seizing on the odd text or the

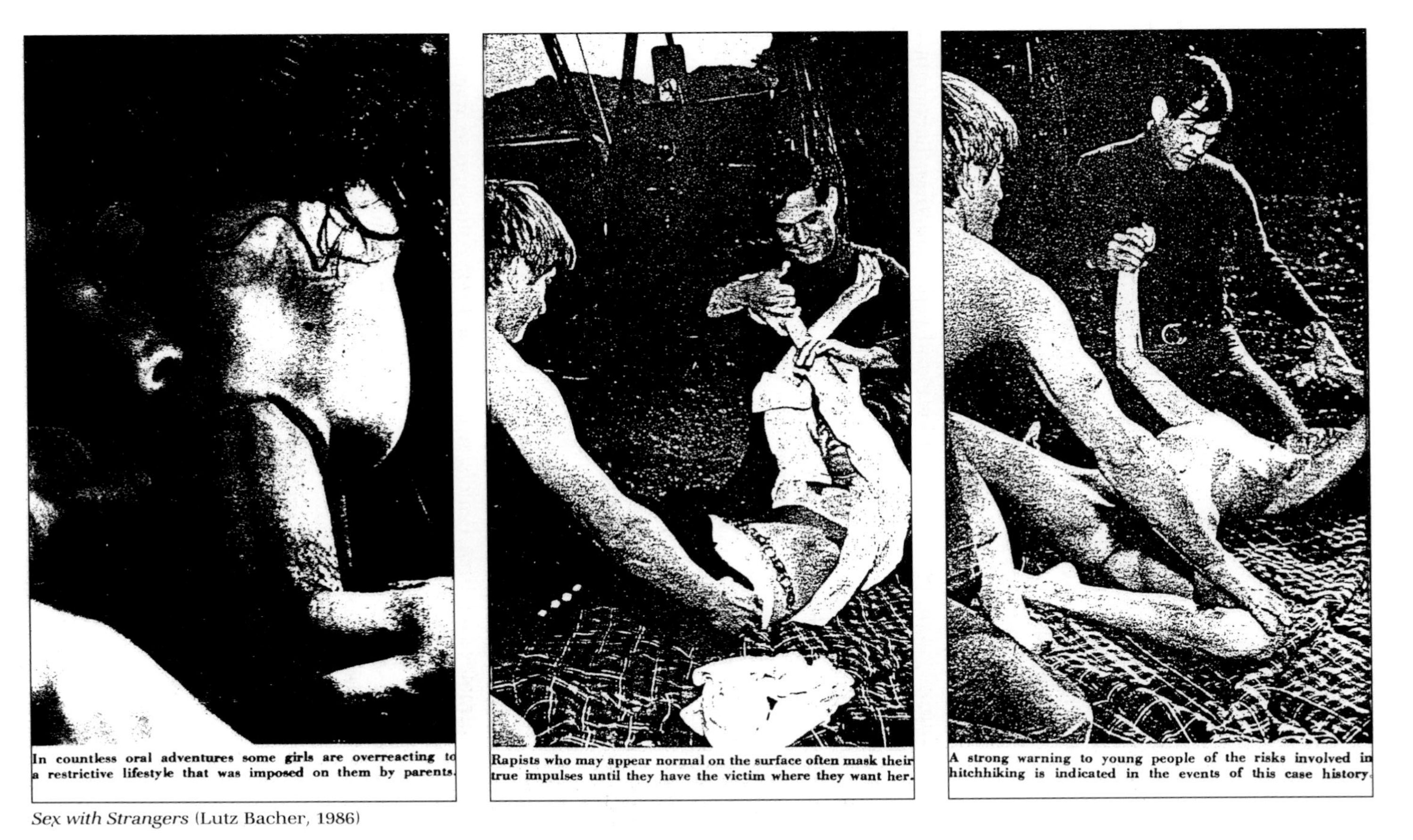

Sex with Strangers (Lutz Bacher, 1986)

extreme moment, Bacher analyses how these 'language systems' themselves create and produce the very masculine desires they record and circulate. The key question, in Bacher's installation pieces, is what it means for a female artist to be doing such work, to be 'taking on' the male voice so forcefully.[34] Porn in this analysis is an apparatus of male subjectivity, a technology of gender; yet by focusing on such 'marginal' texts – porn books, a masturbation manual, texts in the generic interstices of sociology, 'self-help' and pornography – Bacher insists on the inseparability of pornographic representations from other, more 'acceptable' but equally normative cultural practices.

Obsessively exploring these sites of misogyny (all culture is a site of misogyny – porn, *pace* MacKinnon and Dworkin, has no special status), Bacher insists on the impossibility of actually transcending or exiting these warped registers of desire. Explicating the untenability of 'sex positive' or naively intimate images of sex which would claim to evade or undo the complex implication of sexuality, power and representation, Bacher has stated, in reference to *Sex with Strangers*:

> As a woman, I pretty much understand that sex is not a safe situation, that the occasion of sex, the speaking of sex, the way in which sex comes up, is always in effect with strangers, always in that area of pleasure and danger. ... If I was setting up my friends or myself and taking pictures and so on, that would be about some notion of totally free sex, the innocent body, an innocent image world that doesn't exist. This work assumes that bodies aren't innocent, images aren't innocent and language isn't innocent. As for what they're about – who(ever) owns these images gets to say that and make use of them.[35]

What strikes home about *Sex with Strangers* is not just the intense awkwardness of the images, but the *oscillation* between desire and subjugation they embody, and the unstable subject position they invite – a strategy which animates much of Child's work as well. Of course, one reading would be simply to see the materials as completely repellent, and to refuse to accept that any viewer, male or female, could find them a turn-on. Yet what Bacher seems interested in is precisely such moments of *problematic identification* – especially when women take up the position designed for male spectators.

In Bacher's case, the masculinity being appropriated is both homo- and heterosexual, representing a complex response not only to straight male misogyny but also to a gay male aesthetic itself sometimes modelled on the refiguring of culturally normative 'femininity'. Positions of 'masculine' and 'feminine', Bacher's work seems to insist, are themselves unstable and transversal, capable of generating an intense back-and-forth movement. Rather than attempt to enforce the stability and autonomy of these positions – invoking the 'authenticity' of 'identities' as one strain of both feminist and gay politics would advocate – Bacher's 'extreme examples', joining minimalist and pornographic tropes, work to unfix these positions

Mayhem (Abigail Child, 1987)

through obsessive repetition and displacement. For it is through this repetitive cataloguing of awkward instances of male fantasy and desire that Bacher explores heterosexuality as what Butler has termed 'an incessant and panicked imitation of its own naturalised idealisation'. As Butler notes, 'That heterosexuality is always in the act of elaborating itself is evidence that it is perpetually at risk, that is, that it "knows" its own possibility of becoming undone.'[36] Intuitively honing in on these instances of risk and rupture, Bacher picks apart some of the artifices and instabilities of male subjectivity, in effect appropriating them for the female viewer. The point is not to close down or consolidate these positions of 'male' and 'female' but to keep them open to new and unanticipated significations.[37]

In a project linked to Bacher's critical excavation of male subjectivity, Abigail Child's series *Is This What You Were Born For?* probes how 'masculinity' and 'femininity' are figured in Western cinematic representation. Like Bacher, Child works with the destabilising of familiar images, sequences and tableaux, insistently exploring the artifices which structure narrative for moments of rupture and excess. Her focus is on the body, not as narrated in the confessional discourse, but as visually and corporeally enacted through gait, gesture, rhythm and repetition. Influenced by the strategies of language poetry and the avant-garde musical work of John Zorn, Christian Marclay and Zeena Parkins (all of whom have collaborated on her films), she uses rapid editing, disjunctive juxtaposition and multi-layered sound-cutting to reframe and reposition highly charged images and materials. Contrapuntally rechoreographing these fragments of action, gesture and ritualised movement (what Butler has termed 'the array of corporeal theatrics understood as gender presentation'[38]), Child makes a kind of music out of this 'noise'.[39]

Mayhem, the penultimate film of the series, focuses on *film noir*, teasing apart its complex threads of sexuality and violence, narrative and voyeurism. Drawing on a rich collection of archival footage and historical materials, Child fragments and intercuts sequences to confuse and disorder contemporary regimes of gender and sexuality, playing up the troubling interpenetration of male and female (and heterosexual and homosexual) desires embedded in her dizzying array of borrowed and recreated materials. As Child describes the film:

> Perversely and equally inspired by de Sade's *Justine* and Vertov's sentences about the satiric detective advertisement, *Mayhem* is my attempt to create a film in which sound is the character and to do so focusing on sexuality and the erotic. Not so much to undo the entrapment (we fear what we desire, we desire what we fear) but to frame fate, show up the rotation, upset the common, and incline our contradictions towards satisfaction, albeit conscious.[40]

The film opens with a classic *noir* scenario. A woman in 40s attire waits in a darkened room. Her face is barred by diagonal shadows, created by the light through a Venetian blind. The music suggests fear, foreboding. She looks up, startled, awaiting an intrusion. It then cuts to a scene of two men peering menacingly, suggesting malice – except that the sequence is lifted from a postwar spy thriller. Veering between historical periods and locales, the film catalogues types of action, codified gestures, ways of presenting the body, as men and women shift positions constantly. Two men pursue a woman through an urban landscape; just when things look menacing, she turns to watch them as they suddenly embrace, introducing slippages between heterosexual and homosexual desires that reverberate through the text. Yet simply describing sequences cannot do the film justice, for *Mayhem* is a deeply kinetic experience, one in which the images slip from the viewer's grasp before being fully registered – a strategy which heightens their almost subliminal apprehension, their capacity for slippage and deferred action. As it repeatedly sets up and then redirects its melodramatic encounters, *Mayhem* plays on the fine line between threat and fascination; rather than attempting to separate out pleasure and danger (or straight and gay scenes), the film reworks what is fearful or pathologised as a turn-on.

As film scholar Madeline Leskin has noted, '*Mayhem* meticulously employs the language of noir: the lighting, the camera angles, even the latent sadism, but takes noir to the next level by drawing the connections between sex and violence.'[41] With its frenzied cataloguing of allusive glances, awkward pursuits, disguised identities and threatened poses, all forced into a breathless pitch, Child's film suggests a world in which such melodramatic gestures, while full of meaning, do not lend themselves to any sure decoding.[42] Instead, they form an endless series of detours and diversions, disruptions and deviations, as their intimations of violence and suspense take on delayed impacts, detonating at different moments within the film instead of setting up linear continuities of cause and effect.[43]

As the film embraces sexual ambiguity and the relationality of sexual identities, it combines a multiplicity of gazes and forms of desire; the collisions between them give *Mayhem* density and movement. There is a loose progression in the film, from sequences of fear and foreboding towards more playful and comic scenes; this is paralleled by a movement from strictly heterosexual scenes to more mixed encounters, but the film does not lend itself to a reductive or utopian reading about lesbian or gay sexualities. Instead, like the collage and theft-based strategies of the gay fanzines that critic Matias Viegener has written about,[44] Child's found footage and reconstructed materials offer a strategy of appropriation and erotic reinscription of pleasurable *and* problematic images from an array of (sometimes deeply misogynist) mass cultural sources – a strategy based on reconstructing and refiguring these images, rather than trying to produce an 'affirmative image' of female sexuality.

In so doing, Child's representational strategy engages a more critical, contemporary understanding of sexual identity, one not based on somehow 'celebrating' gay identity but actively exploring and interrogating it. Drawing on the historical articulation of gay identities as inseparably liberatory *and* regulatory, work by Judith Butler, Diana Fuss, Jeffrey Weeks and other gay theorists has compellingly argued that any efforts to produce stable, unified identities – even marginal ones – will inevitably be regulative. Attempts to ground lesbian and gay politics or cultural practices in a similarly conceived model of stable, autonomous and 'authentic' sexual identities all too easily fall into the same trap, reactively defined in relation to their heterosexual opposites which they must continually seek to exclude (and based on gender identities that are themselves products of a heterosexual matrix). Instead, theoretical projects such as Butler's propose that the imitative and parodic effects of lesbian and gay cultural practices, by embracing and exploiting their implicit relation with heterosexual norms and practices, can indeed unwrite the very 'originality' of their heterosexual models – the idea that such 'repetitions' and 'reinscriptions', rather than reproducing or reinforcing existing regimes of identity and gender, may potentially act to disrupt and subvert them.[45]

The potentially threatening ambiguity with which this process of reinscription works can be seen in the porn sequence that ends *Mayhem*, and which provides a sort of epilogue or coda to it. These final scenes, taken from a 1920s porn film of unknown origin, feature two women furiously making love; vaguely oriental, it is shot with apparently mock-Japanese setting and characters, but because of the degradation of the image the particulars are difficult to make out. The pair are interrupted by a thief, who masturbates to the women's lovemaking and is then discovered by them and 'forced' at gunpoint to join in. As the voyeuristic dimensions of noir are enacted, very literally, the conventions linking sex, violence and control are stripped bare. Yet as a representation of lesbian sexuality, the sequence is far from reassuring. It offers no safe place, no nostalgic retreat, from the voyeurism and entrapment of dominant cinematic codes. Instead of offering reassurance or the illusion of an uncorrupted sphere of representation, the sequence instead seems to propose a series of questions which reflect back on the film as a whole. Who was this meant for? Who is turned on? What kinds of images are disturbing? What is erotic?

By closing on such a 'corrupt' lesbian image, one not 'free' but completely embedded in histories of oppression and resistance, *Mayhem* implicitly questions the production of sexual identities that are 'stable, natural and good'[46] – as well as questioning the privileged position of a feminist 'critique' which seeks to authorise its own status as rational analysis, somehow outside such histories of distortion, entrapment and desire. Instead it presents a kind of alternative map through its idiosyncratically assembled film history, offering a *proliferation* of sexual identities, pleasures and dangers. As the film constructs a range of positions from which to identify with its male *and* female characters, homo *and* hetero desires, Child, like Bacher, explores just what happens when these limits are tested, when these identities are confused or made ambiguous.[47]

Conclusion

Reflecting a deeply immersed fascination with popular genres, styles and devices, these projects of course participate in a wider tendency within contemporary feminist art-making, one which involves the entry of comic books, soap opera, photo novella and pornography into high art practice. Yet I want to make a distinction, one which seems critical, between works which use such pop cultural or pornographic images as material, as the surface for yet another critical reading – a strategy which seems all about reassuring the viewer in her own superiority and distance – and works which, like Bacher's and Child's, appropriate these warped documents on a much more structural level, engaging with their mechanisms of entrapment and probing the notoriously restless operations of desire and identification.[48]

In their refusal – perhaps even suspicion – of the clarity and authority of a more avowedly critical art, both Bacher and Child explore an admittedly ambiguous position for feminist representation, one committed to exploring the subjugation, inhabiting the distortions, engaging and perhaps even identifying with the sense of pathology. It is work about complicity, and for good reasons it may make some viewers uncomfortable. In threatening our own position as spectators, our forever thwarted desires to escape the entrapments of our culture, these artists enact a deep-seated engagement with psychic mechanisms of fantasy, obsession and obsessive repetition.

Exploring sites of trauma and exploiting the very instability inherent in repetition, Bacher and Child tap into the power of this psychic 'compulsion to repeat' which can work toward potentially conservative or profoundly destabilising ends. In this, the political valency of their work is not always clear. Yet it is perhaps precisely this psychically and politically charged ambivalence that gives their works their aesthetic power. For, as Hal Foster notes, writing on the contradictory nature of the surrealist image in terms that could well be used to describe Bacher's and Child's art-making, this very structural ambivalence can be seen as 'an effect of a repetitive working-over of fantasmatic scenes by a mobile subject, a working over that is never purely involuntary and symptomatic *or* controlled and curative.'[49]

Notes

1. Sections of this article have been published in 'Lutz Bacher: Sex with Strangers', *Artforum*, September 1992; and 'An Unrequited Desire for the Sublime: Looking at Lesbian Representation Across the Works of Abigail Child, Cecilia Dougherty, and Su Friedrich', in Martha Gever, John Greyson and Pratibha Parmar (eds.), *Queer Looks* (New York and London: Routledge, 1993). Thanks to John Archer, Jennifer Kabat, Matias Viegener and Alys Weinstein for commenting on drafts of this article, and to the artists for extensively discussing their works with me.
2. Kaja Silverman, *The Acoustic Mirror: The Female Voice in Psychoanalysis and Cinema* (Bloomington: Indiana University Press, 1988).
3. Ibid., p. 227. Silverman goes on to elucidate what she sees as the usefulness, or even necessity, of relying on male characters to express certain fantasies of gender dismantling:

> This (desire for discursive power) is a necessary desire for the female subject, even as it dreams of a moment beyond it: of the moment when, having acceded to power, the female subject can divest herself of it. ... Cavani is obliged to rely on male characters to express this dream because they alone occupy a position from which divestiture is possible. Her constant return to male subjectivity speaks to the desire to participate in a renunciation which is not yet possible for the female subject (which indeed can only be seen as a dangerous lure at this moment in her history) – the renunciation of power in all its many social, cultural, political and economic guises (p. 231).

4. Ibid., p. 217. However, she cautions that these two terms – gender 'within' and 'outside' the text – can neither be conflated nor completely severed. While Silverman wants to claim such moments of slippage as at least potentially transgressive (implicitly arguing against feminist analyses that would ascribe to such strategies purely colonising or complicitous operations), she does not disavow their problematic status, but instead points to the *complexity* of such unstable gender identifications, which are by no means limited to straightforward reversals or substitutions:

   > At the same time, this libidinal masculinity or femininity must be read in relation to the biological gender of the biographical author, since it is clearly not the same thing, socially or politically, for a woman to speak with a female voice as it is for a man to do so, and vice versa. All sorts of cultural imperatives dictate a smooth match between biological gender and subject position, making any deviation a site of potential resistance to sexual difference.

5. In *Gender Trouble: Feminism and the Subversion of Identity* (New York and London: Routledge, 1990), Butler performs a series of provocative readings of Lacan, Freud and Joan Riviere, among others, analysing their competing versions of how gender identifications work – 'indeed, of whether they can be said to "work" at all.' Butler queries the viability of any unitary, univocal 'gender identity':

   > Can gender complexity and dissonance be accounted for by the multiplication and convergence of culturally dissonant identifications? Or is all identification constructed through the exclusion of a sexuality that puts those identifications into question? In the first instance, multiple identifications can constitute a non-hierarchical configuration of shifting and overlapping identifications that call into question the primacy of any univocal gender attribution (p. 66).

6. 'Phantasmatic Identification and the Question of Sex', presented at the Fifth Annual Lesbian and Gay Studies Association Conference, 1–3 November 1991, Rutgers University.
7. Like Butler, Silverman conceives of gender as perpetually troubled, perpetually endangered. Yet while Butler's reading will focus on the kinds of *pleasure* produced by the instability of these categories, Silverman instead seems to focus on gender as a kind of *anxiety*: as a series of displacements, a set of relationally defined terms uneasily resisting an enormous amount of anxiety, which perpetually threatens to undo these very terms.

   Such a model of gender as anxiety, as perpetually unfinished 'work', is by no means unique to Silverman, and indeed underpins many feminist readings of Lacan and of the oedipalised 'acquisition' of gender. See, for example, Juliet Mitchell, *Feminism and Psychoanalysis* (London: Allen Lane, 1974) and Jacqueline Rose, *Sexuality in the Field of Vision* (London and New York: Verso, 1986). The often British-based Lacanian-inflected psychoanalytic feminist theories radically diverge from more sociologically based and empirically oriented American feminist models, such as those of Nancy Chodorow (in *The Reproduction of Mothering: Psychoanalysis and the Sociology of Gender*, Berkeley: University of California Press, 1978), which tend to rest upon the assumption that the acquisition of gender actually *works*, that it actually achieves any stability and normativity.

8. Butler, *Gender Trouble*, pp. 30–1.
9. Arguing against a more traditional Lacanian reading of the Law of the Symbolic as fixing identity in a rigid and universal determinism, Butler notes:

   > The alternative perspective that emerges from psychoanalytic theory suggests that multiple and coexisting identifications produce conflicts, convergences, and innovative dissonances within gender configurations, which contest the fixity of masculine and feminine placements with respect to the paternal law. In effect, the possibility of multiple identifications (which are not finally reducible to primary or founding identifications that are fixed within masculine and feminine positions) suggests that the Law is not deterministic and that 'the' law may not even be singular (*Gender Trouble*, p. 67).

10. Butler, *Gender Trouble*, p. 71. Such a disaggregation of what 'counts' as gender then in turn underpins Butler's discussion, in subsequent work, of the potential disaggregation and dispersal of the elements of what appear to us as consolidated sexual identity categories. Questioning the possibility of such identities to be adequately constituted and expressed through strategies of disclosure such as 'coming out', Butler asks:

    > If a sexuality is to be disclosed, what will we take as the true determinant of its meaning: the phantasy structure, the act, the orifice, the gender, the anatomy? And if the practice engages a complex interplay of all those, which one of these erotic dimensions will come to stand for the sexuality that requires them all? (Imitation and Gender Insubordination', in Diana Fuss, ed., *Inside/Out: Lesbian Theories, Gay Theories* [New York and London: Routledge, 1991], p. 17).

11. Andrew Ross, *No Respect: Intellectuals and Popular Culture* (New York and London: Routledge, 1989), pp. 171–208.
12. See Lew Thomas (ed.), *Photography & Language* (San Francisco: Camerawork Press, 1986).
13. Loosely titled 'A Birth of the Reader', the project will involve female-authored 're-creations' of canonical male art pieces, from a Robert Morris process piece to a series of Warhol paintings.
14. Critical writings on Child include Marjorie Keller, 'Is This What You Were Born For?', and Charles Bernstein, 'Interview with Abigail Child', *X-Dream* (Autumn, 1987); Maureen Turim, 'Childhood Memories and Household Events in the Feminist Avant-garde', *Journal of Film and Video*, no. XXXVIII (Summer/Fall 1986); Barbara Hammer, 'The Invisible Screen: Lesbian Cinema', *Center Quarterly* (Spring 1988); Dennis Barone, 'Abigail Child', *Arts Magazine* (September 1990); as well as Child's book of experimental writings, *A Motive for Mayhem* (Hartford, Conn.: Potes & Poets Press, 1989).
15. See, for instance, Susan Sontag's 'Notes on Camp', for a depoliticised and yet in some instances quite useful reading of camp, in *Against Interpretation* (New York: Farrar, Straus & Giroux, 1966). For critiques of Sontag by theorists emphasising the critical, denaturalising, or defamiliarising strategies embedded in camp practices, see Michael Moon, 'Flaming Closets', *October* no. 51 (Winter, 1989) and Andrew Ross, 'Uses of Camp', in *No Respect: Intellectuals and Popular Culture* (New York and London: Routledge, 1989).
16. This function can be seen across very different works: the video installation *My Penis* (1992), a two-hour tape loop of a short utterance from William Kennedy Smith's televised trial testimony, uses both duration and repetition to keep shifting the viewer's reception and apprehension of the utterance. On her relation to cinematic minimalism, specifically structural film-making, Bacher herself has noted that her earlier work *Huge Uterus* (1989), a six-hour video installation, 'could not have been made without Michael Snow's *Wavelength*' (conversation with the

author, December 1991). Overall, Bacher's disparate projects could be unified through their use of topical materials in structures derived from minimalism; in turn, it is this use of minimalist repetition, serial structure, and duration that tends to distance them radically from more conventional 'topical' or 'political' art, since these strategies orient the viewer off the specific event onto basic structures.

17. Structural film-making, a movement associated with Michael Snow, Peter Gidal, Hollis Frampton, Paul Sharits, Ernie Gehr, the early work of Tony Conrad, and others, constitutes an analogous movement of minimalism within experimental film culture (just as the earlier 'expressionistic', 'poetic', and 'personal film-making' of Maya Deren, Stan Brakhage and others saw itself as roughly allied with Abstract Expressionism). According to an early assessment of structural film by P. Adams Sitney, 'Theirs is a cinema of structure in which the shape of the whole film is predetermined and simplified, and it is that shape which is the primal impression of the film (*Visionary Film: the American Avant-garde 1943–1978* [New York and London: Oxford University Press, 1979], pp. 369–97).
18. As Anna Chave has suggested in her controversial article 'Minimalism and the Rhetoric of Power', high minimalist art of the 1960s, in its engagement with the visual vocabulary of industry and technology, can indeed be read as a paradigmatic discourse of power and of masculinity. As critically reassessed in the 1980s, minimalism at times came to stand for a quintessentially straight male practice (often defined in opposition to Pop Art, many of whose major practitioners were gay men) in its evisceration of content, politics, emotion or pleasure, as conventionally understood, from visual art-making. See Anna C. Chave, 'Minimalism and the Rhetoric of Power', *Arts Magazine*, January 1990, pp. 44–63. For a response to Chave, see Brian Wallis, 'Power, Gender and Abstraction', in *Power: Its Myths and Mores in American Art 1961–1991* (Indianapolis Museum of Art/Indiana University Press, 1991). For a look at contemporary, more politicised reinscriptions of minimalist practices, see Kathryn Hixson, 'The Subject is the Object: Legacies of Minimalism', *New Art Examiner* (May 1991) and '... and the Object is the Body', *New Art Examiner* (October 1991).
19. And, as her recent piece 'Menstrual Extraction Kit' (1991) suggests, the charge produced by the possibility that this relation is itself transversal, that art could slip out of the frame and back into use – 'menstrual extraction' being of course a euphemism for home-made abortion devices.
20. As Silverman notes, in her exploration of the unstable relation of female 'authors' to their male characters:

    > Foucault is correct to suggest that there is a more crucial project than determining the relation between the author and what he or she says, and that is to establish the position which the reader or viewer will come to occupy through identifying with the subject of a given statement. That position is indeed 'assignable' (or reassignable). All of this is another way of saying that the reader or viewer may be captated by the authorial system of a given text or group of texts. (*The Acoustic Mirror*, p. 233.)

21. Hal Foster, 'The Crux of Minimalism', in *Individuals: A Selected History of Contemporary Art, 1945–1986*, ed. Howard Singerman (Los Angeles: Museum of Contemporary Art/Abbeville Press, 1986), p. 163.
22. Ibid., p. 179. Foster elaborates: 'It is not the "anti-illusionism" of minimalism that "rids" art of the anthropomorphic and the representational, but its serial mode of production: for abstraction *sublates* representation, preserves it even as it cancels it, whereas repetition, the (re)production of simulacra, *subverts* representation, undercuts its referential logic.'
23. Ibid., p. 180.
24. Abigail Solomon-Godeau, 'Reconsidering Erotic Photography: Notes for a Project of Historical Salvage', from *Photography at the Dock* (Minneapolis: University of Minnesota Press, 1991), p. 220.

25. This accusation, that feminist projects critiquing pornography inevitably invite the very pruriently interested forms of spectatorship they endeavour to condemn, has plagued many undertakings, with anti-porn critics almost routinely claiming that supposedly anti-porn films, such as the Canadian documentary *Not a Love Story*, will bring in the 'raincoat crowd' – not to mention the perversity of a document such as the Meese Commission report, itself an amazing compendium of pornographic scenarios. While in anti-porn discourse this phenomenon is clearly seen as a problem, to me it represents a provocative instance of the instability and indeterminacy of subject positions, the very multivalency of porn that Child and Bacher both exploit to more artistic, and to my mind more politically useful, ends.
    I was struck by this phenomenon while recently reading, in Susan Suleiman's *Subversive Intent*, a section on Andrea Dworkin's rewriting of Bataille's 'The Story of the Eye'. While Dworkin's rewrite, as Suleiman rather predictably asserts, flattens Bataille's 'exquisitely' elegant French prose and the 'frisson' produced by bringing it to such coarse and vulgar subject matter, Suleiman completely misses what to me is a far more interesting effect: Dworkin's rewrite, in its direct, crude, street-smart way, reminds me of nothing so much as mid-1970s Kathy Acker. That *Pornography: Men Hating Women* and *The Childlike Life of the Black Tarantula*, two apparently opposed 1970s feminist projects, should exhibit such hidden, and probably unintentional, intertextuality strikes me as very interesting. Acker has in fact stated that she admired Dworkin's work prior to Dworkin's current political commitment to anti-porn censorship; various commentators have noted how the very anti-porn legislation Dworkin has advocated could ironically be used to suppress some of her own books.
26. Judith Butler, 'The Force of Fantasy: Feminism, Mapplethorpe, and Discursive Excess', *differences*, vol. 2 no. 2, 1990.
27. Ibid., pp. 109–10.
28. Lutz Bacher, Statement, 6 July 1990.
29. Phase three of the fantasy – 'Some boys are being beaten (and I am watching)' – being the primary psychoanalytic narrative of female masochism. As Silverman poses the relation: 'For what is the exchange that occurs between Cavani as the author "outside" the text and those male characters who represent her within the text if not a restaging of that fantasmatic drama whereby a girl turns herself into a group of boys only in order to position them as female, i.e. to "castrate" them?' (*The Acoustic Mirror*, p. 232).
30. Silverman, *The Acoustic Mirror*, pp. 220 and 225.
31. See Maria Porges, 'Lutz Bacher', *Artforum*, March 1991, pp. 136–7; Liz Kotz, 'Lutz Bacher, *Men in Love*', *Shift*, Spring 1991, pp. 62–3; and Robert Mahoney, 'Lutz Bacher', *Arts Magazine*, January 1992.
32. This terrain – the mapping of masochistic, marginal or impaired masculinities as a site of resistance to phallic norms – has been a crux of radical male art-making, as represented by Vito Acconci and others, since the early 1970s. See Kathy O'Dell, 'The Performance Artist as Masochistic Woman', *Arts Magazine*, June 1988, and her Ph.D. dissertation, 'Toward a Theory of Performance Art: An Investigation of its Sites' (The Graduate Center, City University of New York, 1992), and my own 'Pathetic Masculinities', *Artforum*, November 1992. For critical readings of masculinity in contemporary art, see Wallis, 'Power, Gender and Abstraction', note 18, and Laura Cottingham, 'Negotiating Masculinity and Representation', *Contemporanea* (October 1989). See also Kaja Silverman, *Male Subjectivity at the Margins* (New York: Routledge, 1992).
33. Hung somewhat low, at 5 feet, I was the right height to read them without stooping – Bacher implicitly positions these narratives for a presumed female viewer. Such stories, she correctly assumes, are not particularly transgressive when framed (in the porn manual) for private male consumption, but become so when reframed, in the gallery, for public female consumption – an intuition borne out more empirically by observing viewers at two installations of the project, one in San Francisco and one in New York: when women entered, men would often leave the room, as if

co-occupying this formerly 'private' space of fantasy with female viewers provoked discomfort and embarrassment.

34. One risk is a potentially straightforward reappropriation by the male. Bacher's work, long neglected by many feminist critics, was later frequently promoted by gay male artists and curators and purchased by gay male collectors – a phenomenon that potentially short-circuits the complex female-to-male-to-female circulation of desire in the work, producing a situation instead where the female artist becomes the mediator between masculine positions of production and consumption.
35. Renny Pritikin, 'Interview with Lutz Bacher', San Francisco, 6 July 1990.
36. Butler, 'Imitation and Gender Insubordination', p. 23.
37. Working from an examination of drag as a sometimes controversial practice of gender imitation, one which 'enacts the very structure of impersonation by which *any gender* is assumed', Butler has asserted the importance of abandoning 'proprietary' notions of gender, and argues instead that *all* gender identities operate by processes of imitation and impersonation. Proposing that 'there is no "proper" gender, a gender proper to one sex rather than another, which is in some sense that sex's cultural property,' Butler asserts that 'where that notion of the "proper" operates, it is always and only *improperly* installed as the effect of a compulsory system.' 'Imitation and Gender Insubordination', p. 21.
38. Butler, 'Imitation and Gender Insubordination', p. 28.
39. In this investigation of gesture and the body, Child is of course deeply influenced by post-Judson Church dance, and the early work of Yvonne Rainer, Simone Forti, and other choreographers who abandoned the classical 'dance' body to turn towards everyday movements (walking, vacuuming, shutting a door, etc.) as an inspiration for modern dance. See Yvonne Rainer, *Works 1961–73*) (Halifax: The Press of the Nova Scotia College of Art and Design, and New York: New York University Press, 1974).
40. Child, 'Program Notes', San Francisco Cinematheque, 22 February 1990.
41. Madeline Leskin, 'Interview With Abigail Child', from *Skop* (West Berlin, February 1988), reprinted in *Motion Picture*, vol. 3 no. 1/2, Winter 1989–90 (New York: Collective for Living Cinema).
42. As Peter Brooks has noted, 'Melodrama operates by an *overdetermination* of signs, it tends towards "total theatre", its signs projected sequentially or simultaneously on several plains' (Brooks, *The Melodramatic Imagination: Balzac, Henry James, Melodrama and the Mode of Excess*, New Haven: Yale University Press, 1976, p. 46). These signs are then played across a number of registers – music, acting style, costumes, decor, visual tableaux – which can reinforce and also relay each other. In *Mayhem*, Child uses such overdetermination to play her registers against each other, more contrapuntally, to open up or scatter the meanings they create.
43. In his article 'Convulsive Identity' (*October*, no. 57, Summer 1991) Hal Foster, drawing from Dominic La Capra and Peter Brooks, suggests the importance of understanding how effects of 'deferred action' operate within and between texts, in order 'to complicate readings of influence, the effectivity of the present on the past' (p. 21). See also Peter Brooks, *Reading for the Plot: Design and Intention in Narrative* (New York: Vintage Books, 1984).
44. Matias Viegener, 'There's Trouble in That Body', *Afterimage*, January 1991. Reprinted in David Bergman (ed.), *Camp Grounds* (Amherst: University of Massachusetts Press, forthcoming, 1993).
45. In Butler's model, identity does not pre-exist such performance but is constituted by it; there is, she remarks in *Gender Trouble*, 'no doer behind the deed'. Instead, in 'Imitation and Gender Insubordination', she conceives of the psyche itself *as compulsive repetition*:

    If gender is drag, and if it is an imitation that regularly produces the ideal it attempts to approximate, then gender is a performance that *produces* the illusion of an inner sex or essence or psychic gender core; it *produces* on the skin, through the gesture, the move, the gait (that array of corporeal theatrics understood as gender presentation), the illusion of an inner depth. ... To dispute the psyche as *inner depth*, however, is not to refuse the psyche altogether. On the contrary, the psyche calls to be rethought precisely as a compulsive repetition, as that which conditions and disables the repetitive performance of identity (p. 28).

46. See Viegener, 'There's Trouble in That Body', p. 12.
47. In her final film of the series, *Mercy* (1990), Child focuses on the endangered *male* body, bringing together 'encyclopedic ephemera – industrial, promotional, tourist films of the 60s, military training films, etc. – to explore the body in social landscape, and particularly, through these images of men, in machine-like poses, the kind of masculinity formed around mimesis of the machine' (artist's statement, 1990).
48. For an analysis of the inseparability of 'lesbian' and 'heterosexual' identifications as they operate in North American fashion photography, see Diana Fuss, 'Fashion and the Homospectatorial Look', *Critical Inquiry*, vol. 18 no. 4 (Summer 1992), pp. 713–37.
49. Hal Foster, 'Convulsive Identity', *October*, no. 57 (Summer 1991), p. 52.

LAURA KIPNIS

She-Male Fantasies and the Aesthetics of Pornography

In Chicago, where I live and where, like most places, pornography is a thriving business, it's illegal to sell magazines such as *Guys in Gowns, Gender Gap, Transvestites on Parade, Feminine Illusion, Masquerade, Petticoat Impostors, Great Pretenders, Femme Mimics* and *She-Male Rendezvous*. Adult book stores are crammed full with all variety of what is often referred to as perversion: sadomasochism, for example, is freely traded, but you cannot buy magazines which eroticise female dress worn by men.[1] You can sell magazines showing naked men, naked women, and any combination of them doing very acrobatic, unexpected or violent things to each other, but if one of the men is wearing a garter belt you would be subject to arrest and prosecution in the state of Illinois.

The nuances and the microdistinctions of this state's obscenity code (you can sell transvestite [TV] newspapers and videos, but not TV magazines, for example) might suggest that it is the act of regulation and deployment of state power over sexuality rather than the specifics of what's regulated that is crucial.[2] And, as is frequently pointed out, anti-pornography feminism shares a highly questionable alliance with the Right and the state to the extent that both see sexual representation as a potential site of regulation and law, and work to criminalise consumers of pornography (whether juridically or through feminist condemnation and ignominy). I had to cross the border into Wisconsin to purchase TV magazines and did, in fact, transport them across state lines to Illinois. I probably committed a crime in order to write this article – against the state, and before I'm through, some might say, against feminism. You may be abetting one by reading this.

The more pornography I look at, though, the less feminist certainty I have about what exactly it is and what, if anything, defines it. There's been general feminist consensus that pornography concerns gender relations. Susan Gubar, for example, defines pornography as 'a gender-specific genre produced primarily for men but focused obsessively on the female figure' and distinguished by its dehumanising effect.[3] So what pornography both portrays and endeavours to perpetuate is the deployment of male power over female bodies; while violating women through representation is just one instance of the male desire to violate women generally, it is the sole purpose of porn.

But what about the pornography of male bodies? There seems to have been a reticence on the part of both pro and anti-porn feminist theorists to discuss, for example, gay male porn, as either not concerned with and not addressed to women, thus none of our business (Linda Williams),[4] or because it is heterosexuality and its institutions that are the problem (Andrea Dworkin).[5] Perhaps one of the reasons there's been a certain under-theorisation of pornography of male bodies is that it might throw that certainty about what pornography as a category is, and does, into question. Yet the vast market share of pornography of male bodies makes this form of the genre not merely not anomalous, but central. Take transvestite porn. The majority of the bodies portrayed are male, a large number are even *fully clothed*. And while gender is certainly at issue, it doesn't follow any of the standard presumptions of how porn works and at whose expense. Yet this material is unproblematically classed, even criminalised in some areas, as pornographic.

These magazines are fairly generic in form – I'll describe a typical one for my non-TV readers. Each issue generally features one or two short stories, in which typically an unwilling man is forced through a variety of circumstances to dress in women's clothes, which are described in elaborate detail. Sometimes this leads to sex in various configurations with either another man or a dominant woman. There are also advice columns in which similar narratives are presented in the guise of letters. Then there are, of course, pictorials of crossdressed men, usually a posed male or (pre-operative) transsexual model in female outfits or articles of clothing, often lingerie.[6] Some display their genitals, others are fully clothed. Sometimes the models are engaged in sex, alone or with others, sometimes the partners are other men, other transvestites, or sometimes women. Some are in a sadomasochistic vein and sometimes other types of fantasy scenarios are enacted – the French maid, the sexual novice. While clinical literature typically insists that TVs are heterosexuals (transvestism is distinguished by fetishism of the female clothing, as opposed to gay drag), bisexuality tends to be the sexual norm in these magazines: pictorial captions or short stories might insist that a man is heterosexual, but he often finds himself enticed by a beautiful transvestite or transsexual.[7] There seems to be a fairly casual back and forth between males and females as sex partners, with the use of hormones by some men additionally blurring the distinction.

Then there are numerous advertisements: for hormone supplements, make-up and dress advice, sexual services, videos and other pornography, an array of expensive and probably useless products like breast enhancement cream, vitamin tablets formulated from various glands which claim to soften skin, and a myriad of prosthetics, supplements and depilatories. As in traditional women's magazines, there appears to be a large market in female anxiety, whatever the sex of the subject experiencing it, and

Transvestite and Transsexual
PERSONALS

'GIRL' ON FIRE
CA-TV With passion and desire - wants to fill your nights with heavenly delights and sexual pleasure we both will treasure. All answered. See photo.
T905182-CA

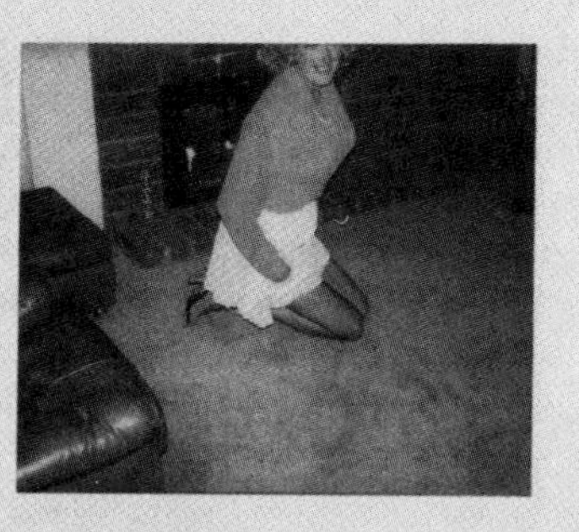

wherever it can be aroused there's soon a product to capitalise on it. It's clear from advice columns and stories that many of the readers experience great anxiety over not being (or imagining they're not) successful as women – that is, seamlessly feminine. As in women's magazines, femininity is viewed as something to be worked at and achieved. Any creeping traces of masculinity – unwanted hair growth, rough skin, figure problems – or harsh judgments by others about one's clothes, appearance or demeanour, or even worse, not being thought universally sexually attractive, comprise the everyday trauma of womanhood. It's quite an interesting cultural indicator that regardless of biological sex, femininity and anxiety are so closely allied.

Perhaps it's also worth mentioning that the TV community seems to have assimilated a number of the forms of contemporary women's culture (much of which I'd interpret historically as the residue of early feminism). These tend to be non-politicised versions of consciousness-raising that have trickled down to the culture at large as strategies for dealing with female anxiety, and are now in their second incarnation as commercial forms. If that other staple of commodified female culture, the daytime talk show, can be seen as the media-commodity annexation of the C.R. group, these magazines, too, advertise a number of for-sale versions of what were once local types of female coping and sublimating mechanisms and are now products – self-help and self-acceptance literature; advice columns; and special telephone lines for make-up and clothes advice, networking, introductions and support.

And lastly, the magazines contain a large number of photographic personal ads. In fact, some of the magazines have no editorial content at all, but consist solely of advertisements and photo classifieds. It's this last aspect of these magazines, the photo classifieds, which I want to discuss here. I'd add that with such a large and growing number of these photos in circulation – around 50–75 photos in each issue of, currently, perhaps twenty-five different magazines just in the US – they clearly have to enter into any discussion of pornography, as one of its *disparate practices*.

These personal ads are basically amateur self-portraits. Many seem to be taken with time-lapse devices or remote shutter cables (which can sometimes be seen in the photos), although it's usually not possible to say when there might also be another person actually taking the photo. Most are reproduced in grainy black and white, although some are in colour. They're most often of a single figure, a man, in a variety of dress and undress, almost always articles of female clothing or lingerie. Most of the men face the camera frontally, gazing into the lens, although expressions and poses vary considerably. The majority are full-figure. Sometimes genitals are showing, sometimes an erection is prominent, sometimes the man makes a point of concealing his genitals between his legs and feminising himself. In many cases the man is dressed completely as a woman and strikes a pose suggestive of various feminine stereotypes – the movie starlet, the slut, the matron, the shy virgin, the maid, 'the good ole girl'.

Unlike most pornography, however, these images aren't produced for monetary gain: the posers and/or photographers aren't paid (although publishers and distributors of the magazine are obviously profiting). So a question might be asked immediately about the status of these images as pornography in relation to feminist analyses of the porn industry as exploitative of women. The relations of production of these images involve no exploitation that I can discern, and generally no biological women either (though there are scattered ads by professional female dominatrixes who grudgingly admit to being willing to consider applications from submissive men who need training and discipline).[8] One of the generally undiscussed issues in the porn debates is how or why sexual images of men work differently from sexual images of women – and clearly there's an assumption that men are positioned differently because, to my knowledge, it's solely images of women that have been the focus of feminist anti-pornography efforts. All the anti-pornography legislation that feminists are attempting to enact across the US and Canada speaks of the violation of *women's* civil rights. So if these TV self-portraits or gay male porn images are not seen as exploitative or degrading to the male models, and are not seen as causing detrimental effects to men at large, it would seem to be due to a somewhat tautological line of reasoning: porn is seen as genericising women alone; men as a class don't suffer ill effects from male pornographic images because porn victimises women.

The ostensible purpose of these photos is to meet other people (they all list box numbers and the state the poser hails from, along with a brief caption and description), often for explicit sexual purposes, but at times simply requesting friendship, advice or correspondence. Often what the poser claims to be advertising for, however, seems highly unlikely to meet with a response. For example, some ads consist simply of a torso, a body part, or the poser from behind, and in some the language is so vague – 'Write and tell me about yourself' – that it is unclear who, and what sex, is meant to respond. Some of the photos seem, to me anyway, deliberately comic, or at least carnivalesque, with garish make-up jobs and precariously top-heavy outsize prosthetic breasts. My speculation is that, to some degree, these ads are forms of self-display rather than, necessarily, attempts to meet others. But instead of trying to guess at the motives behind the practice, I'd like to consider some other, similar forms of bodily display as a device to approach the transvestite classifieds and, through them, larger questions about pornography generally. How might it disturb and perhaps unsettle the category 'pornography' if I were to wrench these photos out of definitional certainty by bringing other discourses to bear on them, if I were to consider them, say, within the category of the self-portrait, a sub-genre of Western art and aesthetics with antecedents in painting as far back as the fifteenth century, which as critic and historian Barbara Rose puts it, records:

> the artist's subjective feelings about himself – his conception of how he is perceived by his world and how he experiences himself within a specific social, political, economic, moral and psychological context.

Self-portraits often include revealing subconscious clues to the artist's emotional state and inner drama.[9]

So what if I were to conjecture that the motive of transvestite self-portraiture is, as our culture tends to understand self-portraiture in general, an aesthetic act of self-definition, and to suggest that we might come to these images with the same kinds of anticipation we bring to the museum or gallery: of aesthetic shocks and visual pleasures, of a descent into symbolic language, of access to another consciousness, or a revealing exposure of our own lives and culture.

To establish the case for so treating TV self-portraiture, I'd like to detour through the work of a well-known contemporary artist who has herself made a career of photographic self-portraiture, or at least of recirculating its codes. Cindy Sherman became known in the early 1980s for a series of photographs called 'Untitled Film Stills'. In them, she transforms herself into a variety of female types – 'The Girl Detective, America's Sweetheart, The Young Housewife, The Starlet, The Whore With a Heart of Gold, The Girl Friday, The Girl Next Door' *et al.* – posed within the *mise-en-scènes* of non-existent B-movies. To call them self-portraits raises an immediate dilemma: although they are all 'of' Sherman, who the 'self' is, is open to question. As Arthur Danto puts it in his definitive critical essay on Sherman's work, the introduction to a coffee table-size book of her photographs: 'They are portraits at best of an identity she shares with every

Untitled Film Still 11 (Cindy Sherman, 1978)

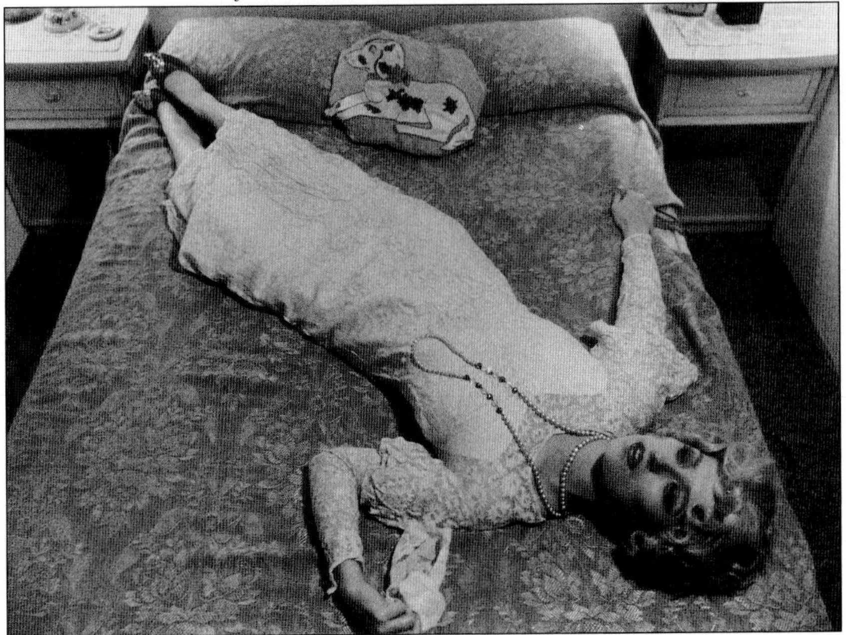

Untitled Film Still 14 (Cindy Sherman, 1978)

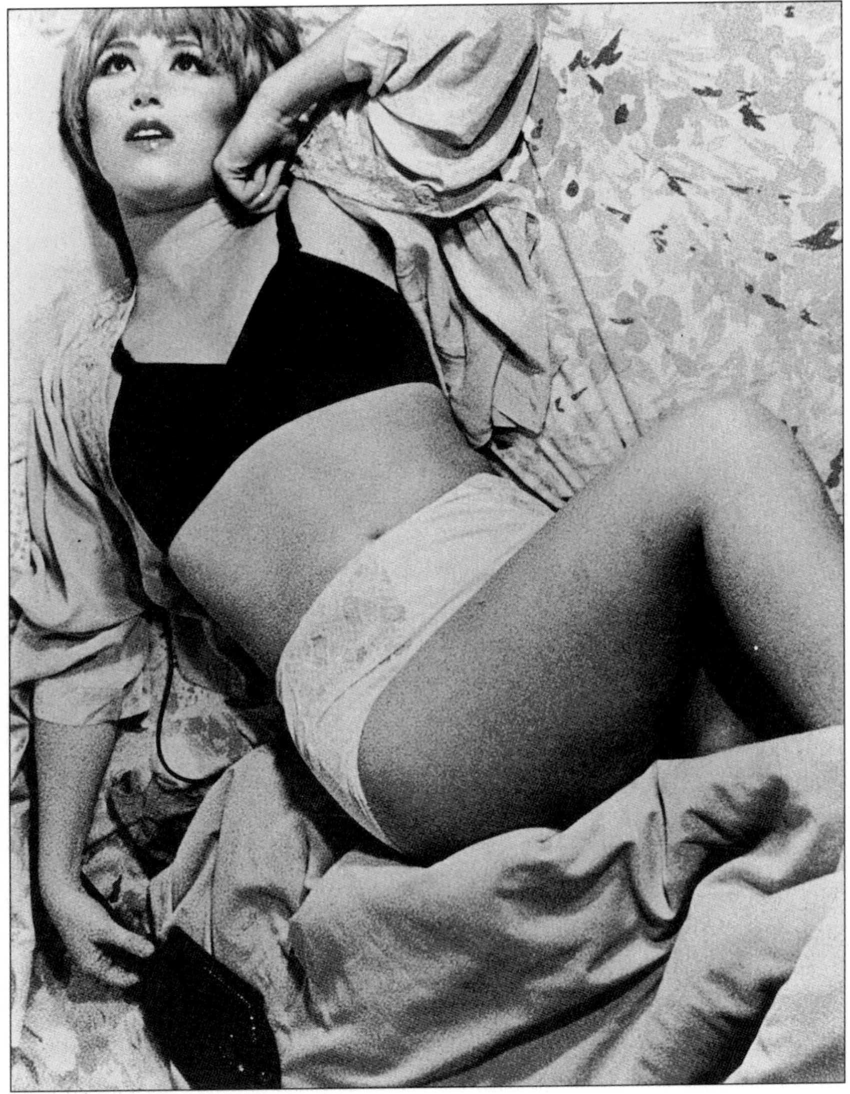

Untitled Film Still 6 (Cindy Sherman, 1978)

woman who conceives the narrative of her life in the idiom of the cheap movie.'[10]

At first glance, the similarities between Sherman's work and the TV self-portraits are striking: both put categories of identity into question by using the genre of the self-portrait to document an invented 'self'. And both are centrally and crucially concerned with femininity and its masquerades. Danto, however, as aesthetician and critic, is concerned with categories and classifications in the arts. Although he doesn't bother with the regulation question, 'Is it art?', instead he asks 'Is it photography?' Sherman isn't particularly concerned with the standard concerns of the art photograph – print quality, and so on – and further, the genre she chooses to appropriate, the film still, is what Danto labels 'working photographs', that is, photographs which have a *purpose*, are meant to perform some labour, and are 'subartistic'. Danto finally concedes on two different grounds, however, that Sherman *is* a photographer. First because the camera is central to her work; it doesn't 'simply document the pose: the pose itself draws on the language of the still.' Secondly, Danto admits that the prejudice against 'working photographs' is the basis of a *class system* in photography with an 'aristocracy of proto-paintings allowed into the precincts of high art, and a proletariat of working photographs playing productive roles in the facilitation of life.'

It was the upheavals of the 60s (Danto confines himself to upheavals in art, by which he means Warhol) that allowed the working photo to be perceived as a vehicle of meaning, and allowed 'photographs of common life [that] had little to do with the artistic ambitions of fine photography ... to find their way into the space of art.' These commonplace photos – baby pictures, graduation photos – carry a 'powerful charge of human meaning'; they 'condense the biographies of each of us', and it was the 60s that taught us to be able to 'recognize the deep human essence with which these lowly images were steeped, aesthetics be damned.' So by extension, Danto seems to imply that refusing to perform critical labour on non-aristocratic, non-high art photographs, or refusing to work at extrapolating the same kinds of meaning and affective impact from, say, TV self-portraiture as from, say, Sherman's work, would mean that one was both forgetting the lessons of the 60s, and imposing a class system on the field of photography – perpetuating inequalities which presumably reverberate through other social spheres as well.

Having established to his satisfaction that Sherman can be considered a photographer, Danto plumbs the work for meaning, not in terms of its aesthetic qualities, but in its thematics and relation to its culture and audience. Through her photographic self-reflexivity, Sherman achieves

> a oneness with her means, a oneness with her culture, a oneness with a set of narrative structures instantly legible to everyone who lives this culture, and so a oneness with her presumed audience. The stills acquire consequently a stature as art which draws together and transcends their artistic antecedents. ... [They] condense an entire drama.[13]

Given the licence Danto has established to look more deeply at non-art photography, I have to ask: in what sense is his assessment of how Sherman's photos operate on an audience not true of TV self-portraiture as well? Don't their photos resonantly (and self-reflexively) call up in each of us a deeply internalised cultural memory-bank of images and codes of 'feminine' poses – in that these photos are only 'legible' to the extent that the viewer recognises and shares the gender and dress codes in operation? Within Western culture they're instantly legible as an act of defiance against the 'naturalness' of the set of arbitrary signifiers – dress, hair, make-up – which tend to be taken as evidence of the equivalence of sex and gender, and legible as an assault on the almost universal assumption that you can tell a person's sex by looking at their clothes and gender presentation.

So the viewer of these photographs – even more so than in Sherman's work – is made critically aware of the cultural construction of the feminine, in that the poser, the bearer of the codes of femininity, is (and often explicitly displays the fact that he is) biologically male. Doesn't this work very evocatively 'condense an entire drama' – most obviously, the drama of gender assignment, a universal and sometimes disastrous drama, as is brought home by TV self-portraiture's brief glimpses into the occasional yet recurring schism between biological sex and binary gender? Sherman's work, Danto tells us, 'rises to the demand on great art, that it embody the transformative metaphors for the meaning of human reality.' Could we actually refuse transvestite self-portraits the opportunity to embody transformative metaphors? Or is it that the transformations embodied here actually surpass the threshold of what Danto names and values as 'disturbatory art', which seeks 'real transformations through charged artistic enactments', 'requires great courage' and 'set[s] up perturbations across a social field.' (Or when great art seeks 'real transformations', are these expected to be confined to art institutions and their specific audiences?)

And as a postmodern critic, I have to add that we would also want to consider the TV self-portraits, like Sherman's work, in their contemporaneity, in the context of other examples of postmodernist representational practices that appropriate and recirculate genres and idioms – the self-portrait, in these cases – of previous styles and epochs. In that context I might be led to deduce that the 'self' presented in these self-portraits *is* just that, a self in quotation marks rather than the stolid Cartesian self-certainty displayed in the self-portraiture of a Rubens or a Rembrandt. The ceaselessness of all this transvestite self-representation, read in the aggregate, seems not dissimilar to certain other relentless preoccupations and repetitions of postmodernist representation which return, like Sherman's work, again and again to the same sore tooth, probing those no longer viable humanist fictions of self, nature and truth.

Sherman's work, somewhat surprisingly, propels Danto into a tizzy of humanist hyperbole rather than post-humanist gloom: 'I can think of no body of work at once so timeless and yet so much of its own time as Cindy

Sherman's stills, no oeuvre which addresses us in our common humanity ... no images which say something profound about the feminine condition and yet touch us at a level *beyond sexual difference* [my emphasis].' Perhaps Danto is so cheery about Sherman's work only because he seems to be in a certain state of denial about its sexual and gender politics, because he prefers to think he's being addressed 'at a level beyond sexual difference' in his 'common humanity'. While Danto seems unable to take sexual difference seriously as a category, the psychoanalyst Louise Kaplan, who does, points out that the transvestite *also* desires a position beyond sexual difference.

Kaplan's general view of perversions in both men and women is that rather than being sexual pathologies, they're pathologies of gender role identity – an inability to conform completely to the gender conventions and gender stereotypes of the dominant social order. Kaplan defines perversions as mental strategies that use

> one or another social stereotype of masculinity and femininity in a way that deceives the onlooker about the unconscious meanings of the behaviors she or he is observing. Were we to think about perversion solely in terms of manifest behaviors without going into the motives that give meaning to those behaviors, we could simply conclude that the male perversions are quests for forbidden sexual pleasures and nothing more.[11]

So Kaplan would tend to overlook the sexual motives of the TV personals to look at their narratives of gendering. All 'perverse scenarios', for Kaplan, are ways of triumphing over childhood traumas; male perversions allow men to cope with forbidden and humiliating feminine strivings and longings. Perversions are a series of deceptions: the perverse strategy is to give vent to one forbidden impulse as a way of masking an even more shameful or dangerous one. The desire that is out in the open distracts the viewer from the thing that's hidden. So a male transvestite, in Kaplan's view, doesn't want to *be* a woman, but is coping with forbidden feminine longings and the insurmountable anxiety they cause by demonstrating that he *can* be a woman, but a woman with a phallus, a woman who hasn't been castrated. Crossdressing is a performance of a *script* that allows the man to allay the anxiety of his feminine wishes, and of his incomplete assimilation to the social gender binary of masculinity. So, as with Danto, transvestites are attracted to elaborate, theatrical forms of feminine display (I'm speaking of Danto's choice of Sherman's work as subject matter) as a way of *denying* sexual difference. This is no aspersion on the estimable Arthur Danto: one of the things I hope we'll begin to see is that wherever there is art, or even art criticism, there is also perversion, or as Kaplan would put it, perverse *strategies*.

Much of Kaplan's study is devoted to defining and detecting female perversion (perversion has generally been thought to be a male domain) in behaviours that exaggerate femininity, behaviour often seen as 'normal' female behaviour. So, for example, were Cindy Sherman's adoption of stereotypically feminine behaviours, poses and clothing presented outside the distancing device of the art gallery, the clinical term 'homovestism' – a gender impersonation of the same-sex person – might apply, a term coined by Canadian psychoanalyst George Zavitzianos to describe gender conflicts expressed through dressing in exaggerated or ritualised versions of same-sex clothing.[12] Sherman, in her repetitive return to the same 'script', and without the art world, outside the gallery, would seem as perverse in her preoccupations as any crossdresser.

According to psychoanalyst and gender researcher Robert Stoller, the 'scripts' behind the perverse scenarios are similar to *all* instances of sexual excitation. Behind every erection, male or female, are fantasies ...

> ... meanings, scripts, interpretations, tales, myths, memories, beliefs, melodramas, and built like a playwright's plot, with exquisite care, no matter how casual and spontaneous the product appears. In this story – which may take form in a daydream as one's habitual method of operation for erotic encounters, in styles of dress and other adornments, in erotic object choice, and in preference in pornography (in brief, in any and all manifestations of erotic desire) – I shall keep insisting that *every detail counts*.[13]

So for Stoller, sexual excitation, whether perverse or quotidian, has an *aesthetics* which is as complex, coded and meaning-laden as other forms of narrative, theatre or art. And perverse scenarios are particularly tightly constructed, with every detail and element fraught with narrative significance.

We might note, interestingly, that the language used to delineate the aesthetics of perversions, to trace their etiologies and describe their psychobiographical raw materials, is almost identical to the type of psychocritical language used to describe the aesthetic and creative process of the modern artist. Artistic activity, and the specific repetitions within an individual artist's oeuvre that constitute style, thematics, even medium, are often said to have their formation in unconscious, unresolved conflicts, traumas and torments that are expressed, returned to and repeated in art and literature. It may be something of a critical cliché in the age of the 'death of the author', but the artist as suffering neurotic is still one of the most prevalent discourses of artistic production. This art historian's analysis of Mondrian's abstractions is typical:

> Mondrian's aesthetic choices emerged from his unconscious conflicts; as he translated these choices into his painting, wielding his ruler and applying his brush, these conflicts guided his hand. He found sensuality so frightening that it was his dread of desire, rather than the desires themselves, that ultimately shaped his abstract designs. No sentiment, no curves, no touching – that is how he lived and that is what his paintings proclaim. ... [They] offer impressive evidence just how much beauty

> the talented can wrest from fear... Painting was, for Mondrian, the aesthetic correlative for his repressions, his way of coming to terms with himself – at once an expression of his problem and an embodiment of his solution.[14]

And who among us hasn't made some sort of casual inference about an artist, writer or film-maker's unconscious life and preoccupations read through the symptom of his or her work? One has only to think of say, Hitchcock, and the cottage industry in linking his psychosexual quirks to the thematics of his films. So *sublimation*, which in its pop psychology form means 'working something out' through other means, is tacitly acknowledged by both professional and casual critical enterprise as the key to artistic production: socially unacceptable impulses and contents are channelled through and buried in the artistic work for future critics and historians to elicit and decode. As perversion starts to appear more aesthetic – 'every detail counts' – don't aesthetics, conversely, start to seem more perverse?

In Freudian theory proper, the *what* that gets channelled elsewhere, into more socially valued forms, is sexual energy. And for Freud, too, the connection is explicitly made *between art and perversion*: 'The forces that can be employed for cultural activities are thus to a great extent obtained through the suppression of what are known as the *perverse* elements of sexual excitation.' These are what Freud called the component instincts, which are anarchic, polymorphous and infantile, and which, when they fail to achieve successful integration into normal adult sexuality, are most likely to become sublimated into other aims.[15] (And the connection between the terms 'sublimation' and the sublime shouldn't be forgotten.) So art and perversion are similar in origin, dissimilar in that art rechannels the same impulses and energies into a socially acceptable or elevated idiom: aesthetic language.

So clearly this rechannelling will mean that, at a surface level, art tends to *look* different from perversion, or its media form, hard-core pornography. Stoller defines pornography as material that intends to be pornographic, that is to produce a certain response – arousal – in its audience. But for Stoller, art and pornography are formally similar: erotic response is as complex a phenomenon as aesthetic response, and the distinctions between the two come down to differences in their respective contents.[16] But as we've seen, the two are also quite proximate: art is also libidinal, perverse; perversions have their aesthetics, and both are structured according to the imperatives of the unconscious. It's perversion which, having undergone transformation through the psychic processes of sublimation, then *elicits, produces* aesthetic response.[17] The energy devoted to keeping aesthetics and perversity – art and pornography – so discursively sequestered begins to make more sense when you see that the aesthetic response is actually completely *dependent* on perversity, only produced in the alchemy of sublimation.

What Stoller also neglects to mention are the class aspirations behind these content differences – that the competence necessary to do the work of translating the energies of compulsion and perversion into the lofty heights of aestheticism and the language of form is, to a large degree, an educated response, a cultural competence.[18] It presupposes a degree of intellectualisation and the 'distance from the world' which, Pierre Bourdieu writes, is the basis of the bourgeois experience.[19] There may be upper-class aesthetes using porn or lower-class abstract artists producing gallery art, but as Bourdieu puts it:

> The aesthetic disposition, understood as the aptitude for perceiving and deciphering specifically stylistic characteristics, is thus inseparable from specifically artistic competence. The latter may be acquired by explicit learning or simply by regular contact with works of art, especially those assembled in museums and galleries.[20]

This aesthetic competence, produced largely through the vehicle of what Bourdieu calls 'educational capital', is a form of cultural capital, a mechanism for enforcing class distinctions. So also at stake in maintaining the absolute discursive distinction between art and pornography are the class divisions that a distinctively high art works to maintain, as well as the necessity of reproducing the requirement for sublimation – so crucial for the bourgeois project of producing distance from the body, the unconscious and the materiality of everyday life.[21]

And perhaps there's another stake: art's potential *as* 'disturbatory', *as* political. For art historian Francis O'Connor, also writing about self-portraiture, Mondrian's translation of his conflicts into *abstraction* 'from symbol to sign ... denies the aesthetic a world other than itself'. A similar argument has been advanced by Peter Burger, also writing of the twentieth-century avant-garde, that in modernism and twentieth-century art generally art lost any political edge as it became increasingly self-referential, increasingly mediated by art institutions, and increasingly cordoned off from praxis and everyday life.[22] O'Connor adds that what Mondrian has done is to relegate art to 'a mode of moral etiquette'. So both writers appear to be saying that the work of translation and transmogrification of perversion, neurosis, social conflict and artistic rebellion into self-referential art – into *gallery art* – is precisely what strips art of social meaning: for Burger, of its political potential; for O'Connor, of the possibility of being something other than mere moral etiquette. So this seems to be an argument *against* sublimation, against aesthetics as an exercise in decorousness and the social niceties. It seems to be an argument, then, for pornography over art.

If the discursive distinctions between art and pornography come largely down to issues around sublimation and the class imperative to produce and reproduce it, the problem with pornography appears to be its failure to translate one set of contents into another. The problem is that it produces a body of images that are too *blatantly* out of the unconscious, too *unaesthetically* written in the language of obsession, compulsion, perversion, infantile desires, rage, fear, pain and misogyny; too literally about sex and power rather than their aesthetically coded forms in the works of any number of famous and adulated artists and writers who treat similar themes (or the socially coded but equally ritualised forms through which they're expressed at gallery openings and academic conferences). Too *potent* for art. It might appear that the interest of the state in regulating pornography is that it *meets* the criteria for 'disturbatory art', as Danto calls it, which seeks 'charged artistic enactments' and sets up 'perturbations across a social field'. And as art has moved to appropriate – or return to – pornographic idioms, in the work of Robert Mapplethorpe, Karen Finley, Holly Hughes, to name a few, the government has been very quick to step in.

As the distinctions between art and perversion begin to unravel, perhaps some of the certainty about what pornography is and how it functions does so too. This isn't necessarily an argument for moving pornography into the art galleries and museums. Aesthetics may rely on perversity, perversity may be aesthetically complex, but sublimation isn't imaginary: the pornographic response is still viscerally and experientially distinct from aesthetic response. It *is* an argument, however, for regarding pornography (when we regard it theoretically) *as* we do artistic production rather than as discursively distinct, and for applying the same degree of critical, interpretive acumen to it; for understanding porn, as Stoller suggests, as imbued with theatrical and semiotic complexity, far from lacking in nuance. It's not *only* a naked woman, it's not *transparently* a pair of lace panties, it's a condensation of narratives of the entry into the social order, the passage from infancy to childhood to adulthood, the prison-house of binary gender role assignment, of mother-dominated child-bearing *and* the oppression of women. But as Kaplan indicates, the woman in the porn pictorial is as likely to represent the female side of the male viewer he wants to subjugate as it is to express, in some literal way, his desire to oppress me. There's no reason to assume that pornographic images function any more literally (or produce more literal effects) than other more socially elevated images that we're accustomed to reading for their symbolic and latent meanings – no reason other than class prejudice against 'working photographs' or pure censoriousness against sexual pleasure.

So as I began trying to look as closely at TV self-portraiture as the art establishment would at Cindy Sherman's work, I began to examine the *mise en scène* of the photos: the spaces around the bodies instead of the distracting flash of the bodies themselves. Rather than posing themselves against a blank wall or backdrop (although a few do), most of the men choose to pose themselves within their domestic space, affording a voyeuristic glimpse into their decor and environs. The juxtapositions of the body and its social geography condense, in tableau, the lived experience of gender distress and its familial melodramas: the burden of liminality and otherness and their by-product secrecy and shame. They force the viewer onto intimate terms with the small forms of social tyranny and the too often, too taken-for-granted policing of everyday life that none of us – however putatively gender-normative – ever escapes.

These self-portraits are very much dramas of the home. They tell stories. Living rooms and bedrooms are both popular scenarios, but a lot of men choose to pose themselves in their kitchens as well – perhaps in their minds the most feminine space in the house. The image of a glamorous yet virile blond in four-inch heels perched seductively on the kitchen counter – the shiny kitchen appliances, dish soap, cute spice rack and harvest-motif wallpaper competing visually with her erect penis – suggests the American sit-com suburban mom as imagined by David Lynch or perhaps John Waters, and the absent presence of a 'real' wife as well. The wife-impersonator, gazing impudently into the camera, usurping the rightful occupant (and her narrative), verifies the complaints of many TV wives that their husbands are competitive as women: spending more time on looks, more money on clothes, making the wives feel dumpy and inferior as women. The kitchen as a gendered turf conveys that both the wife we see and the wives we don't are equally padlocked into social gender stereotypes and their domestic spaces.

The image of a beefy man in lingerie pouting into the camera, posed in front of a Swedish-modern breakfront displaying a neatly arranged collection of Time-Life books and china figurines – with perhaps even a wedding photo in the background – says everything about carefully compartmentalised secrets and the fantasy of seamless 'normal' surfaces, with this insistent display of all the props and set-pieces of happy American home life. It's an image that almost makes you understand the popularity of Ronald Reagan – the carefully constructed, pomaded and overproduced surface, that cynical (and of course completely fictive) promise of sit-com family normalcy, of docile mothers and strong fathers who will bomb us out of perversity and back to the fantasy of God-given sex roles and their respective, separate, wardrobes.

Sometimes the self-portraitist will send in not just one photo, but an entire layout in which he poses himself in every room of the house, giving you the guided tour – the formal dining room, the rec room with the CD collection and component stereo system, the master bedroom suite. As is common throughout the history of portraiture, he pictorially surrounds himself with his property and possessions. What mute assertion or appeal is being made here? Schooled by John Berger in 'ways of seeing' early oil painting, we're alerted that these objects supply us information about the poser's position in the world – his class status and material wealth obviously – but also about what *possession* itself implies: entitlement, citizenship, the assertion of a right.[23] Given what we know about the disdain heaped on the male transvestite in our society, this self-protective gathering of one's possessions around oneself seems sadly talismanic. (Interestingly, for Berger, pictorial qualities such as these are gendered: a man's presence is dependent on displayed forms of external power and possessions, whereas a woman's presence is in her physical appearance. These TV self-portraits, not surprisingly, walk right down the middle. Even

SEXY BLONDE TV

MO-TV Send photos and letter expressing interests for further correspondence. See photo. T905146-MO

28

Berger has no aesthetic analysis that isn't binary in its gender assumptions.)

The more of these photos I looked at, the more curious I began to be about why so many transvestites seem to have matching bedspreads and curtains in their bedrooms. Had I stumbled onto the missing link in the etiology of transvestism through my close reading of transvestite home decor? Something about matching fabric? I finally realised that what I was looking at were motel rooms, and began to notice the further clues (most of these photos are quite grainy): a suitcase in a corner, those backbreaking slab-of-wood headboards that no one would dream of putting on their own bed, an occasional rate card on the door, the motel-type plumbing fixtures in the bathrooms.

These *mise-en-scènes* narrate a fairly obvious tale of secrecy – a compulsion to cross-dress that the man has managed to keep secret from a wife and family. So, a small drama, a brief glimpse into what fear and pain must accompany the deception of being unable to reveal the most central thing about yourself to your mate, and the catastrophe that exposure would mean in a life carefully constructed around a sexual secret.

One thing to add about this evident sexual secrecy is that it flies completely in the face of Robert Stoller's account of the essential role of women in the causation and maintenance of transvestism. According to Stoller, who has written extensively about transvestites and transsexuals, 'the women of transvestites ... all share the attribute of taking a conscious and intense pleasure in seeing males dressed as females. All have in common a fear of and a need to ruin masculinity.' The cooperation of women is essential for 'successful' transvestism – and the fact that some men are able to pass as women is 'almost invariably due' to women and girlfriends – 'succorers', Stoller calls them, who, because of their own concealed rage at men devote themselves to teaching the transvestite how to dress, walk and use make-up.[24]

These motel room photos stand in silent rebuke to the clinical literature and, of course, to its blame-the-woman line. As with feminist art, which consciously appropriated the power to define and narrate women's lives against dominant and dominating discourses – including, frequently, the male-dominated medical and psychiatric professions – so may these TV self-portraits be forms of defiance and self-empowerment for another oppressed minority.

I've chosen to discuss a form of pornography that may seem, to a certain extent, anomalous. TV classifieds are something of a folk practice, hand-crafted and artisanal in relation to other more mass-produced forms of porn. And I've chosen to discuss a form of pornography that doesn't depict biological women's bodies either – largely in order to be able to talk about porn without all the usual red flags going off, and to avoid reproducing all the usual gender assumptions of the porn debates. But in conclusion I want to suggest that perhaps in reading all pornography more closely we might uncover other histories, other narratives, perhaps crudely written, and perhaps, as Kaplan says of perverse scenarios, exposing one thing to distract you from thinking about another. The perverse strategy hides *through* exposure, it works overtime to deflect your attention from what's really at stake. Pornography exposes a lot of naked bodies, but perhaps this is as distraction: the repetitions of all pornography, the return again and again to the same scenarios and scripts, have the compulsive character that is the mark of material emanating from the unconscious.

In seeing pornographic images of women as so transparently about male erections and female disempowerment, what remains hidden? As with the TV self-portraits, closer reading may provide glimpses into the forgotten (repressed) histories that all gendered subjects share, and from which some have emerged more unscathed than others. Perhaps there is some understanding to be gained – for women, and maybe men too – that will be the wedge into male power, perhaps a realisation that so often what looks like power is props, compensatory mechanisms and empty signifiers. I suggest that in looking at pornography we should not be so distracted by surfaces, and that like art critics, we're alert for meaning, to what we don't yet know, are threatened by, or may have forgotten.

Notes

1. My use of the word 'perversion' throughout this essay should not be read as derogatory. I've retained the term primarily because it's used throughout the clinical literature I refer to; however, it will become clear that my attitude towards that literature is ambivalent. The word perversion obviously implies its distinction from so-called 'normal' sexuality, but this should be understood as referring to social norms, and not implying some form of natural or a priori sexuality.
2. For example, bestiality is another such regulated area. This means you can freely slaughter and eat animals, you just can't photograph sex with them, which is surely not any *less* humane.
3. Susan Gubar, 'Representing Pornography: Feminism, Criticism, and Depictions of Female Violation', in Susan Gubar and Joan Huff (eds.), *For Adult Users Only* (Bloomington: Indiana University Press, 1989), p. 48.
4. Linda Williams, *Hard Core: Power, Pleasure and the 'Frenzy of the Visible'* (Berkeley: University of California Press, 1989), p. 6.
5. See Andrea Dworkin, *Intercourse* (New York: Macmillan Press, 1987).
6. The term 'transvestite' refers to men (I don't discuss female transvestism here) who dress in women's clothing. The term 'transsexual' denotes men who through hormones or surgery have physically changed their primary or secondary sexual attributes, most typically in these magazines men who have developed breasts through hormone use. For clinicians, the difference additionally is that transvestites see themselves as men and want to be men, albeit men dressed occasionally as women; transsexuals actually want to be women.
7. It's not my purpose here to try to distinguish between heterosexual and homosexual transvestism, or otherwise categorise practices, but I do want to point out that these magazines do seem to belie the clinical literature on transvestism, which defines transvestism as heterosexual. Both Stoller and Kaplan define male transvestism as a man fetishising female clothing as a path to arousal but in which the sexual object choice is a woman; both define homosexual drag as non-fetishistic cross-dressing. What the magazines indicate, though, both in the stories and in the

personal ads which I discuss here, is that many men who cross-dress and define themselves as heterosexual *are* interested in sex with other men or cross-dressed men when they themselves are cross-dressed (although they may see themselves and even their bodies and genitalia as female in those encounters), and that their sexuality, at least as far as the biological sex of their object choice goes, is much more multivalent than the clinicians suggest. There also *does* seem to be homosexual fetishism of female clothing. But I make no assumption that any of these images or writings represent actual practices, but that, as with all porn, this may strictly represent fantasy.

8. It should be noted, though, that feminists have repeatedly expressed resentment of the fact that the transvestite male may foray into femininity while in no way relinquishing any of the prerogatives of male power. It has also often been said of transvestites that they caricature the 'worst' aspects of femininity and are, deep down, actually hostile to women; so some analysts may be inclined to read some degree of coded misogyny in these images. For a feminist analysis of transvestism, see Annie Woodhouse, *Fantastic Women: Sex, Gender and Transvestism* (New Brunswick: Rutgers, 1989), which, as the author says, 'is not a study which is particularly sympathetic to transvestism' (p. xiii). See also Marjorie Garber, *Vested Interests: Cross-Dressing and Cultural Anxiety* (New York: Routledge, 1992), which, though primarily concerned with the figure of the transvestite across Western culture, also analyses the gender and sexual politics of transvestism from a feminist vantage point.
9. Barbara Rose, 'Self-Portraiture: Theme with a Thousand Faces', *Art in America*, January–February 1975, pp. 66–73.
10. Arthur Danto, 'Photography and Performance: Cindy Sherman's Stills', in Cindy Sherman, *Untitled Film Stills/Cindy Sherman* (New York: Rizzoli, 1990), pp. 5–14.
11. Louise Kaplan, *Female Perversions* (New York: Doubleday, 1991), p. 9.
12. See also Joan Riviere, 'Womanliness as a Masquerade', in Cora Kaplan (ed.), *Formations of Fantasy* (New York: Methuen, 1986), pp. 35–44.
13. Robert J. Stoller, M.D., *Observing the Erotic Imagination* (New Haven: Yale University Press, 1985), p. 49.
14. P. Gay, *Art and Act: On Causes in History – Manet, Gropius, Mondrian* (New York: Harper & Row, 1976), pp. 225–6. Quoted by Francis V. O'Connor, 'The Psychodynamics of the Fronted Self-Portrait', in Mary Mathews Gedo (ed.), *Psychoanalytic Perspectives on Art* (New Jersey: The Analytic Press, 1985), p. 197.
15. J. Laplanche and J.-B. Pontalis, *The Language of Psychoanalysis* (New York: Norton, 1973), p. 432.
16. Stoller, *Observing the Erotic Imagination*, chapter 2, 'Erotics/Aesthetics'. The content argument actually gets harder to support as more and more artists appropriate pornographic idioms. For example, as I write, novelist Nicholson Baker's new book *Vox*, which is composed entirely of a two-way phone sex conversation, is third on the *New York Times Book Review* hard-cover bestseller list.
17. See also Janine Chasseguet-Smirgel, *Creativity and Perversion* (New York: Norton, 1984), p. 89.
18. On the class basis of anti-pornography sentiments see Laura Kipnis, '(Male) Desire and (Female) Disgust: Reading *Hustler*', in Lawrence Grossberg, Cary Nelson and Paula Treichler (eds.), *Cultural Studies* (New York: Routledge, 1992), pp. 373–91.
19. Pierre Bourdieu, *Distinction: A Social Critique of the Judgment of Taste* (Cambridge, Mass.: Harvard University Press, 1984), p. 54.
20. Ibid., p. 51.
21. See Norbert Elias, *The History of Manners* (New York: Urizen Books, 1978).
22. Peter Burger, *Theory of the Avant Garde* (Minneapolis: University of Minnesota Press, 1984).
23. John Berger, *Ways of Seeing* (London: Penguin, 1972).
24. Robert J. Stoller, M.D., *Sex and Gender: On the Development of Masculinity and Femininity* (New York: Science House, 1968), pp. 206–17.

LYNDA NEAD

'Above the pulp-line'[1]

The Cultural Significance of Erotic Art

Introducing the Erotic

> Up to the point of obscenity, art consecrates and purifies all it touches.
> Charles-Augustin Sainte-Beuve, as quoted by Peter Webb, 1975.[2]

> The advantage of erotic art over the common run of hard-core pornography is that ... like all good art ... it quietly *educates* while it entertains. It may arouse our senses and stimulate desire – it is meant to do so and would fail if it didn't – but it will do so by making us *think* as well as *feel*.
> Drs P. and E. Kronhausen, 1973.[3]

These quotations introduce the central terms of this discussion: obscenity, pornography, art and the erotic. Both are drawn from publications which appeared in the early to mid-1970s, a moment when, as will be argued at the end of this essay, the attempt to draw meaningful distinctions between these terms and to assert the value of erotic art had a particular urgency. Webb and the Kronhausens represent different aspects of sexual liberalism, itself only one voice within the polyphony of sexual discourses in the 1970s. Webb uses the words of Saint-Beuve to assert the mutual exclusivity of art and obscenity. Obscenity appears as a given or intrinsic quality of an object or representation; it is the point at which the sacred powers of art are rendered useless. If art represents here the domain of pure culture, then obscenity symbolises the profane, where culture disintegrates and the subject is strictly beyond representation.

The Kronhausens express a more pragmatic view. Hard-core pornography lacks cultural distinction, its function is merely and solely that of sexual arousal and sensual gratification. Erotic art, on the other hand, takes on the didactic role of high art and lifts the depiction of desire to a higher cultural plane. Desire is thus contained and controlled by the aesthetic. Erotic art arouses, but it is a reflective and enriching form of arousal.

The opposition of art and pornography, or the aesthetic and the obscene, is one which has structured much modern cultural discourse. It has worked to classify acceptable and unacceptable forms of culture and to differentiate the licit and the illicit, the ennobling and the forbidden. In 1972, Lord Longford, one of the main British campaigners of the period for the restoration of 'traditional' moral values and the family, organised an investigation of pornography and its effects on contemporary British society. The report of the Longford Committee was published in the form of a mass-market paperback and launched in a blaze of publicity. Among the many expert witnesses called before the Committee was Lord Kenneth Clark, a key figure within British arts administration and one of the Western world's best-known art historians through his presentation of the television series *Civilisation* (1969–70). His formulation of the art/pornography opposition usefully summarises the view inherited from Enlightenment aesthetics:

> To my mind art exists in the realm of contemplation, and is bound by some sort of imaginative transposition. The moment art becomes an incentive to action it loses its true character. This is my objection to painting with a communist programme, and it would also apply to pornography.[4]

For art to be art it has to engage the mind rather than the body; it has to involve the faculty of imagination and bring about a still, contemplative state in the viewer. Propaganda and pornography shatter the unified subjectivity of the viewer and incite, or more accurately excite, the body to action. What is clear from this kind of formulation is that the artistic and the pornographic are not simply properties of any given representation, but are also, and perhaps more significantly, classifications of those who view the images; they are social, cultural and moral designations of people as well as objects.

Clark's definition recalls the work of Steven Marcus, whose classic study of Victorian pornography, *The Other Victorians*, was published in 1966. For Marcus, literary writing is characterised by multiplicity, narrative complexity and a concern with human relations; but pornography is essentially repetitive, literal and unmetaphoric, and interested in organs rather than people.[5] Although this is primarily an account of formal characteristics, it too may be taken as a description and ranking of audiences as well as texts.

As views such as these demonstrate, pornography is seen to be essentially non-creative; in its urgency to bring about sexual arousal in the viewer, its singular onanistic intention, it sweeps aside all the formal and imaginative preoccupations which are seen to be at the heart of artistic creativity. But perhaps the terms of this cultural debate need to be recast or refocused. What about other categories within this system, categories such as the erotic? Within both mainstream and alternative cultural politics the focus has been on producing objective criteria for the designation of pornography. Although this has produced competing definitions, involving both the extension and narrowing of the boundaries of the pornographic, essentially this exclusive preoccupation with pornography, seen as a discrete cultural category rather than as part of a broader system of cultural distinction, perpetuates the view of cultural production and consumption polarised between art and pornography, the pure and the profane. It fails to recognise the significance of the mid-terms within this system which, as I will argue, are the principal means by which meaning is produced.

It is easy to conceive of art and pornography in their most extreme forms, forms which we might situate securely at the centre of each category; it is harder, though, to specify where one category ends and the other begins, and yet this is surely the critical place of judgment. It is at the limit, at the framing edge of the category, where differences are most emphatic and where the finest distinctions between inclusion and exclusion, acceptability and unacceptability are made. So we might begin to alter the focus, away from the polarisation of art and pornography and towards a re-examination of erotic art, where art most nearly succumbs to the pornographic and brushes up against the obscene. Erotic art defines the boundaries of allowable sexual representation in modern Western culture and is where the depiction of sex can be given moral and social value. How, then, is the erotic differentiated from the pornographic or the obscene?

The etymology of pornography is from the Greek words for harlot and writing; the *Oxford English Dictionary* therefore gives the primary definition as writings of or about prostitutes and their patrons. The word has subsequently taken on the additional meaning of the expression of obscene or unchaste subjects. The derivation of erotic is from the Greek 'eros', sexual love – its *OED* definition is given as 'of or pertaining to the passion of love'. Significantly, one of the references given in the *OED* is from George Steiner's *Language and Silence* (1967): 'Above the pulp-line ... lies the world of erotica, of sexual writing with literary pretensions or genuine claims.' The pulp-line is an apt metaphor for the boundary between illicit and licit sexual representation. Pulp connotes unbounded matter, possibly the body reduced to unformed flesh, the body as it is addressed by pornography, void of moral or intellectual regulation. Erotic art, then, is above the pulp-line, for it implies a form of contained cultural consumption which, whilst carrying the exciting risk of failure, succeeds in addressing the viewer as a unified and rational subject. Clearly there are significant areas where the two terms dissolve into each other, for if pornography is the domain of forbidden sexual representation, then erotic art must always carry the traces of this possibility in order to retain its distinctive identity and not simply be absorbed into the realm of art.

As we can see from the etymology of pornography, the term has always connoted a form of commodified sex; sex for a mass market and sold for a profit. The erotic, however, carries none of these associations; its etymological roots are with love. Erotic art seeks to transcend the market-place, and it is this absence of concern with commercialisation and money which makes the concept of 'erotic art' possible.

Cultural Distinction

> Taste classifies, and it classifies the classifier. Social subjects, classified by their classification, distinguish themselves by the distinctions they make, between the beautiful and the ugly, the distinguished and the vulgar...
>
> Pierre Bourdieu, 1984[6]

The judgment of erotic art should be seen, in Bourdieu's terms, as an act of cultural distinction which carries particular social significance. Bourdieu's survey of taste takes the form of a critique of Kantian notions of the aesthetic. Kant sought to distinguish the condition of disinterestedness, which is the only guarantee of aesthetic contemplation and which differentiates it from the interests of reason and the senses. Bourdieu suggests that the Kantian notion of the detached and pure gaze asserts a life free from economic necessity which functions at all levels of social life:

> Although art obviously offers the greatest scope to the aesthetic disposition, there is no area of practice in which the aim of purifying, reforming and sublimating primary needs and impulses cannot assert itself, no area in which the stylisation of life, that is, the primacy of forms over function, of manner over matter, does not produce the same effects. (p. 5)

Although Bourdieu could justly be accused of having a romanticised perception of an uncorrupted, honest working-class culture, his general theoretical framework offers a particularly helpful way of understanding the cultural significance of erotic art. For Bourdieu, the cultural sphere is maintained by the evacuation of vulgar, coarse and venal pleasures and the assertion of pure, disinterested and sublimated ones. This hierarchy is commonly expressed by the prioritising of form over function and of manner over matter. According to Bourdieu, those who are satisfied by purified pleasures are assured social superiority; cultural consumption thus fulfils the function of legitimating social differences.

When this model is applied to the judgment of erotic art, we can see that this form of classification might yield a special legitimating force. If the sacred sphere of culture is characterised by the expulsion of the appetite, then what could be more risky, but potentially more rewarding, than to classify the venal, sex, itself? What better way to demonstrate your cultural disinterestedness and superiority than to come into contact with the erotic and to be – practically – unmoved? Erotic art legitimises the representation of the sexual through the assertion of form which holds off the collapse into the pornographic. Erotic art takes the viewer to the frontier of legitimate culture; it allows the viewer to be aroused but within the purified, contemplative mode of high culture. Arousal and contemplation – erotic art must remain for ever between these two conditions for it to function as the point of distinction between art and pornography. This flirtation with the sexual can be seen at work in Kenneth Clark's evocation of the eroticism of the painted nude:

No nude, however abstract, should fail to arouse in the spectator some vestige of erotic feeling, even although it be only the faintest shadow. ... The desire to grasp and be united with another human body is so fundamental a part of our nature, that our judgment of what is known as 'pure form' is inevitably influenced by it; and one of the difficulties of the nude as a subject for art is that these instincts cannot lie hidden, as they do for example in our enjoyment of a piece of pottery, thereby gaining the force of sublimation, but are dragged into the foreground, where they risk upsetting the unity of responses from which a work of art derives its independent life. Even so, the amount of erotic content which a work of art can hold in solution is very high.[7]

The publishing success of Clark's *The Nude*, from which this extract is drawn, makes it worth looking at in detail. The text takes us through a series of steps which negotiate the issue of erotic art. The uneasiness of its tone is apparent, particularly towards the end where Clark describes the way in which sexual instincts are 'dragged' into the open by the nude and 'risk upsetting' the purity of the aesthetic faculty. In fact throughout the extract Clark emphasises the magnitude of the risk which faces the intrepid connoisseur. Beginning with vestiges and shadows of erotic feeling, the sexual body makes itself ever more present until, towards the end, the response verges on the kinaesthetic. But the entire passage asserts the mastery of the body, the triumph of the mind over the baser senses and instincts. It is the enactment of cultural distinction, announcing the social and cultural superiority of the connoisseur art historian and the putative reader.

The Primacy of Form and Sound Economics

We have seen that to maintain its function as arbiter of the pulp-line, erotic art must be seen to foreground the concern with form. Whereas pornography is believed to reduce language to its most basic forms or to cliché and stereotype, erotic art pursues the dual preoccupations of love and linguistic exploration. In Steiner's essay on contemporary erotic writing, he describes pornographic vocabulary as the '"stripped naked" of language', brought about by the reduction of privacy and individual imagination within a mass consumer society. 'Where everything can be said with a shout,' he observes, 'less and less can be said in a low voice.'[8] Pornography is presented as the genre of function and necessity, the language of the sexual body, for which style is simply an obstacle to its primary task of arousal. Good erotic art, on the other hand, is the genre of individualism, of the subtle and enchanting whisper rather than the yells of the mob.

There is of course a paradox in this conception of pornography as stylelessness, or of style reduced to the utmost degree. For language – written or visual – to give the reader a sense of stylistic absence demands extreme stylisation. It requires conventions of representation, narration, contextualisation which say to the reader or viewer: this is representation 'stripped naked', which abandons superfluous details of style and form and takes you directly, without formal interference, to the realm of the sexual. Erotic art cannot easily take this risk with style but has to neutralise obscenity through a range of creative forms. As one aesthetician puts it:

> The erotic elements may be treated metaphysically. In this case sex is regarded as the absolute or related to some other absolute. ... Second, the sexual may be poeticized, that is, invested with emotional charge. ... Third, the description of sex may be intellectualized through a distancing of the characters from their behavior. ... Finally, the most frequent method, aestheticization, that is, the accenting of such values as sound, color, shape, movement etc.[9]

In all these cases the content undergoes a formal manoeuvre which distances the sexual and transforms it into culture. Of course, this transmutation cannot be guaranteed or permanently secured, the erotic may devolve into pornography and all these classifications are subject to competing and historically specific claims. What is most constant is the connotation of eroticism as style made manifest, even if it is parodic style which mimics the stylelessness of pornography. Style is a signifier of the aesthetic and necessitates an engagement which is non-sensual and unconcerned with gratification.

Within the discipline of art history this process of aestheticisation of the sexual has been explored to the point at which the medium itself, regardless of content, is seen as an expression of sex. Comparing a female nude and a landscape by the painter Pierre Bonnard, Janet Hobhouse writes:

> The landscape is by far the sexier painting, with its trees and leaves pulsating in the wild, emotive colouring of Bonnard's palette. Nature is voluptuous, enticing, opulent, beckoning the painter in the same manner as did his early nudes.[10]

The aesthetic disposition is thus able to purify and sublimate the sexual to the extent that form and medium alone are able to convey the wild, expressive sexuality of the painter. The language of connoisseurship ensures that this does not become a vulgar display; instead, the response serves as an indication of the viewer's refinement and taste.

The concepts of art, pornography and the erotic are constituted through moral and cultural discourses, and they are also economic categories. Pornography is the product of mass culture; it is, as we have seen, sexual representation made solely for the purpose of profit. But pornography represents a wayward form of economics; it circulates covertly, 'under the counter', and seems to transgress the system of differential value established in the field of culture. In 1972 the report of the Longford Committee emphasised the huge sums of money being made through trading pornography and the disparity between its cost and its cultural value:

> Glossy art books sell for £6 or £7 a time, and *Private*, an internationally notorious erotic magazine – printed in four languages – costs no less than £5 an issue in Britain. From the same source colour pictures cost £4 for a set of eight, or £80 for 'all 27 sets'.[11]

What kind of economic system is this, in which a porn magazine costs nearly as much as a well-produced glossy art book and in which 'pin-ups' go for the price of masterpieces? Pornography is thus characterised by disparity between economic and cultural value, whereas erotic art is altogether a sounder product which confirms the parity between these two fields of value. Erotic art never evades the question of market value altogether, however; rather it occupies a particular place within the specific economic conditions of the art market.[12] Art as a commodity is priced according to quality and rarity, and as a part of this system erotic art is set apart from other commodities and the trash of mass-produced porn.

Pornography testifies to the loss of economic management which is an apt paralleling of the loss of moral management. This relationship comes together most forcefully in the notion of 'permissiveness', a metaphor which emerged in the political context of the 1960s and 1970s.[13] Used most frequently by the advocates of traditional and authoritarian morality, permissiveness was a term which connoted loose moral standards and sexual promiscuity leading to a general decline in social life. From the perspective of legislation, permissiveness encapsulates a series of legal reforms concerning issues such as obscenity and censorship, abortion, contraception and divorce. But in its wider context permissiveness can be applied to a much more generalised set of social changes arising from the boom in the world capitalist economy following the Second World War. The 1960s, then, seemed to be an age of economic affluence and moral liberalism. There is a long and complex association between transformations in the economic field and in sexual morality; in the mid-nineteenth century the metaphor of 'spending' carried the sense of both economic and sexual expenditure and implied the need for careful self-management in both spheres. In terms of the development of this metaphor in the 1960s, Jeffrey Weeks comments: 'There is no doubt that the prolonged boom depended in part upon a switch in moral attitudes away from traditional bourgeois virtues of self-denial and saving ("prudence") towards a compulsion to spend.'[14]

Perhaps the most visible feature of this growth in economic and sexual consumption was pornography. Although there was undoubtedly an increasing eroticisation of social life in the major cities of Western Europe and the United States and a manifest expansion in the pornography industry, it is equally true that pornography – or, more precisely, the representation of the sexual – took on symbolic importance in the 1960s and early 1970s. It became the battleground for competing definitions of sexual and social acceptability, and it was precisely in this historical context that attention was turned to erotic art as the site where new ground might be won for sexual freedom within legitimate culture, or which confirmed the corruption of traditional public life through permissiveness. In order to exemplify some of the issues discussed so far, it is worth looking in more detail at the formation of erotic art during the historical moment of the late 1960s.

The First International Exhibition of Erotic Art

This exhibition of erotic art opened in a public gallery in Sweden on 3 May 1968, more or less to the day when student revolts in Paris and in campuses across Britain and the USA reached a peak. From Sweden, the show moved on to a gallery in Denmark and then sought a private venue in the USA. The exhibition was largely the work of two people, the Drs Phyllis and Eberhard Kronhausen, psychologists who had pioneered new techniques in psychotherapy and had published on various aspects of sexual psychology, sex and censorship. The Kronhausens also had an extensive personal collection of erotic art, which formed the nucleus of the show. The exhibition received substantial publicity in Sweden and in other European countries and the implications of public funding for the display of sexually explicit material were fought out by various moral and political factions.

As well as the exhibition itself there was an accompanying catalogue, two substantial volumes which included an essay by the Kronhausens on the nature and value of erotic art, transcribed interviews with visitors and experts and illustrations of the exhibits. Both the show and the catalogue promoted the Kronhausens' view of the liberatory and therapeutic effects of erotic art and of sexual behaviour freed from the conventions of bourgeois authoritarianism and repression:

> Erotic art expresses the demand for sexual freedom – a freedom vital to individual happiness and mental well-being. In that sense, erotic art carries a truly revolutionary message: it demands no less than extension of freedom, not only in the sexual area, but in every sphere of social life.[15]

For the organisers, the significance of the exhibition was that it gave the public an opportunity to look at pictures about sex without looking at pornography, without feeling embarrassed or ashamed. Indeed, although it is not specified, the implication of their position is that the pornographic and the erotic are largely defined in terms of their means of distribution and consumption and their place within the cultural spectrum. If representations of sex are placed on the walls of a public art gallery, they are more likely to be understood within the discourse of art than that of pornography.

> In the case of pornography, most people will feel that they are looking at something they shouldn't perhaps be looking at. But here in the museum they can look at erotic pictures that are beautiful and artistic and they can do so in an atmosphere of social acceptance, social approval. (p. 16)

From P. and E. Kronhausen, *Erotic Art: A Survey of Erotic Fact and Fancy in the Fine Arts*, vol. 1 (New York: Grove Press, 1968), p. 9

This partial recognition of the discursive formation of pornography is perhaps the most lasting radical aspect of the exhibition; otherwise the commentary and exhibits are marked by an exclusive concern with heterosexuality and a romantic view of sexual freedom as a state of pre-Fall bliss.

The poster which advertised the exhibition begins to demonstrate how the primacy of form is deployed by the Kronhausens (see below). This poster raised particular problems for the organisers since, by its very function, its circulation was less circumscribed than the exhibition and it was more likely to transgress the boundaries of acceptable and unacceptable public display. Although the exhibition included a wide range of Western and non-Western art, contemporary and historical, the image used on the poster is a seventeenth-century Japanese woodcut. This image exemplifies the concept of primacy of form, discussed earlier; the depiction of pattern and surface decoration is visually at least as important as the representation of sexual intercourse. Formally, the bodies are a continuation of the lines and shapes of the surrounding drapery. Moreover, the woodcut is historically and geographically distant and, wrenched from its cultural specificity, it can become a timeless, aesthetic evocation of sexual love. Elsewhere in the catalogue, this process of aestheticisation is repeated:

> We had occasion, in fact, to watch the transformation of pornography into art before our own eyes when Hans Bellmer one day worked in our presence, making a complicated and highly erotic engraving from a series of common pornographic photographs. (p. 3)

The erotic artist is thus perceived as an alchemist who transmutes the base matter of pornography into the gold of high culture.

According to the organisers, erotic art is a force for liberation, aesthetically valuable and a better product than pornography. Bringing sexual representation out into the open as legitimate culture would, they claimed, produce more discerning consumers who, in turn, could impose their taste and choice on the pornography industry. Denmark and Sweden could thus lead the way in the production of erotic art, 'as they once did with modern furniture and household design.'[16]

'The First International Exhibition of Erotic Art' was made possible by the lifting of censorship laws in Sweden and Denmark during the second half of the 1960s. In 1967 Denmark removed all restrictions on written forms of pornography, and what became known as the 'Danish experiment' was assessed on both sides of the Atlantic as part of the reshaping of obscenity and censorship legislation. In September 1970 the report of the American 'Commission on Obscenity and Pornography' was published, rejecting any clear correlation between pornography and acts of sexual violence and advocating a liberalising of sex education in order to foster 'healthy' sexual development. The report resulted in a split between members of the Commission and was rejected by the Senate and President Nixon. In June 1970 an interim report was produced which contradicted the conclusions of the Commission. The 'Obscenity Report' came down strongly on the side of moral authoritarianism and, in a brash dismissal of cultural distinction, situated images of the unclothed body in high art on a sexual continuum with pornography:

> In galleries from Washington, D.C., to San Francisco, pictures of naked people are regularly displayed and in Europe the situation is even more deplorable. Sometimes these pictures masquerade as culture – for example the projected Kronhausen tour through the United States of notorious erotic paintings from Europe. But a naked body is naked, whether it be in oil or in the flesh.[17]

In Britain there was a cluster of prosecutions for obscenity in the early 1970s; the National Viewers and Listeners Association organised a popular campaign against immorality in broadcasting, and in 1972 Lord Longford published his report on pornography. Longford concluded that exposure to pornography did adversely affect social behaviour and moral standards, and cited the Danish and American situations as evidence that the state alone could not be relied upon to protect moral standards.

What we find during this period is a number of different interests trying to redraw the lines around forms of sexual representation. To look at this situation solely from the perspective of pornography is to misunderstand how these debates occupy the whole of the cultural sphere rather than one discrete area. I have been arguing that in many ways erotic art, as the boundary of legitimate culture, is a more significant site of judgment and contestation than pornography, a view which is borne out by more recent debates. In 1989, in the United States, Senator Jesse Helms spearheaded a campaign to prohibit the use of public funds from the National Endowment for the Arts for work which might be deemed obscene. During his campaign, Helms targeted an exhibition by the photographer Robert Mapplethorpe, denouncing his photographs of 'homosexual erotica' as pornographic and obscene.[18] In these cases the entire spectrum of culture is recast; to redefine erotic art is necessarily to redefine art and pornography. So one way out of the current impasse within discussions of pornography is to reintegrate our examination of culture and sexual representation, to bring together the high and the low, the world of the aesthetic and the pornographic, precisely at the point of the erotic. And it may be that with a careful and critical re-examination of this category, there is a way forward for a progressive and exciting form of sexual representation.

Notes

1. The quotation in the title is from George Steiner, *Language and Silence: Essays 1958–1966* (London: Faber & Faber, 1967), p. 91.
2. Charles-Augustin Sainte-Beuve (1804–1869), literary critic, novelist and poet; as cited in Peter Webb, *The Erotic Arts* (London: Secker & Warburg, 1975), p. 1.

3. Phyllis and Eberhard Kronhausen, *The International Museum of Erotic Art* (New York: Ballantine, 1973), p. 6.
4. Quoted in Lord Longford, *Pornography: The Longford Report* (London: Coronet, 1972), pp. 99–100.
5. Steven Marcus, *The Other Victorians: A Study of Sexuality and Pornography in Mid-Nineteenth Century England* (London: Weidenfeld and Nicolson, 1966), pp. 278–80.
6. Pierre Bourdieu, *Distinction: A Social Critique of the Judgement of Taste*, trans. Richard Nice (London and New York: Routledge and Kegan Paul, 1984), p. 6.
7. Kenneth Clark, *The Nude: A Study of Ideal Art* (London: John Murray, 1956), p. 6.
8. Steiner, *Language and Silence*, p. 89. The essay, 'Night Words', from which these quotes are taken, is in fact a critique of modern American erotic fiction. The details of this argument about the 'Great American Novel' cannot be addressed within the scope of this article.
9. Stefan Morawski, 'Art and Obscenity', *Journal of Aesthetics and Art Criticism*, vol. XXVI no. 2 (Winter 1967), p. 204.
10. Janet Hobhouse, *The Bride Stripped Bare: The Artist and the Nude in the Twentieth Century* (London: Jonathan Cape, 1988), p. 44.
11. Longford, *Pornography*, p. 37.
12. See, for example, discussions such as 'A Passion for Collecting: Erotic Art comes out of the Closet and into the Auction Rooms', *Economist*, no. 302 (10 January 1987), p. 82.
13. This discussion is particularly indebted to the account given in Jeffrey Weeks, *Sex, Politics and Society: The Regulation of Sexuality since 1800* (London and New York: Longman, 1981), pp. 248–72. See also John Selwyn Gummer, *The Permissive Society: Fact or Fantasy?* (London: Cassell, 1971).
14. Weeks, *Sex, Politics and Society*, p. 250.
15. Phyllis and Eberhard Kronhausen, *Erotic Art: A Survey of Erotic Fact and Fancy in the Fine Arts*, vol. 1 (New York: Grove Press, 1968), p. 8.
16. Ibid., p. 7.
17. *The Obscenity Report: The Report to the Task Force on Pornography and Obscenity* (New York: Stein and Day, 1972), p. 32. See also 'Report of the Commission on Obscenity and Pornography, September 1970' (Washington, D.C.: Government Printing Office, 30 September 1970).
18. For further discussion of the Helms amendment, see Carol S. Vance, 'Misunderstanding Obscenity', *Art in America* (May 1990), pp. 49–55.

CHRIS STRAAYER

The Seduction of Boundaries

Feminist Fluidity in Annie Sprinkle's Art/Education/Sex

Annie Sprinkle's post-porn modernist art surpasses revision and crossover via an autoerotic straddling of fences. Her fusional play engages multiple discourses from pornography, feminism, art, spirituality, sex education, advertising, political activism, performance art, body play, and the self-help health, prostitutes' rights and safe sex movements. As a 'nurse' she prescribes sex as an analgesic; as a porn star she sells pubic hair, soiled panties and urine; as an artist she exhibits her cervix; as a slut/goddess she pisses/ejaculates. Offering her wrist to Spider Webb on the steps of the Museum of Modern Art in 1981, Sprinkle successfully defied Manhattan's prohibition against tattooing. Despite an arrest in the late 70s for 'conspiracy to publish obscene materials, conspiracy to commit sodomy, and sodomy', Sprinkle has prospered as a photographer, performer, writer and producer of erotic art. Her Sprinkle Salon in Manhattan has been touted as the 1990s' version of Warhol's factory. Her book *Annie Sprinkle: Post Porn Modernist*, which provides the personal history in this essay, is an autobiographical artwork in which self-actualisation relies on artifice as much as origins.

Within this multiplex creativity, numerous boundaries are licked clear. Art melts into porn, porn accommodates life, life becomes art. Breathing orgasms into non-genital sex, and spirituality into orgasms, Sprinkle seduces deconstruction. Exercising a 'queer' ideology arising from contemporary gay and lesbian subculture, she confounds pornography's boundaries, transgresses ours, and wraps us in her own. Pornography's naturalist philosophy spreads outward, merging private and public realms, simultaneously intensifying and diffusing the pornographic sensibility. In this essay, I'll track these multiple confluences in Sprinkle's social intercourse to their denaturalised climaxes. In her self-conscious photography, performance art and film/video work, I will locate a demystification of sexiness, an affirmation of fluid identity, and a visualisation of female orgasm. Finally, I will argue that Annie Sprinkle's sex-life-art challenges the hegemonic categories of 'heterosexual' and 'male'.

First, I want to underscore the intersection of feminist art and porn discourses in Sprinkle's 'arthole' activities. My juxtaposition of two photos graphically suggests Sprinkle's vital link to 70s feminist performance art, no doubt augmented by her summer camp training with life-artist Linda Montano. The first photo shows Carolee Schneemann in a 1975 performance asserting the propriety of personal experience as content for art by reading a diary scroll withdrawn from her vagina. The second photo shows Annie Sprinkle in 1991 douching on stage in preparation for her 'public cervix announcement' in which, aided by speculum and flashlight, she allows audience members to look at her cervix (see figures 1 and 2). Just as feminist artists such as Montano, Schneemann, Suzanne Lacy, Judy Chicago and many others injected women's everyday experience (from housework to menstruation) into art, Annie injects the everyday into porn. Like Schneemann, Sprinkle uses her body to unsettle gendered knowledge. Ultimately, Sprinkle foregrounds gender as the performance of roles.

In 'Anatomy of a Pinup Photo' (1991), Sprinkle dissects another form of body art to display the constructed 'nature' of sexiness (see figure 3). This demystification of the sexual object is a motif in Sprinkle's work from her admission that she can't walk in her six-inch heels to her design for a paper-doll Annie with cock, finger and tampax accoutrements. In her Transformation Salon photos, Sprinkle demonstrates the coexisting potentialities of 'regular person' and 'sex star' in a series of before/after snapshots/portraits. Sluts and sex goddesses are readily 'revealed' in a variety of ordinary women via make-up, costume, studio lighting, and direction. As Sprinkle explains to her female audience, 'Maybe there's a little porn star in you. Maybe not. But I can tell you from experience … there's a little of you in every porn star' (p. 91). The codes of soft porn constitute a Pygmalion discourse which women can deploy as strategically as men.

In 'The Most Prevalent Form of Degradation in Erotic Life', Freud explains how the psychology of male love commonly necessitates a good-bad binary opposition for women:

> In only a very few people of culture are the two strains of tenderness and sexuality duly fused into one; the man almost always feels his sexual activity hampered by his respect for the woman and only develops full sexual potency when he finds himself in the presence of a lower type of sexual object; and this again is partly conditioned by the circumstance that his sexual aims include those of perverse sexual components, which he does not like to gratify with a woman he respects. Full sexual satisfaction only comes when he can give himself up wholeheartedly to enjoyment, which with his well-brought up wife, for instance, he does not venture to do. Hence comes his need for a less exalted sexual object, a woman ethically inferior, to whom he need ascribe no aesthetic misgivings, and who does not know the rest of his life and cannot criticize him. It is to such a woman that he prefers to devote his sexual potency, even when all the tenderness in him belongs to one of a higher type. (p. 64)

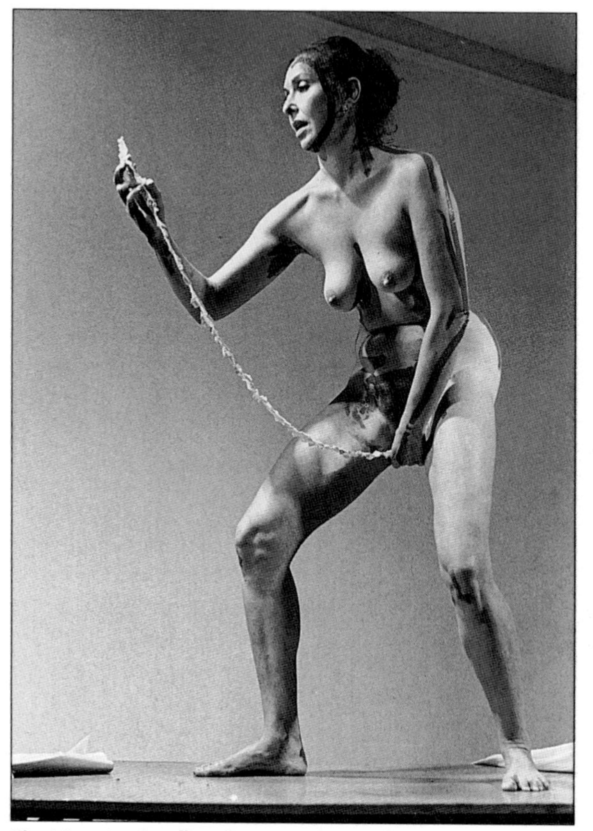

Fig. 1 *Interior Scroll* performance by Carolee Schneemann, 1975. Photo by Anthony McCall

In addition to the implicitly classist dichotomisation of sex and ethics in this statement, the sequestration of sexuality from the rest of life draws a protective line between private and public. For this reason, I submit the quotation here as a symptomatic text rather than a theoretical foundation. In the essay, Freud describes psychoanaesthesia, a behaviour (in love) of the psychically impotent type, widespread in civilised society. He offers a number of factors contributing to a man's dependence on a lower object for full sexual gratification, for example the early incestuous fixations of childhood (the original impetus for phantasies in which boys 'degrade the mother to the level of prostitute'); the nearly equal prohibition of sex with persons outside the family during adolescence; the tension between animal excitation, arising from the contiguity of erotic and excremental organs, and its necessary sublimation into cultural achievement. What remains less clear is the etiology of a woman's lower status. Is her ethical inferiority God-made or man-made?

Fig. 2 Annie Sprinkle douching in her one woman show, *Post-Post Porn Modernist*

Where such men love they have no desire and where they desire they cannot love. In order to keep their sensuality out of contact with the objects they love, they seek out objects whom they need not love; and, in accordance with the laws of the 'sensitivity of complexes' and the 'return of the repressed', the strange refusal implied in psychical impotence is made whenever the objects selected in order to avoid incest possess some trait, often quite inconspicuous, reminiscent of the objects that must be avoided.

The principal means of protection used by men against this complaint consists in *lowering* the sexual object in their own estimation, while reserving for the incestuous object and for those who represent it the overestimation normally felt for the sexual object. As soon as the sexual object fulfils the condition of being degraded, sensual feeling can have free play, considerable sexual capacity and a high degree of pleasure can be developed. (p. 62)

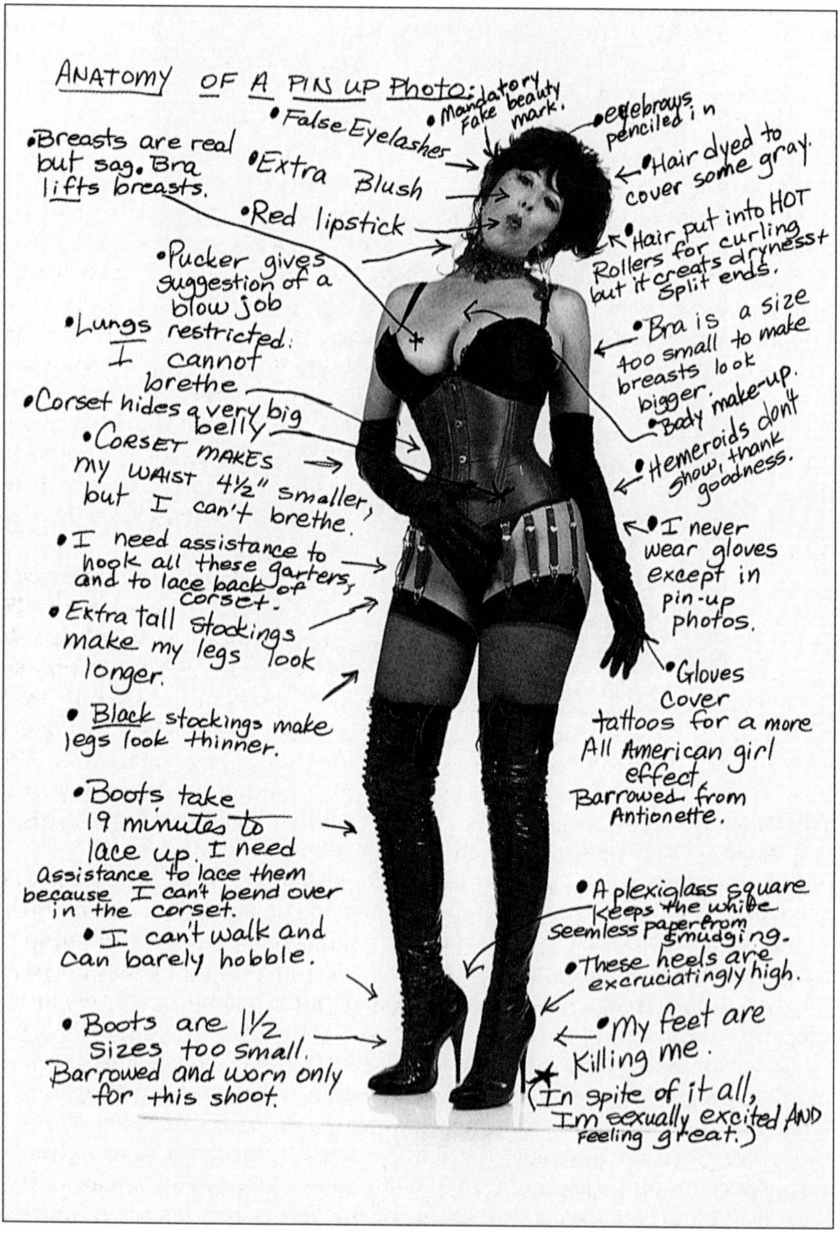

Fig. 3 *Anatomy of a Pin-up* by Annie Sprinkle, 1991. Photo by Zorro, 1981

In Freud's argument, (a) woman's lower status is both attributed and assigned to her. This corresponds to the relation of unchastity to both impurity and defilement identified by Gail Pheterson in 'The Social Consequences of Unchastity', a critique of the gendered stigma of 'whore'. Women of colour and working-class women (with dirty hands) are especially vulnerable to the 'whore' stigma. But experience also, especially that which veers away from virginity and monogamy whether by desire or abuse, can defile girls and women and condemn them to the 'whore' stigma. Whether their own or men's, sexuality degrades women.

In 'Speaking the Body: Mid-Victorian Constructions of Female Desire', Mary Poovey argues that mid-Victorian debate over prostitution inadvertently provided opportunity for the discussion of female sexuality. Contradictory discourse simultaneously positioned 'the prostitute' as wanton and fallen, as revelling in sexual delight and victim of her originally passionless, positive love of self-sacrifice. The prostitute is understood as innately sinful and made sinful by her desperate actions. This discordant representation was deployed for middle-class interests to allow, but regulate, prostitution. At the same time, however, it became available for use by women differently positioned in the social formation. As Poovey states, 'If the limits of female self-representation were initially set by the dominant representation of women, however, this representation could not finally dictate how individuals with a different investment in it would elaborate the contradictions it contained.' (p. 43)

These views of prostitution and women's sexuality remain today ready for an exploitation of their 'contrariness'. Within her creative porn discourse, Annie Sprinkle certainly retains a feminine 'heart of gold'; but she inextricably fuses it with active female sexual desire and audacious sex positivity. Furthermore, she seeks and values personal change through sexual encounters. Through her assertion of desire, she consciously claims prostitution and pornography as her own sexual experiences. The tricks, the experiments, the knowledge, the exhibition, the pornographic discourse, the pleasure belong to her. Her aim to please the client is not in conflict with her other sexual aims.

Typically, the pornography genre deploys the articulation of female desire in the service of a reassuring address to male viewers. Such address circumvents anxiety over masculine performance and competition; the viewer need only be male to be desirable. Sprinkle both exploits and extends this effect. In his essay 'When Did Annie Sprinkle Become an Artist?', Chuck Kleinhans describes Sprinkle in her early porn performances as already a performance artist, who constructs simultaneously generous and ironic personae: the teacher, the nurse, the mother.

> In (decidedly non-Lacanian) Oedipal terms: she enacts the nurturing mother who encourages sexual exploration: a figure who allays performance anxiety while encouraging voyeurism as part of the acquisition of knowledge that can create a new straight male sexual subject. In brief, she prepares boys (i.e., an infantile/juvenile/adolescent uncon-

scious formation in all adult males) to be (het or bi) men that (het or bi) women can (at least tolerably) live with and have sex with.

This subject position, Kleinhans argues, offers a positive alternative to 'the aggressive sadist voyeur model which has dominated discussion of heterosexual male spectatorship of pornographic imagery'. Freud's mother vs. prostitute dichotomy, therefore, is effectively collapsed in the 'mothering prostitute'.

In Monika Treut's independent feature film *My Father is Coming* (Germany, 1991), in which a bisexual's straight father arrives for a visit from Germany, it is Annie Sprinkle who initiates the older generation in the pleasures of New York City's Lower East Side/ Times Square sexual culture. Annie's character enthusiastically and genuinely seduces this older man, who is not conventionally attractive in either physical appearance or narrative agency (see figure 4). Although unusual for mainstream cinema, this is not unusual for pornography. But, as Kleinhans has suggested, Sprinkle's performance is as much nurturing as reassuring. As such, her pan-sexuality displays a challenging array of sexual desires, activities and objects.

In her 'personal' life, which frequently occurs onscreen, Sprinkle pursues even less conventional sex partners: a gay man, a female amputee, a 43-inch-tall man. In her tape *Linda/Les and Annie – The First Female to Male Transsexual Love Story*, Annie enjoys sex with her lover Les, a lesbian

Fig. 4 Alfred Edel and Annie Sprinkle in *My Father is Coming* (Monika Treut, 1991)

separatist-turned-macho transsexual who has a constructed penis but also retains his female genitals – a male hermaphrodite with a clitoris enlarged by excessive hormone ingestion. In 1989, Annie exhibited Les as a freak show at Coney Island. People could enter the hermaphrodite's tent with flashlight in hand and examine the genitalia. This exposure of 'the curiosity' as a mirror for our own curiosity was too much for the Coney Island management, who closed it down. Sprinkle has also photographically transformed Les into a 'sex slut'; supposedly it took three hours of transformative (cross)dressing to 'bring out [Les's] femininity to the hilt'.

Sprinkle exercises a polysexual desire which ultimately foregrounds traditional desires as codified. The male viewer who accepts Annie's unconditional positive regard is grouped implicitly with her other objects of desire and hence complies with her confrontation of these codes. When he knows of her life/art/work, he cannot simply appropriate her reassuring discourse for himself; this discourse also calls for rethinking the economy of desire.

In her contribution to this anthology, Linda Williams analyses in detail Sprinkle's 1981 porn film *Deep Inside Annie Sprinkle*. She describes a scene in which Annie fingers a man's anus while addressing the (extradiegetic) viewer with 'dirty talk' instructions. Here, Williams argues, Sprinkle raises new questions about the gendered nature of address.

> Is she telling and showing a hypothetical 'him' how to finger another man's ass? If so, the film insidiously transgresses 'normal' heterosexual taboos against males penetrating males. Is she telling and showing 'him' how *she* likes to finger a man's ass? If so, the pleasure depicted casts her in the role of the active penetrator and him in the role of penetrated, again a switch in expectations for the conventionally posited heterosexual male viewer. Or is she perhaps telling and showing a hypothetical 'her' how to finger a man's anus? After all, this is 80s porn and women are included in its address. If so, the original rhetoric of the female-whore addressing the male-client breaks down. Any way you look at it, Annie has played with the conventions of who gives pleasure to whom.

I agree with Williams but also believe that the above viewer, male or female, is encouraged to identify with Annie *as a woman* – with her heterosexual activity and female sexual pleasure – as well as with the onscreen man. In other words, Sprinkle is not only reversing traditional subject-object sexual and viewing positions, but is also engaging us in what will become, in her later video work, a virtual identity orgy.

By now it seems mandatory to claim Annie Sprinkle as an exemplary proponent of 'queer' aesthetics, sexualities and politics. Indeed, she deserves the compliment. In contemporary sexual politics, 'queer' embraces a population far larger than lesbians and gay men: bisexuals, transsexuals and various non-straight heterosexuals; tranvestites, S&M enthusiasts, fetishists, and so on. In theory, more than in practice, 'queer' also embraces diversity in race, class and ethnicity. When conceptualised most radically, the category 'queer', to my mind, does not necessarily contain all lesbians and gay men. In other words, I endorse a 'queer' politics which is deconstructive *as well as* non-normative. Although 'queer' has been praised and berated for its (potential) inclusiveness, I feel its theoretical framework allows a more critical stance. Annie Sprinkle puts 'queer' theory into practice. And, in representations of herself and her younger and older queer-peers and partners, she demonstrates that 'queer' mentality is not the sole jurisdiction of youth. Most importantly, Sprinkle extends a 'queer' celebration of differences to contest the very straight-and-narrow referent itself – that illusory but nonetheless pure heterosexual.

In 'Misreading Sodomy: A Critique of the Classification of "Homosexuals" in Federal Equal Protection Law', Janet E. Hallery describes how US sodomy laws, which in almost half the states determine anal intercourse, fellatio and cunnilingus to be criminal behaviour for heterosexuals and homosexuals alike, are discriminately applied to homosexuals only. Felony sodomy virtually becomes homosexual sodomy. The act of sodomy is conflated with and comes to define homosexual status. Homosexuals, then, are those identified by this act while all others remain unmarked and presumed heterosexual.

> Sexual orientation identities are produced in a highly unstable public discourse in which a provisional default class of 'heterosexuals' predicates homosexual identity upon acts of sodomy in a constantly eroding effort to police its own coherence and referentiality. (p. 352)

Inadvertently containing both sexually inactive homosexuals and secretive homosexual sodomites, the default category of nonhomosexuals, or heterosexuals, encourages closeted behaviour and internalised homophobia. Of course this category also contains heterosexuals who engage in anal intercourse, fellatio and cunnilingus, but, as Halley states, 'The criminality of sodomitical acts involving persons of different genders is simply assumed out of existence' (p. 357). Within these terms, the unity of heterosexual identity relies on both the knowing of homosexual sodomy and the unknowing of heterosexual sodomy.

In *Epistemology of the Closet*, Eve Sedgwick ascribes as much potency to unknowing as to knowing.

> I would like to be able to make use in sexual-political thinking of the deconstructive understanding that particular insights generate, are lined with, and at the same time are themselves structured by particular opacities. If ignorance is not – as it evidently is not – a single Manichaean, aboriginal maw of darkness from which the heroics of human cognition can occasionally wrestle facts, insights, freedoms, progress, perhaps there exists instead a plethora of *ignorances*, and we may begin to ask questions about the labor, erotics, and economies of their human production and distribution. Insofar as ignorance is

> ignorance *of* a knowledge – a knowledge that may itself, it goes without saying, be seen as either true or false under some other regime of truth – these ignorances, far from being pieces of the originary dark, are produced by and correspond to particular knowledges and circulate as part of particular regimes of truth. (p. 8)

Annie Sprinkle reinscribes sodomy into heterosexuality. By expanding the understanding of heterosexuality to acknowledge innumerable and diverse desires and practices (including certain activities shared by homosexuals and bisexuals), Sprinkle effectively contests the equation between homosexuality and deviance as well as the boundaries between homosexual, heterosexual and bisexual.

Sprinkle's contestation of boundaries is further elaborated by her creative participation in four avant-garde film/video texts: *ANNIE* (Monika Treut, US/West Germany, 16mm, 1989), *25 Year Old Gay Man Loses His Virginity to a Woman* (Phillip B. Roth, US, video, 1990), *Linda/Les and Annie* (Albert Jaccoma, John Armstrong and Annie Sprinkle, written by Sprinkle, US, video, 1990), and *The Sluts and Goddesses Video Workshop, or How to Be a Sex Goddess in 101 Easy Steps* (Maria Beatty and Annie Sprinkle, written by Sprinkle; Spiritual Advisor, Linda Montano; Inspiration, Carolee Schneeman; dedicated to Joan of Arc, US, video, 1992). In these film/videos Sprinkle combines and integrates numerous subcultural figures and widely diverse discourses. This constructs a liberationist sexual ideology in complex relation to and against notions of identity. Annie's explicit visual presence is complemented by her intense diaristic, instructional and seductive verbal activity. Pornography's naturalist presumption must make way for crucial teaching and sharing of sexual information. Tantric symbols and anatomical diagrams are integrated with porn iconography to conjoin what Foucault has distinguished as *ars erotica* and *scientia sexualis*.

With slides and re-enactments, *ANNIE* 'documents' one of Sprinkle's performance art works in which she combines codes from feminist body art, diary, science, pornography and erotic stripping. Encouraging the sexual dimension of voyeurism but discouraging distance, Sprinkle creates a performance arena in which audience members (film viewers as well as the diegetic audience) can look at the female body with both desire and curiosity. Annie relates her personal history, plays 'Tit Art' with her large bare breasts, bends over and spanks her ass, lectures on the female reproductive system, and shows the audience her sex. 'Isn't it beautiful,' she says over a close-up of her cervix. 'I have my period today so it might be a bit bloody. But that's OK. Isn't it great!'

25 Year Old Gay Man Loses His Virginity to a Woman documents videomaker Phillip Roth and Annie Sprinkle having sex. The tape begins with Phillip confessing his fear; he's afraid that a heterosexual experience might alter that part of his identity which is gay. Annie advises him simply to decide to stay gay regardless of their upcoming intercourse. For herself, fluid identity holds no threat. 'I just became a lesbian myself. ... It's a real

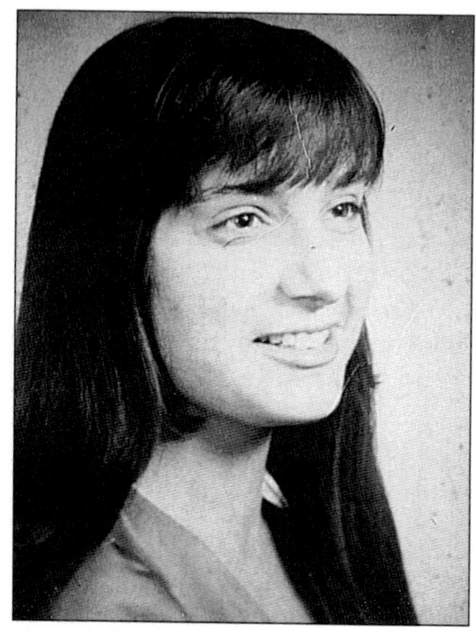

Fig. 5 Linda Nichols

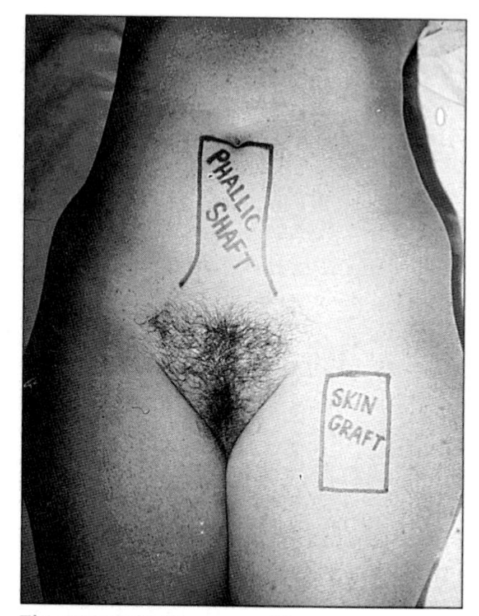

Fig. 6 Mapping transexuality

adventure to change your identity, I think.' Later Phillip adds, 'I wouldn't ever want to give up men.' 'No,' Annie replies. 'I wouldn't either.' Annie proceeds to demonstrate how a tampax is used, engages Phillip in wrestling, teaches him how to stimulate her clitoris, and initiates various positions for intercourse. During all this, they affectionately discuss their emotional and physical feelings, Annie explains who Grafenberg was, and they both occasionally look at and talk to the cameraperson. Wishing Phillip love and prosperity, Annie then presents him with a small box for his altar in which they place his condom and one of her pubic hairs.

Linda/Les and Annie begins with Annie sitting in a wooded location wearing a girlish outfit and writing in her diary. In voice-over, she expresses her excitement about her new lover. 'He's really different than the other guys,' she says as the image cuts to Les Nichols in black jeans and tank top, with long sideburns and tattooed arms, drinking beer and smoking a cigarette. As the lyrics to 'Best of Both Worlds' suggest and the delayed title confirms, Les is a female-to-male transsexual. 'I'm a big man on the outside but you know he was a she. Yes you know I'm hard and nasty, but I'm sweet and sassy too.' Later we see Les neatly groomed in a pressed blue workshirt and red tie. 'This is America,' he states. 'And I made the choice.' We learn that his choice cost $50,000 and multiple surgery. Medical pictures accompany Annie's voice-over explanation of phalloplasty procedures. We also see Les making his penis erect first by inserting a plastic rod and then by inserting his thumb. Despite humorous contrary narrative evidence, Annie declares, 'It felt free not to worry about getting it up and keeping it up.' Both Les's male and female genitals are explicitly demonstrated during the love-making that follows (see figures 5–8).

Fig. 7 Les Nichols

Fig. 8 Linda/Les and Annie

Les reports that as a male now he has more privilege and gets more respect – as if he were 'born to ask'. He refers to his male genitalia as phallus rather than penis. This framework, perhaps inadvertently, lends attitude and meaning to his description of his earlier female body as 'nothing down there'. By contrast, Annie cleverly credits hermaphroditism to Les's body when writing and narrating their story: 'He had large succulent nipples – the kind made for feeding babies. ... When I informed Les that I was having the last day of my period, he just said, "No problem". What man could be more understanding and less intimidated by a little blood than a man who used to menstruate? ... His skin was soft and smooth like a woman's, yet he had hair on his chest. His hands were small and delicate with a woman's touch, yet he wore men's rings.' Annie finds sex with Les a positive mind-fuck as she sucks both 'his clit' and his 'new sex toy'.

In *The Sluts and Goddesses Video Workshop*, Annie acts as host with seven facilitators who are transformed for our instruction into ancient sacred prostitutes via facials, clay baths, make-up, masks, wigs, hair ornaments, body jewellery, false fingernails, body paint, tattoos, piercings, high heels, new names, new clothes, sexercises and sex. High tech video effects create natural and cosmic backgrounds, provide graphs and illustrations for sex education, and allow Annie to 'emerge' full body from a close-up vulva. Later, these newly constructed sacred prostitutes facilitate two orgasms 'of, by, and for' women (of Annie, by them, and for us). Both these orgasms are visually evidenced, the first by female ejaculation (which the subtitles name 'Moon Flower Drops of Wisdom'), the second by a running orange line superimposed over live footage of Annie which charts her five-minute ten-second orgasm. In the latter, orgasmic codes of pornography such as the woman's face and open mouth are combined with indexical sweating and a didactical tracing of subjectivity. Of course, these visual representations can only provide problematic evidence. Representation always remains inconclusive. Although Annie feels her experience, we do not. Nevertheless, the mixing of sexology/porn/feminist discourses in these ejaculation and graphed orgasm scenes adds considerable envy to any remaining doubt (see figures 9–10).

In her book *Hard Core: Power, Pleasure, and the 'Frenzy of the Visible'*, Linda Williams locates within the genre a quest for a visible truth of female pleasure. Although a productive reading of pornography texts, this does not adequately explain the industry's scarce use of female ejaculation as a possible signifier of orgasm. The current shock wave resulting from representations of female ejaculation in tapes such as Blush Entertainment/Fatale's *Clips* marks this quest in the bulk of pornographic texts as self-imposed and pseudo. Obviously, many pornographers actually avoid available visible evidence. Censoring the image of female ejaculation, one might argue, maintains a male standard by a deliberate unknowing that consciously re-produces female 'lack'.

In 'Feminist Ejaculations', Shannon Bell cites sporadic references to female ejaculation from Hippocrates in 400 BC to Grafenberg in 1950, then notes that it was ignored by dominant scientific discourses defining female sexuality from 1950 to 1978. Sexologists and physicians either denied its existence altogether or (mis)diagnosed it as urinary stress incontinence. In 1978, J.L. Sevely and J.W. Bennett published 'Concerning Female Ejaculation and the Female Prostate', upon which Bell relies heavily. In this article, the authors use historical and anatomical texts to

Fig. 9 From *The Sluts and Goddesses Video Workshop* (Maria Beatty/Annie Sprinkle, 1992)

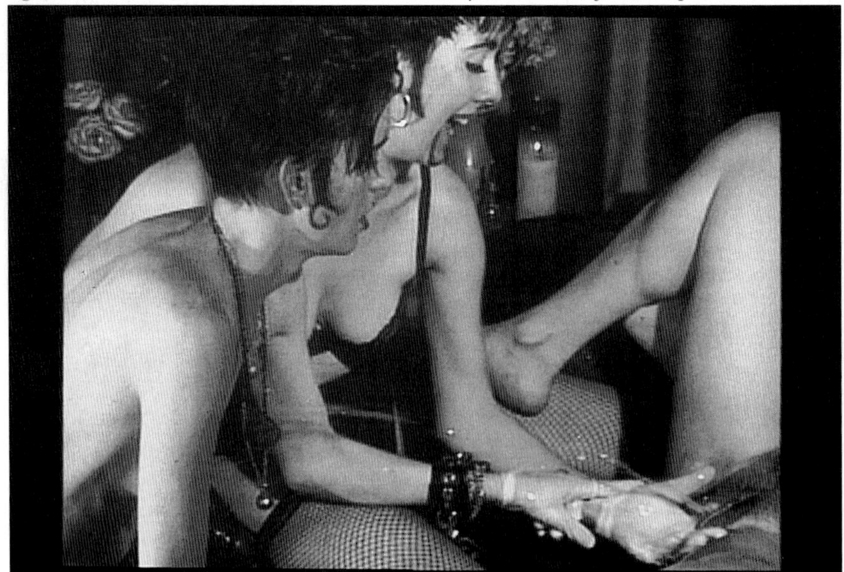

assert that: a) both males and females have active prostates; b) a wide variation in size and distribution of this gland occurs among women; c) the male prostate produces much of the fluid expelled during ejaculation (the testes contribute only a small volume which contains the procreative sperm); and d) at least in some women, the female prostate (also known as the para- and peri-urethral glands) allows for ejaculation through the urethral meatus of a fluid not identical with urine. They argue that the erasure of female ejaculation is supported semantically by a) the often improper use of adjectives such as 'vestigial' and 'atrophied' to describe the less developed homologue of an organ found in both sexes, a naming which serves to emphasise sexual bipolarity, and b) the Aristotelian discovery that female ejaculate, which Galen and Hippocrates had called 'semen' and assumed procreative, was in fact not.

> With the resolution of the Aristotelian argument, the language that had been previously used to describe the fluids of both sexes was allocated in the scientific literature to the male alone. Since female ejaculatory fluids did not contain 'seed', these fluids were left without a word to describe them. The apparent solution was to drop the notion of a female 'semen', which simultaneously meant the loss of the concept of female ejaculation. (p. 17)

Language misuse and insufficiencies therefore produced an ironic invisibility of female ejaculation.

Fig. 10 From *The Sluts and Goddesses Video Workshop* (Maria Beatty/Annie Sprinkle, 1992)

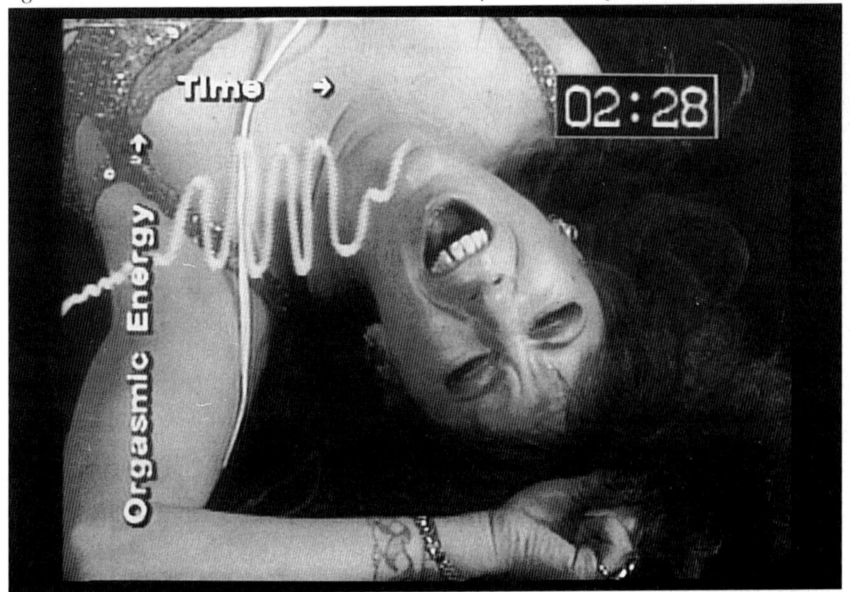

Shannon Bell suggests a more interested reason for the continuing invisibility of female ejaculation despite significant research and debate following Sevely and Bennett's article. Specifically, she questions why feminists have failed to speak about female ejaculation, and postulates the reason to be that female ejaculation challenges the fundamental assumption in feminism of sexual difference.

> The ejaculating female body has not acquired much of a feminist voice nor has it been appropriated by feminist discourse. What is the reason for this lacuna in feminist scholarship and for the silencing of the ejaculating female subject? It has to do with the fact that the questions posed, and the basic assumptions about female sexuality, are overwhelmingly premised on the difference between female and male bodies. ... The most important primary differences have been that women have the ability to give birth and men ejaculate. Women's reproductive ability has been emphasized as a central metaphor in feminist critiques of partriarchal texts and has been theorized into a 'philosophy of birth' and an economy of (re)production. Feminists, in their efforts to revalorize the female body usually devalued in phallocentric discourse, have privileged some form of the mother-body as the source of écriture féminine: writing that evokes women's power as women's bodily experience. ... The fluids, reappropriated in feminine sexual discourse and theorized by French feminist philosophers such as Luce Irigaray and Julia Kristeva, have been the fluids of the mother-body: fluids of the womb, birth fluids, menstrual blood, milk: fluids that flow. Ejaculate - fluid that shoots, fluid that sprays – has been given over to the male body. To accept female ejaculate and female ejaculation one has to accept the sameness of male and female bodies. (pp. 162–3)

Although I agree that equating motherhood with womanhood is dangerous, I strongly disagree with Bell's monolithic representation of feminism. Not all women are or want to be mothers, nor do all women ejaculate; but scholarship and political practices relating to both these (and many other) experiences have been intellectually provocative, perhaps even earthshaking. We can see that the use of maternity as a essential metaphor for womanhood sustains the historical elision of female sexual desires and pleasures. However, even cultural feminism (which best describes the subgroup of feminists attacked by Bell) has always included women who deployed 'sexual difference' for purposes other than mythologising women's birthing capacity, for example to idealise lesbian sex. Bell's articulation of her argument reinforces a currently popular although reductive dichotomisation of sex-positive women and feminists. I would argue that not only does the category 'feminist' contain an enormous range of intellectual and political practices and positions on motherhood, sex, sexuality and gender, but the contemporary stance of sex-positivity was made possible by, and builds on, feminism's reclaiming of women's bodies to empower women. In other words, the current sexual rebellion, depending on, as much as attacking, feminism's investigation of sexual difference, is a *feminist* sexual rebellion of benefit to and properly credited to 'both sides'. (From the 'feminist' in her title 'Feminist Ejaculations', I doubt that Bell and I totally disagree about this.) Certainly Annie Sprinkle finds no incompatibility between feminism and active female sexuality, between menstrual blood and ejaculate. Her slut-goddess, divine prostitute and mothering sex partner exemplify such (non-re) productive discursive intercourse. Feminism must be and is an expanding discourse that responds to and initiates critical self-reflection and continuing political debate.

Nevertheless, although I would replace her term 'sameness' with 'similarity', I agree strongly with Bell's primary argument. Female ejaculation pierces a culturally constructed and enforced boundary between 'males' and 'females'. It is not just that its existence corrects the mistaken assumption that only men have prostates. It is one leak that solicits further inspection of the more generally leaky system of binary sex. For starters, we might consider the article immediately following Sevely and Bennett's in *The Journal of Sex Research*, entitled 'Multiple Orgasms in Males'. Here, Mina Robbins and Gordon Jensen describe multiple orgasms in men which they note correlate physiologically to multiple orgasms in women. These orgasms, which are generally non-ejaculatory except for the final one in a series, establish an independence between orgasm and ejaculation and, moreover, can probably be learned. Annie Sprinkle's exaltation of multiple orgasms in Les Nichols may not be so (positively) 'freaky' as she supposes. We might also consider a 1984 essay on female ejaculation by Desmond Heath in which embryological and histological research supports a consideration of the anterior vagina, urethra, glands, vulva and clitoris as a single organ, a concept more 'naturally' associated with male sexuality. (This of course is subject to attack as in Irigaray's critique of men's projection of sameness – that is, unitary sex – onto women. However, as the following discussion of Laqueur's work demonstrates, a system of difference can erase women's eroticism as much as sameness can.)

In his book *Making Sex*, Thomas Laqueur identifies a shift in knowledge occurring in the eighteenth century from a one-sex to a two-sex human model, a shift not scientifically determined but rather resulting from an epistemological and social-political revolution. Galen's description in the second century AD of women as essentially the same as men, having the same genitalia inside their bodies that men's bodies held visibly outside, has been upstaged by a now dominant understanding of women as men's opposite (and of woman as 'lack'). Laqueur argues that near the end of the Enlightenment, the noted irrelevance of female orgasm to human reproduction opened the way for a new concept of female passionlessness. 'The presence or absence of orgasm became a biological signpost of sexual difference' (p. 4). Scientific progress is not to be credited for this shift in conceptualising sex. For example, the embryological homologies of penis and clitoris, labia and scrotum, ovaries and testes, which were not identified until the 1850s, could have supported a one-sex model as much as adult genital anatomy might earlier have supported a two-sex model. As Laqueur states, 'To be sure, difference and sameness, more or less recondite, are everywhere; but which ones count and for what ends is determined outside the bounds of empirical investigation' (p. 10).

What we know does not necessarily derive from what we see. But neither can language contain all possible knowledge. Female ejaculation, experienced by some women and perhaps often wrongly known, witnessed by many women and men but perhaps wrongly named, challenges hegemonic difference but cannot replace it with totalising sameness. What it can do is happen. And for those who 'know' (or even consider) this, female ejaculation invites a re-collection of 'feminist conceptions' in all their nurturing, erotic and intellectual dimensions.

I would like to conclude by examining one more blurring in Annie Sprinkle's feminist-porn-art. This concerns a 'confusion' between golden showers and female ejaculation. According to Sprinkle, a golden shower is 'the art of erotic urination during sex-play', a creative scene for which she is well known. She elaborates: 'Women can pee while getting fucked, and it's an incredible sensation for both partners.' Although in her film *Deep Inside Annie Sprinkle* she calls it 'squirting pussy juice', Annie reports that the film is no longer available for sale because of a 'peeing scene'. This scene, which Linda Williams refers to as a female 'money shot', was read (at our 1992 Society for Cinema Studies conference panel) by Linda Williams and myself as ejaculation, but by Chuck Kleinhans as urination. In marketing her mail-order Golden Shower Ritual Kit 5019 (in *Love Magazine* 83, co-edited with Veronica Vera), Annie again uses the term 'pussy juice'. And in the accompanying text that guides the user through a fantasy ritual, she writes, 'I'd like to slide your finger up into my hole so you can feel it before it comes out.' Although, I'm frankly at a loss as to *which* hole she means and what *it* is, this confusion hardly seems problematic under the conditions of mail-order sex. The term 'golden showers' comes from porn discourse and itself functions to excite. However, despite all her feminist demystification, I feel Annie's slippery discourse can support an erasure of female ejaculation. Viewers are given the authority to interpret these scenes to service their own pleasure and comfort. But perhaps this is just the point. Once again, representation allows rather than ensures any 'preferred' readings.

To my knowledge, the only explicit reference to women ejaculating in Annie's published work occurs in a utopian vision of the future.

> I have a vision for the future, of a world where all the necessary sex education will be available to everyone, thus, there will be no more sexually transmitted diseases. … Fetish lingerie and sex toys will be freely distributed to all people. People will be able to make love without touching if they choose. Men will be able to have multiple orgasms without ejaculating, so that they can maintain erections for as long as they want. Women will ejaculate. It will be possible to make love anywhere in public, and it will not be impolite to watch. …

Fig. 11 *Deep Inside Porn Stars* by Club 90 and Carnival Knowledge. Photo by Dona Ann McAdams

> On second thoughts; the world is really PERFECT just the way that it is. (p. 117)

When I presented an earlier version of this article at the Society for Cinema Studies conference, I concluded that Sprinkle's blurring of 'golden showers' and ejaculation effectively contributed to the medico-scientific erasure of female ejaculation. Since that time I have expanded my position to recognise also that Sprinkle's discourse contains a subtextual attack on one more binary. Discussing my project with Sprinkle while selecting the photos to accompany this piece, I learned that she actually does *not* see a distinct line between ejaculation and urination – a position that resonates significantly with the anatomical-physiological descriptions outlined earlier and graphically illustrated in the Federation of Feminist Women's Health Centers' *A New View of a Woman's Body* (pp. 46–57). Sprinkle describes (and prescribes) at least four kinds of erotic female fluids: vaginal secretions, 'golden showers', the squirting or dribbling of non-urine fluid through the urethral opening (which can occur with or independently of orgasm), and erotically induced urination. The fourth type, which falls into the overlap of the second and third, Sprinkle finds most clearly evident when, after a group discussion on sexuality (or a performance by Annie, I might add) the women's restroom is 'flooded'. At the LUST Conference ('Lesbians Undoing Sexual Taboos', 17 November 1992,

New York City, attended by approximately 500 women), Sprinkle asked those women in the audience who ejaculated to raise their hands. Approximately one third did so. She reported that in 1982 she ejaculated in a porn movie but had assumed it was a 'golden showers' scene. Acknowledging that female ejaculation is all the rage, she announced that she is currently more enthusiastic about 'energy orgasms', for which she proceeded to provide instructions.

It has not been my purpose here to defend or critique sex-liberationist ideology but rather to analyse the ends towards which Annie Sprinkle develops and deploys a particular brand of it. In her post-porn modernist art, Sprinkle not only attempts to break down barriers among people but also challenges the arbitrary and assumed boundaries among/between pornography, art and everyday experience, spirituality and sexuality, queer and straight, homosexual and heterosexual, male and female, desirable and undesirable, slut and goddess, prostitute and mother, 'golden showers' and female ejaculation. She effects this purposeful aesthetics by 'self'-exposure, by displaying her tools and methods for sexy encoding and her unconventional attitudes, desires, practices and pleasures. She enacts a fluidity in which lesbian and heterosexual identities are not mutually exclusive. Exhibiting sodomy within heterosexuality, she probes the legal/semantic basis by which heterosexuality is constructed as a default class in opposition to 'sodomites'. Her demonstrations of lengthy, multiple and ejaculating orgasms cross-examines pornography's generic 'transcendental' money shot, a signifier that I would argue relies on an interpretive editing of man's 'little death'.

Whether Annie Sprinkle is acting (and/)or experiencing orgasms in her performances cannot be determined by us. Similarly, the possibility of non-ejaculating orgasms in men allows that we may not always have (or want) visible evidence of male orgasm. In video porn, fluid has been injected into vaginas to produce images of female ejaculation (*The Grafenberg Spot*), and realistically functioning penis-like prostheses have been used (on women) to image male ejaculation convincingly (*Bi and Beyond*). Nevertheless, it is interesting that the current visibility and widespread discussion of female ejaculation have resulted from films and videos made by women. The refusal to read signs can produce misrecognition as much as can 'lying' signs. To utilise Sedgwick's terminology, with regard to its elision of female ejaculation and its continuing investment in the invisible female orgasm, the regime of pornography has exercised a long-standing 'privilege of unknowing'.

Works Cited

Bell, Shannon, 'Feminist Ejaculations', in Arthur and Marilouise Kroker (eds.), *The Hysterical Male: New Feminist Theory* (New York: St. Martin's Press, 1991), pp. 155–69.

Federation of Feminist Women's Health Centers. *A New View of a Woman's Body* (West

Hollywood: Feminist Health Press, 1991).
Foucault, Michel. *The History of Sexuality Vol. 1*, trans. Robert Hurley (New York: Vintage Books, 1980).
Freud, Sigmund. 'The Most Prevalent Form of Degradation in Erotic Life (1912)', in *Sexuality and the Psychology of Love* (New York: Collier Books, 1963).
Halley, Janet E. 'Misreading Sodomy: A Critique of the Classification of "Homosexuals" in Federal Equal Protection Law', in Julia Epstein and Kristina Straub (eds.), *Body Guards: The Cultural Politics of Gender Ambiguity* (New York: Routledge, 1991).
Heath, Desmond. 'An Investigation into the Origins of a Copious Vaginal Discharge During Intercourse: "Enough to Wet the Bed – 'That' Is Not Urine"', *Journal of Sex Research*, vol. 20 no. 2 (May 1984), pp. 194–215.
Irigaray, Luce. *This Sex Which is not One*, trans. Catherine Porter with Carolyn Burke (Ithaca: Cornell University Press, 1985).
Kleinhans, Chuck. 'When Did Annie Sprinkle Become an Artist? Female Performance Art, Male Performance Anxiety, Art as Alibi, and Labial Art', paper presented at the Society for Cinema Studies Conference, University of Pittsburgh, May 1992.
Laquer, Thomas. *Making Sex: Body and Gender from the Greeks to Freud* (Cambridge, Mass.: Harvard University Press, 1990).
Montano, Linda. 'Summer Saint Camp 1987', *Drama Review*, vol. 33 no. 1 (Spring 1989).
Pheterson, Gail. 'The Social Consequences of Unchastity', in Frédérique Delacoste and Priscilla Alexander (eds.), *Sex Work: Writings by Women in the Sex Industry* (Pittsburgh: Cleis Press, 1987), pp. 215–30.
Poovey, Mary. 'Speaking the Body: Mid-Victorian Constructions of Female Desire', in Mary Jacobus, Evelyn Fox Keller and Sally Shuttlewo (eds.), *Body/Politics: Women and The Discourses of Science* (New York: Routledge, 1990), pp. 29–46.
Robbins, Mina B. and Gordon D. Jensen. 'Multiple Orgasms in Males', *Journal of Sex Research*, vol.14 no. 1 (February 1978), pp. 21–6.
Sedgwick, Eve Kosofksy. *Epistemology of the Closet* (Berkeley: University of California Press, 1990).
Sevely, J. Lowndes and J.W. Bennett. 'Concerning Female Ejaculation and the Female Prostate', *Journal of Sex Research*, vol. 14 no. 1 (February 1978), pp. 1–20.
Sprinkle, Annie. *Annie Sprinkle: Post Porn Modernist* (Amsterdam: Torch Books, 1991).
Williams, Linda. *Hard Core: Power, Pleasure, and the 'Frenzy of the Visible'* (Berkeley: University of California Press, 1989).
Williams, Linda. 'A Provoking Agent: The Pornography and Performance Art of Annie Sprinkle', in this volume, pp. 176–92.

LINDA WILLIAMS

A Provoking Agent

The Pornography and Performance Art of Annie Sprinkle

> My feminist mother used to come into my room and joke whether I would grow up to be a whore or an artist. She was exactly right!
>
> Annie Sprinkle[1]

The career of Annie Sprinkle is a peculiarly American success story. Beginning her professional performance career as a masseuse, soon after becoming a whore, Sprinkle next expanded into burlesque and live sex shows, then to writing for sex magazines and performing in pornographic films and videos (where she eventually became a director). In a later stage of her career she moved to such venues as the Franklin Furnace, Performing Garage, and other avant-garde performance spaces. In her recent one-woman show entitled *Post-Post Porn Modernist*, she performs a parodic show-and-tell of her life as a sexual performer. This show includes inviting audience members to shine a flashlight at her cervix through a speculum. In 1990, while she was giving this performance in Cleveland, the municipal vice squad forced her to omit the speculum component of her act. It is a fascinating comment on American culture that when Annie Sprinkle performed live sex shows in that same city she was never visited by the vice squad.[2]

Performance artists, especially women performers whose gendered and sexed bodies serve as the basic material of the performance, are often vulnerable to vice squads, or to NEA censorship, because their art and thought occurs through the body. Defenders of performance art have thus often found it necessary to distinguish this art from pornography.[3] While I agree that this art is not pornography, I am suspicious of attempts to draw the line too vigorously between performance art on the one hand and pornography on the other.[4] My tactic in this essay, therefore, will not be to establish the precise moment when Annie Sprinkle became a performance artist, nor to argue, as Chuck Kleinhans has done, that Sprinkle has always been a performance artist,[5] but rather to show how her myriad sexual performances tend to blur the boundaries between the two. This, I shall argue, is the particular genius, as well as the limitation, of Annie

Sprinkle's postmodern feminist agency.

Annie Sprinkle's work demonstrates that the political context in which we ponder the questions of art and obscenity is no longer one in which a secure category of sexual obscenity can be safely confined to the wings of sexual representation. For as gender and sexual identities have become more politicised, and as 'speaking sex' has become as important to gay, lesbian, bisexual, transsexual and sadomasochist activists as it has to Jesse Helms, drawing clear lines between what is dirty and what is clean, what is properly brought on scene and what should be kept off (ob)scene, no longer seems the crux of a feminist sexual politics.[6]

A recent reviewer of *Post-Post Porn Modernist* claims, mistakenly I think, that Sprinkle's performance 'strips away all porn', as if the vehement denial of all pornographic elements purified the art.[7] Such a claim relies on the kind of hierarchical binary opposition between art and pornography, and between artist and whore, that Annie Sprinkle's art *and* pornography challenges. The phenomenon of Annie Sprinkle forces us to ask: what is the political value, in terms of women's agency, of not drawing a firm line between obscene pornography on the one hand and legitimate art on the other?

As the quotation at the beginning of this essay suggests, Annie Sprinkle has a way of defusing and going beyond, rather than directly confronting, familiar oppositions. In this quotation the feminist mother poses the question of her daughter's vocation as an opposition: will her daughter be an artist *or* a whore? Without confronting the mother directly, the 'postfeminist', 'postporn' daughter counters her either/or with a destabilising agreeability: 'My mother was right!' The daughter unsettles the familiar opposition: she is neither artist *nor* whore but artist *and* whore.

Can Annie Sprinkle's performance of the postmodern, 'post-feminist' sexual role 'woman' accomplish the feminist goal of being *for women*? Does she represent a new permutation of feminist agency that moves beyond some of feminism's most troubling binary oppositions – beyond, for example, the opposition that posits pornography as inimical to women; beyond the opposition that posits pornography as inimical to art; beyond the opposition that posits women as powerless victims of male sexual power and thus as colonised in their desires? Or is Annie Sprinkle more simply a symptom of a 'postfeminism' that has been accused, most recently by Tania Modleski, of being an end to feminism, a reversion to prefeminism?[8]

How, in other words, shall we interpret this postfeminist sensibility emerging so agreeably from the 'depths' of a misogynist mass culture? Like Modleski, I reject postfeminism if it is taken to mean that the goals of feminism are either irrelevant or already achieved. However, I understand the political and social realities that have led many women to reject the term feminism, to claim to be beyond it, when to my way of thinking they are still embedded within its struggles. One of the reasons for this rejection has been the association of feminism with an all-or-nothing understanding of what *is* good for women, with often self-righteous positions that know for sure on which side of any binary opposition a 'proper' feminism belongs.

Sex workers, we know, have often found themselves on the 'wrong' side of these binaries. For sex workers have all too often been regarded by feminists as objectified victims of an aggressive, sadistic, masculine sexuality rather than as sexual agents themselves. Anti-pornography feminists in particular have gone so far as to define pornography as 'the graphic sexually explicit subordination of women' in which women are dehumanised sexual objects 'presented as whores by nature'.[9] To the Dworkin-MacKinnon anti-pornography faction, agency can only be located in resistance. Yet in Annie Sprinkle we encounter a whore turned pornographer turned performance artist with more of a stake in the 'post' than in the 'antis' that constitute so much feminist position-taking on this subject. This essay suggests that we take seriously the whore side of Annie Sprinkle's performances by examining, first, her early work as a whore and then how this whore persona informed her later work as a pornographer and performance artist. My hope is that this examination may help us to clarify the nature of a postfeminist sexual agency that has brought obscenity so aggressively on scene.

Another hope is that the case of Annie Sprinkle may be used to clarify a larger argument on the essentialist or non-essentialist meaning of the name 'woman'. In *Am I that Name?*, Denise Riley has argued the value of a poststructuralist refusal of the name 'woman' as reducing women to fixed identities which then work to reduce women's agency.[10] Feminism does not need the fixed category 'woman', Riley argues. Against this post-structuralist position Tania Modleski has argued the importance of keeping the name 'woman' as an essential category.[11] Modleski points out that Riley's title, a quotation from *Othello* in which Desdemona asks Iago if she is the name her husband has given her, ignores the fact that the name Othello actually gave Desdemona was not woman but 'whore'. Riley's point is that the name 'woman' has become an essentialist trap. Her poststructuralist argument is that women lose agency if reduced to the singularity of this name. Modleski, however, suggests that Riley's elision of that other name, 'whore', is an example of why the feminist use of the essentialist name 'woman' is politically important. 'Although women have had to take up the term "women" emphatically to rescue it from opprobrium, they have done so in opposition to patriarchy's tendency to "saturate" us with our sex' (pp. 16–17).

My interest in Annie Sprinkle is that she represents one possible feminist position of agency arising out of the embrace of this saturation. For Annie Sprinkle the postmodern, postfeminist, postporn performance artist has not eschewed the term 'whore' or the sexual saturation of 'woman'. Rather, her sexual performances, firmly rooted within the specific conventions of pornography and the persona of 'whore', are provocative instances of agency that draw upon the performative traditions of the sexually saturated 'woman', without simply duplicating them. By performing sex differently, though still within the conventional rhetoric and form of the genre, Annie Sprinkle demonstrated a provocative feminist agency that would fruitfully contribute to her later feminist performance work.

From Masseuse to Whore

Let's begin with Annie Sprinkle's first sexual performances, the ones she writes about in her early sex magazines, then later in her book *Post Porn Modernist* (not to be confused with her performance piece *Post-Post Porn Modernist*) and in her interview in *Angry Women*. These writings are all versions of Annie Sprinkle's life story, which she has been writing and performing, initially for specialised sex magazines, since the early 70s. In every version of this story, Annie Sprinkle tells us that she did not know she was a prostitute until she was linguistically hit over the head – or in Althusser's terms, 'hailed' or 'interpellated' – by this discourse.

> I was working in a massage parlor. For 3 months I worked and didn't even know I was a hooker – I was having such a good time! The men I saw were referred to as 'clients' or 'massages'. But finally, after about 3 months one woman used the word 'trick' and I realized, 'Ohmigod – they're *tricks*! Oh shit – I'm a *hooker*!'[12]

At first she believed the performance for which she was paid was the massage. The money 'was for the massage plus a tip', while the sex 'was just something I threw in for fun!'[13] 'I just thought of myself as a horny masseuse. I liked having sex with the guys after I gave them a brief massage. When it finally did occur to me that I was a hooker, and I got over the initial shock, I enjoyed the idea.'[14]

Now we could interpret this reasoning as the false consciousness often attributed to sex workers by anti-pornography feminists. But false consciousness assumes the existence of a 'true' or authentic consciousness betrayed by the persona of the 'happy hooker'. It is this idea of an 'authentic', 'true' self that Annie Sprinkle's account of her experience contradicts. For she only recognised herself as a whore – one who performs sex for money – in the word 'trick'. She never chose – in any liberal, Enlightenment sense of the exercise of free will – to become a whore. Annie Sprinkle found herself 'hailed' by an entire system of signification.[15] But her inability to choose does not necessarily mean that she is discursively constructed by a misogynist system over which she has no control, or that she is the victim of misogynist false consciousness. In what sense, then, *can* we speak of Annie Sprinkle's agency in the deeds that make her, first a whore and then, later, an artist?

The answer involves the thorny question of how and in what way there can be agency in the absence of a subject who pre-exists the discourses in which he or she is situated. In other words, if there is no subjectivity prior to discourse, if subjects are constructed in and by an already existing cultural field, and if, as in Annie Sprinkle's case, that cultural field 'interpellates' the woman who performs sex for money as having the identity of 'whore', then what hope is there for that woman's ability to 'act otherwise' if she doesn't act *against* the system that constructs women as whores and objects of pornography?

Feminist postmodern theorist Judith Butler offers one answer to this problem when she writes that 'the question of agency is not to be answered through recourse to an "I" that pre-exists signification.'[16] Rather, Butler argues, agency needs to be reformulated as a question of how agents construct their identities through *resignification*. The rules that enable and restrict the intelligible assertion of an 'I' – rules, Butler reminds us, that are structured by gender hierarchy and compulsory heterosexuality – operate through repetition. Signification itself is '*not a founding act, but a regulated process of repetition* that both conceals itself and enforces its rules precisely through the production of substantializing effects.' Agency is 'located within the possibility of a variation on that repetition.' In other words, there is no self prior to the convergence of discursive injunctions to be something (whore, mother, heterosexually desirable object, and so on). There is only, Butler writes, 'a taking up of the tools where they lie' (p. 145).

For Annie Sprinkle these tools were initially the remarkable opportunity for repetition in the sexual acts performed by a whore. If, as Butler argues, the self is constructed out of the repetition of performances, and if agency occurs within the possibility of variation, then Annie Sprinkle's repetitious performances of sex acts have been the locus of her construction of self throughout her career. In this first instance of sexual performances in which she first wasn't, and then was, 'hailed' as a whore, we can see the discovery of an agency that is not opposed to, but rooted in, the discourse that constructs her. Her agency could be said to consist in the fact that in the repetition of the performance of sex, first for free, then for money, she realises that 'whore' does not fully name who she is. Annie Sprinkle neither denies that she is a whore nor fights the system that so names her. Rather, she accepts the nomination; but in that acceptance also sees room for what Butler calls 'subversive repetition'. This subversive repetition becomes an articulation of something that is not named in 'whore': her own desire. There is no other scene of Annie Sprinkle's agency; the scene of the ob-scene is the place where she is able both to 'act otherwise' and still 'be herself'.

A whore performs sex for pay, usually for a single customer. The sexual performances must please the customer and not necessarily the performer, who may or may not be caught up in its art or excitement. Because the performer is so restricted in the nature of the performance, remarkably little is said about the quality of performance within the customer-whore transaction. Though it is often acknowledged that this performance can be either perfunctory or inspired, it is not an area of performance that is taken very seriously by the traditions of Western art. It is, however, taken seriously in an Eastern, Tantric tradition to which Sprinkle has recently been drawn, as well as in the narratives of pornographic films and videos which are almost obsessively about the quality and quantities of sexual performance.

All of Annie Sprinkle's performances begin by taking this performance of sex for the pleasure of a customer or viewer very seriously and by linking this performance to the fundamental contract by which the whore agrees to please the john by showing him her 'secrets'. When Annie describes herself as a 'hooker with a heart of gold', she does so without mockery, without intending to demean the profession of whore or to subvert the whore's basic function of performing sexual acts that give pleasure.[17] She does not rail against the basic dichotomy that divides women into good girls and whores.[18] The art of her performance consists in what she can do by way of subversive repetition within this basic contract, not in refusing or opposing it but in finding her desire cultivated and satisfied within it. In the 'whore' phase of Annie Sprinkle's careeer, these subversive repetitions consist of an ever-widening range of sexual acts, or 'perversions' which expand the notion of what sexual performance is, and sexual objects, conventionally not regarded as acceptable objects of desire – dwarves, burn victims, transsexuals, persons with Aids, amputees – which allow her to explore her desires in new ways.

From Whore to Pornographer

Deep Inside Annie Sprinkle, the 1981 porno film which Sprinkle wrote and directed, is consistent with her early writings as well as her later performance work in its first-person direct address in the persona of the whore speaking to the client. 'Hi, I'm Annie. I'm glad you came to see me. I want us to become very intimate...' Intimacy here consists, as in the discourse of the whore, in showing and telling sexual secrets that please. Yet intimacy with a flesh and blood client is the one thing that is not possible within the mediated form of porno film and video; the whore-client relation of proximity is necessarily replaced, and in a sense compensated for, by the ideal visibility of sexual performers who are not physically there with the spectators viewing the film. Yet the woman who performs with another performer for the camera remains a kind of whore, replacing sexual performance with and for the pleasure of one with sexual performance for an audience of many. In most contemporary feature-length hard-core film and video this shift to the audience of many entails the abandonment of the female sexual performer's address to the client.[19]

Annie Sprinkle, however, maintains the paradoxical, quasi-parodic rhetoric of intimate address to the client who is no longer really there, in the introduction to each of this film's numbers. Her pornography thus makes a point of retaining the literal voice of the whore whose name is inscribed in the Greek word 'pornography', literally, whore-writing: the *graphos* (writing or representations) by *pornei* (whores). This word needs some explanation.

Though Andrea Dworkin has made much of the word's continuity from antiquity,[20] in fact our contemporary notion of pornography, as writing or images depicting sexual activities with the aim of arousal, bears little relation to the meaning of the word in antiquity. Classicist Holt N. Parker writes that *pornographos* was simply a subcategory of biography – tales of the lives of the courtesans – which may not contain any obscene material at all.[21] Parker notes, however, that another subspecies of literature – *anaiskhunto-graphoi*, literally writers of shameless things – more properly corresponds to the erotic content of contemporary pornography. These works, known today only secondarily and from fragments, correspond to our contemporary sex manuals. They were putatively based on the writer's personal experience describing various methods of heterosexual intercourse.[22]

Though the writing of these manuals was ascribed to women, this was not because of any proven female authorship but because the excesses of sexuality – to the Greeks this included pleasures that rendered participants ecstatically out of control and out of possession of themselves – were conceived in antiquity as feminine. Active, in-control sexuality was associated with the free man who 'penetrated, who moved, who fucked' and who could also abstain from doing so if he chose. Women, on the other hand, like slaves and boys, were the passive penetrated, who did not move, who were fucked and who had no power to abstain. Thus while women were the authorities on shameless things, they had no real authority or agency in speaking them because they were lacking the ultimate cultural value of self-control.[23] Parker borrows Joanna Russ's formulation of the classic double bind applied to this literature: 'No proper woman writes about sex; therefore the writing is not by a woman. And if she does write, she's not a proper woman.'[24] Since this class of writing about shameless things most closely corresponds to the kind of advice-giving that Annie Sprinkle, speaking from her whore persona, offers in *Deep Inside Annie Sprinkle*, it is worth considering whether this same double bind erasing women's sexual agency still operates today.

In traditional pornography, 'whores' (whether literally so or simply women who, because they speak of sex, are automatically 'shameless') write of their experience of sex for the pleasure of men. These experiences must be presented as pleasurable for the genre to function. A whole generation of feminist performance artists has aggressively and angrily broken the contract to provide pleasure and thus grounded their performance art in an attack on pleasure that uses the tools of obscenity. Annie Sprinkle differs from these performers in that she does not rupture the whore's contract to provide pleasure. Instead, she goes back to its roots. In taking on the persona and address of the 'whore' hailed by misogynist culture, she opens up a field of acting otherwise through subversive repetitions of the role. Moving-image pornography, like prostitution, offers the perfect occasion for repetition since it requires some variation of sexual performances to relieve the monotony of the seven-to-ten numbers conventionally offered by the feature-length form.

In this film Annie Sprinkle, self-designated 'porn star', tells the conventional pornographic narrative of her sexual evolution from shy, non-glamorous, non-sexual 'Ellen' to the sexually fulfilled, exhibitionist Annie. The basic structure of this narrative, which is full of advice about what positions are the most pleasurable, thus assumes the educative function that

Annie Sprinkle. Photo by Amy Ardrey; art direction by Leslie Barany extends back to the sex manuals of antiquity. What is different in Annie Sprinkle's 'whore-writing', however, is that she injects elements into this narrative that disrupt the active male, passive female paradigm of conventional pornography.

She begins by displaying a scrapbook with photos which are the 'real' pictures of herself as an awkward girl growing up. These pictures of the ordinary, non-glamorous woman are unsettling. Whereas they do not suggest that this is the true woman while the fetishised Annie is false, nor do they suggest, as conventional 'whore-writing' does, that the 'true' woman is the fetishised desirable one. Instead, they suggest the very constructedness of the woman's identity and Annie's ability to manipulate the codes of glamour. The film also introduces an unusual note of social reality, with photos of Mom and Dad and the family and mention of their efforts to accept Annie's role in the 'sex business'.[25]

Having established that the persona who addresses us is not 'naturally' glamorous and sexy, Annie next asks her absent client-viewer if 'he' would like to see 'what I would love to do to two husky men right now?' Happening across two husky naked men arm-wrestling before a fireplace, she admires their bodies, kisses their muscles and inserts herself between them to initiate a threeway number that ends with the conventional porno 'money shot' – external, and therefore visible, ejaculation by the male.[26] This threesome is perfectly conventional for 80s porn. What isn't conventional is the homoerotic context of the display of glistening male muscles, Annie's verbally articulated delight in their bodies, and her active control of the situation ('what I would like to do').

Moving on to the next number, still addressing an absent 'client', Annie asks if he likes 'big tits'. 'You may have noticed I have rather large ones…' She then introduces Sassy, a 'girlfriend who loves big tits'. The number with Sassy is the conventional 'lesbian' duo interrupted and completed by a male intruder. What isn't conventional is Sassy's very short stature – her mouth reaches as high as Annie's breasts – Annie's use of her breast to stimulate Sassy's clitoris, and Sassy's sustained, body-shuddering (performance of) orgasm, which takes place before the man arrives.

The third number introduces anal intercourse performed on Annie and ending in a conventional 'money shot' on her lower back. What is different in this number is the fact that it begins in Annie's verbal celebration of anal eroticism, in this case her pleasure taken in a man's ass: 'You ever wonder why I keep my middle nail short? Now take this ass for example…' Though we never see the man's face, Annie continues her 'dirty talk' instructions for fingering a man's ass while performing the deed. Only after she has completed her play with his anus does his play with hers commence.

Annie's 'objectification' of the man's ass and her instructions on how to give anal pleasure to a man are unconventional preludes to her own more conventional anal penetration. It is possible to see this as simple table-turning: the objectified woman fragments and objectifies the male body in turn. But perhaps more challenging to the conventional porno form is the fact that here too Annie maintains the first-person address to a hypothetical client, speaking to the camera and thus raising new questions about the gendered nature of her address. Is she telling and showing a hypothetical 'him' how to finger another man's ass? If so, the film insidiously transgresses 'normal' heterosexual taboos against males penetrating males. Is she telling and showing 'him' how *she* likes to finger a man's ass? If so, the pleasure depicted casts her in the role of active penetrator and him in the role of penetrated, again a switch in expectations for the conventionally posited heterosexual male viewer. Or is she perhaps telling and showing a hypothetical 'her' how to finger a man's anus? After all, this is 80s porn and women are included in its address. If so, the original rhetoric of the female-whore addressing the male-client breaks down. Any way you look at it, Annie has played with the conventions of who gives pleasure to whom.

The fourth number is even less conventional; it constitutes one of Annie's specialities, and at least one source of her name. We could call it the female money shot. Annie performs it first alone, then after intercourse with a male partner. This partner performs his money shot as the conventional climax to intercourse while Annie does hers before his, on her own so to speak, and then as a kind of topper after. This exhibitionist display of female pleasures that are usually, in post-70s moving image pornography, internal and invisible is clearly based on the male-competitive 'mine is bigger than yours' or 'anything you can do I can do better' model. 'You want visible proof of my orgasms measured against the standard of yours?' Annie seems to say, 'Well here it is!' In this most spectacular of her performances, the female body might be said to parody the male body's obsession with measurable quantities of ejaculate and the projective force of expulsion, except that, if it is a parody, it is not one that automatically destroys the erotic terms of the performance.

We have seen that Annie Sprinkle's performances take as their starting point the role of the whore, whose first commitment is to deliver the goods: the performance of 'sex' in a culture in which such performances can be bought. I have argued in *Hard Core* that contemporary hard-core film and video pornography particularly locates the climactic pay-off of those goods in the invisible interior of women's bodies. The genre's 'frenzy of the visible' is thus a contradictory desire to see the involuntary, convulsive proof that a woman's pleasure is taking place measured against the standard of a male 'norm'.

However, since 'normally' the woman's pleasure is not seen and measured in this same quantitative way as the man's, and since visual pornography also wants to show visual evidence of pleasure, the genre has given rise to the enduring fetish of the male money shot. One of the first 'corrections' of the new pornography by and for women was to eliminate this convention. The films of the Femme production group offered clean sheets, handsome men and no money shots. Annie Sprinkle's directorial contribution to this effort – a half-hour segment of *Rites of Passions* (Annie Sprinkle and Veronica Vera, 1987) called *The Search for the Ultimate*

Sexual Experience – conformed to this standard as well. But suppression of the masculine standard for the exhibition of pleasure is only one strategy of acting otherwise. Annie Sprinkle's strategy here, in this earlier work, as well as later in *The Sluts and Goddesses Video Workshop, or How to be a Sex Goddess in 101 Easy Steps* (Annie Sprinkle and Maria Beatty, 1992), where she exhibits not only a female money shot but also the performance of a six-minute orgasm, would seem to so spectacularly imitate the male standard of the pornographic evidence of pleasure as to destabilise and denaturalise its 'normal' meaning.

Anyone with experience of hard-core film and video must marvel at these orgasmic performances. We might say that, in an adaptation of Luce Irigaray's terms, recognising the extent to which orgasm is one of the basic 'goods' of porno, Annie Sprinkle decided to market her goods with a difference. This difference is measured in the degree of discrepancy and de-formation produced in repetitions that destabilise the very sense of what delivering the 'goods' is.[27]

At the Society for Cinema Studies Panel on Annie Sprinkle ('Sprinkle, Sprinkle Little Star: Permutations of a Porn Star', May 1992) there was considerable debate about the nature of Sprinkle's orgasmic performances. While I argued that Sprinkle had performed a female version of a money shot, fellow panellist Chuck Kleinhans insisted that I had misconstrued 'golden showers' as female ejaculation.[28] Kleinhans maintained that Sprinkle tells us we are seeing ejaculation for primarily legal reasons, since public urination is legally actionable in some localities. Another panellist, Chris Straayer, also perceived that the liquid was ejaculate but argued a different significance than I had: a liberatory return of the repressed of female ejaculation. Why, Straayer asked, has women's ejaculation been censored in the very pornography that has placed so much emphasis on visible proof of pleasure, if not as a means of continuing to reproduce female 'lack'?

The debate suggests how insistently pornography catches its viewers in the impossible question of the ontological real of pleasure. Each of us has a fantasy of this real corresponding to our ideological investments in pleasure. I see Sprinkle playing with the conventions of the hard-core 'frenzy of the visible' and exhibiting agency in the parody of masculine money shots; Kleinhans sees a greater affirmation of agency in the greater taboo of golden showers; Straayer sees a greater agency in the exhibition of a self-sufficient female sexuality in female ejaculation. The important point, however, is not to determine the truth of what the female body experiences but, rather, the variety of different truths that can be constructed and the fact that they are constructed here by a female pornographer who is clearly in control. Pornography is all about the supposedly true and natural but actually constructed bodily confessions of pleasure. Annie Sprinkle shows the extent to which even the whore locked in the contract to please the customer, making confession of the 'shameless things' of sex, can speak differently – not necessarily more truthfully – of these things.

In a broader sense, however, we might consider the basic marketing of the 'shameless goods' of Annie Sprinkle herself. Sprinkle is the fetishised woman *par excellence*. Though she will later metamorphose into an oscillation between the two equally valued states of slut and goddess, in this earlier pornography the self-conscious masquerade of femininity is of the whore who aims to please. But as we have seen, there is enough of a Mae West-style exaggeration in this persona to alert us to an element of parody. The gap-toothed, big-breasted, slightly chubby woman who addresses us in her sexiest voice and who has already shown us the pre-whore, pre-porn body out of which this new persona was constructed, presents herself as an effect of performance. As in her later how-to-do-it diagrams in which she draws arrows to parts of her body to show how a particular fetish effect was achieved, or in the famous bosom ballet in which she performs a dance with painted, yin/yang breasts, she invites us to admire a performance the truth of which is always elusive.

The gap between the performed imitation of the sex goddess and the 'original' on which that imitation is based creates an effect not unlike that of the drag queen. Although Sprinkle 'is' a woman and doesn't perform otherwise, her exaggeratedly fetishised femme appearance is offered as a performative achievement, not as natural. Judith Butler writes that 'in imitating gender, drag implicitly reveals the imitative structure of gender itself.'[29] Sex and gender are denaturalised in drag by a performance which avows their distinctness and dramatises the cultural mechanism of their fabricated unity.

In a recent documentary about Tantric sexual seekers, *Sacred Sex* (Cynthia Connop, 1992), Annie Sprinkle tells us in an interview that in her *Post-Post Porn Modernist* performance piece she takes on the persona of a 'porno bimbo character'. This could sound as if she performs a demeaning imitation of such a character, as if the parodic repetition criticises the unauthenticity of the original. However, in neither of the performances of this role does Annie Sprinkle assume that there is a 'proper' or 'normal' female identity from which this construction diverges. Her parody of gender and desirability thus reveals, as Butler puts it about drag, 'that the original identity after which gender fashions itself is an imitation without an origin.'[30]

Parody causes laughter. But this laughter does not chide the imitative failure of this character with reference to a better, 'truer' woman. It might be more appropriate, then, to speak of Annie Sprinkle's parody – her subversive repetitions of sexual performances, her 'porno bimbo character' played to the hilt – as more properly a form of pastiche. The term has been invoked in a manner critical of postmodernism by Fredric Jameson, who argues that our contemporary postmodern condition is replete with parodies that have lost their ability to criticise and hence their ability to laugh. Such parodies degenerate to mere pastiche: imitations that mock the very notion of an original. Jameson argues that without the feeling that there exists something normal compared to which what is being imitated is comic, pastiche becomes blank parody, 'parody that has lost its humor'.[31]

It is precisely this notion of 'norm', and 'original', however, that is at issue in a postmodern world of sexual identities and representations.

We have seen that laughter at sexual pleasures which diverge from a 'norm' are familiar features of contemporary culture. All the more reason, then, to welcome the pastiche with humour that does not posit a corrective norm but continuously plays with the terms of norm and perversion. This is what Annie Sprinkle does best. Sprinkle is proof, as Judith Butler puts it, that 'the loss of the sense of "the normal" ... can be its own occasion for laughter, especially when "the normal", "the original" is revealed to be a copy ... an ideal that no one *can* embody.'[32]

From Pornographer to Performance Artist (a Sketch)

These, then, are some examples of the strategy of the 'post' – postmodern, poststructuralist, postfeminist – in the early work of Annie Sprinkle. While this work is not yet performance art and not yet 'post-porn', we can see in it the seeds of an evolution that is beyond, but never against, porn. Annie Sprinkle's persona will go on to include the sex educator, the sex therapist, the sexual fairy godmother and the sex goddess – all personae which are reworked into the *Post-Post Porn Modernist* theatre piece.

In each new permutation, Sprinkle never denies or criticises her whore-porn origins. For example, in *The Sluts and Goddesses Video Workshop, or How to be a Sex Goddess in 101 Easy Steps* Sprinkle becomes a 'legitimate' sex educator proffering more knowledge than pleasure. Yet the interest of the tape is its combination of clinical knowledge and raunchy enjoyment, the participatory hands-on, pornographic nature of this particular sex educator's 'show and tell'. Once again Sprinkle has gone to the roots of the form – sex manual advice on the best positions – and transformed it without directly opposing it.

If, as the classicists tell us, pornographic sex manuals by putative women for the pleasure of men are the true origins of what today we call pornography, then this 'workshop' exclusively by and discursively addressed to women, yet still imbued with all the naughtiness of conventional pornography, is its reappropriation. This reappropriation is certainly not free of the conventions of pornographic sex manuals for men. In this video, for example, Sprinkle repeats her performance of the female money shot, and goes on to measure the duration of an orgasm with a graphic insert of a digital clock (5 minutes and 10 seconds).

This image of the sex-educator flexing her orgasmic muscles is still similar to the whore-pornographer in *Deep Inside Annie Sprinkle*. In both cases duration and ejaculation are emphasised. In both cases a parody pastiche of masculine conventions dominates. Yet in this video, orgasm is no longer performed for the pleasure of a discursively addressed male viewer. Other women in the video facilitate the orgasm and function as audience cheerleaders. In the *Post-Post Porn Modernist* performance piece, the orgasm is a solo and the point is the self-sufficiency of the female body.

We have seen that Annie Sprinkle's spectacular orgasms are the constant feature of each of her pornographic, educative or art performances.

We have also seen the subtle ways in which these orgasms take on new meanings in different contexts. The point about these orgasms is never whether they are real or performed, showered with ejaculate or urine, parodic or sincere, since with Annie Sprinkle there is never an either/or but always a this/and.

These orgasms can be taken as indices of a very different sexual agency from that which obtained for the whore-writers of antiquity. For the Greeks, the rigid dichotomy between passive penetrated and active penetrator corresponded to the feminine and the masculine positions. Pleasure was always on the side of the uncontrolled female and, as in the famous argument between Zeus and Hera about who had the most pleasure in sex, always operated to the detriment of female agency in the social sphere. The woman's pleasure, quantified as inherently greater than the male's, was out of control and in excess, while the masculine pleasure of penetrator was capable of control and not in excess.

The female body remains today the one more 'saturated' with sex. The insatiable, 'excessively' pleasuring woman remains caught in the familiar double bind by which her knowledge of sex invalidates other forms of authority – we can think, for example, of Arlen Specter and the Senate Judiciary Committee's dismissal of Anita Hill's charges against Clarence Thomas as sexual fantasy and displaced desire. Nevertheless, despite the very real operation of this harmful double standard, the sphere of the sexual now occupies so much greater an area of social concern and social power that participation in sexual pleasure no longer automatically signifies the same powerlessness it did for the Greeks. This is why it is important not to conflate today's pornography with that of the ancients, or indeed, with that of any other time. And this is why sex-positive Annie Sprinkle and her spectacular orgasms can suggest quite another strategy for 'acting otherwise'.

I would make no claim for the resisting, subversive potential of Annie Sprinkle's strategies outside the realm of the sexual. And certainly sexual performance is *not* the solution to a great many of the problems of women. But Annie Sprinkle shows that, within the realm of the sexual, performances of bosom ballets, female money shots and six-minute orgasms can sometimes work wonders. For sexuality today is a thoroughly commodified arena of self-help and self-fulfilment requiring levels of self-control and agency that would have baffled the Greeks. While it was once the case that a mind/body split relegated men to the realm of the spirit, women to the realm of the body, placing the blame of male lust on women, today sexual pleasure is far too important a commodity for women not to seek in it their own desire and agency.

Notes

1. Annie Sprinkle, *Love Magazine 83,* p. 4963, n.d.
2. Cindy Carr, 'War on Art: The Sexual Politics of Censorship', *The Village Voice*, 5 June 1990, p. 28. Sprinkle called her performance piece, at the Cleveland Performance Art Festival, a demystification of the female body. She describes the burlesque club where she performed live sex as the 'wildest' place she ever worked, commenting that the vice squad was unconcerned about that obscenity because it was confined to 'the porn ghetto...' 'But now that it's something for me ...' (Carr, p. 27).
3. Art critic Linda Burnham writes, for example, 'I went to Cleveland for this performance [Annie Sprinkle's performance at the Cleveland Performance Art Festival], and performance art critics don't come any more credentialed than I do, and I declare it: Annie Sprinkle is a performance artist and this performance was art, not pornography.' *High Performance*, 1990, p. 13. In his paper at the 1992 Society for Cinema Studies conference, 'When Did Annie Sprinkle Become an Artist?: Female Performance Art, Male Performance Anxiety, Art as Alibi, and Labial Art', Chuck Kleinhans has shown that Burnham's defence of Sprinkle is based both on an appeal to authority and on the location of a specific point in Sprinkle's career when she ceased to be pornographic and became art. Something of the same discriminating assertion occurs in performance artist Linda Montano's 'baptism' of Annie Sprinkle and Veronica Vera as artists while the two were in attendance at Montano's upstate New York summer camp in 1987. See Linda Montano, 'Summer Saint Camp 1987', *The Drama Review*, vol. 33 no. 1 (Spring 1989). The assumption in these defences is that Annie Sprinkle became a performance artist when she began, as she herself puts it, to deconstruct 'mainstream images about what is sexy' (*Los Angeles Times*, 'Queen of Kink not Taking It Lying Down', F 11) rather than simply to arouse. I hope to show, however, that Annie Sprinkle's performances never obey such simple dichotomies.
4. This line drawing, like the line drawing between the erotic and the pornographic, almost always depends on who you are and what turns you on (or off): pornography, as Robbe-Grillet once said, is the eroticism of the 'other'. In other words, if it turns me on it's erotic; if it turns you on it's pornographic. Performance art as a whole has been condemned by the New Right philistines as pornography on the assumption that some creep, not me, gets turned on by the material, or as bogus art. Here is Tony Kornheiser in a recent piece in the *Washington Post* (9 February 1992): 'I'm not exactly sure what it is – other than it seems like everybody who does it gets naked. Does that mean when I'm taking a shower, I'm a performance artist? Because if that's the case I want the NEA to spring for the soap.' At the other extreme of this position is the condemnation of performance art as pornography. Attacks on performance art, like attacks on pornography, oscillate between the assumption that any engagement of the body is excessively obscene (showing what should never be shown) or excessively ordinary (the naked body in the shower).
5. 'When Did Annie Sprinkle Become an Artist? Female Performance Art, Male Performance Anxiety, Art as Alibi, and Labial Art'. Paper given at the Society for Cinema Studies conference, May 1992.
6. See 'Pornographies On/Scene, or "Diff'rent Strokes for Diff'rent Folks"', in Lynne Segal and Mary McIntosh (eds.), *Sex Exposed: Sexuality and the Pornography Debate* (London: Virago, 1992). In this article I suggest that the word obscene, which literally means 'off scene', no longer functions to refer to genuinely hidden things, sexual or otherwise. In our contemporary sexual politics the more proper term is on/scene.
7. Quoted in the documentary film *Sacred Sex* (Cynthia Connop, 1992).
8. Tania Modleski, *Feminism without Women: Culture and Criticism in a 'Postfeminist' Age* (New York: Routledge, 1991), p. 8.

9. These are excerpts from the Minneapolis Ordinance authored by Andrea Dworkin and Catharine MacKinnon. In 'Appendix II' of Varda Burstyn (ed.), *Women against Censorship* (Vancouver: Douglas & MacIntyre, 1985), p. 206.
10. Denise Riley, *Am I that Name? Feminism and the Category of 'Women' in History* (Minneapolis: University of Minnesota Press, 1988).
11. Modleski, *Feminism without Women*, pp. 16–17.
12. Andrea Juno and V. Vale, *Angry Women. Re/Search Publication* (San Francisco, 1991), p. 24.
13. Ibid., p. 26.
14. Annie Sprinkle, *Post Porn Modernist* (Amsterdam: Torch Books, 1991), p. 13.
15. Louis Althusser, 'Ideology and Ideological State Apparatuses (Notes towards an Investigation)', in *Lenin and Philosophy and Other Essays*, trans. Ben Brewster (London: New Left Books, 1971), pp. 122–73.
16. Judith Butler, *Gender Trouble: Feminism and the Subversion of Identity* (New York and London: Routledge, 1990), p. 143.
17. In Juno and Vale, *Angry Women*, p. 26.
18. This is why she is out of place in an anthology called *Angry Women*.
19. Many stag films, however, still retain this discursive address. See Linda Williams, *Hard Core: Power, Pleasure and the 'Frenzy of the Visible'* (Berkeley: University of California Press, 1989), pp. 58–92.
20. Andrea Dworkin, *Pornography: Men Possessing Women* (Chicago: University of Chicago Press, 1979).
21. Holt Parker, 'Love's Body Anatomized: The Ancient Erotic Handbooks and the Rhetoric of Sexuality', in Amy Richlin (ed.), *Pornography and Representation in Greece and Rome* (New York: Oxford University Press, 1992), p. 91.
22. Ibid.
23. Ibid., p. 99
24. Dworkin, *Pornography*, p. 93.
25. It is worth noting that this shot of Mom and Dad is held so briefly that their faces are not actually discernible, apparently out of consideration for their feelings.
26. I discuss the form and function of this money shot in Chapter 4 of *Hard Core*.
27. I am alluding here to Luce Irigaray's notion, in the essay 'When the Goods Get Together', that women as commodities have been prostituted to men as 'goods'. Irigaray suggests that these goods should refuse to go to market. However, she also raises another possibility – which she goes on to reject – that the goods might 'go to market on their own ... enjoy their own worth among themselves, to speak to each other, to desire each other, free from the control of seller-buyer-consumer subjects.' In Luce Irigaray, *This Sex which is not One*, trans. Catherine Porter and Carolyn Burke (Ithaca, NY: Cornell University Press, 1985), p. 197. I have suggested in *Hard Core* that the Femme Productions group of female pornographers, to which Annie Sprinkle belongs, represents a form of the 'goods' getting together to market themselves differently (pp. 248–50). I am suggesting here that Annie Sprinkle's marketing offers a subtle revision of what these goods are.
28. His argument was based on his perception that liquid emerged from the urethra and not, as I thought, the vagina.
29. Butler, *Gender Trouble*, p. 137.
30. Ibid., p. 138.
31. Fredric Jameson, 'Postmodernism and Consumer Society', in Hal Foster (ed.), *The Anti-Aesthetic: Essays on Postmodern Culture* (Port Townsend, WA.: Bay Press, 1983), p. 114.
32. Butler, *Gender Trouble*, pp. 138–9.

GRACE LAU

Confessions of a Complete Scopophiliac

Grace Lau's photography could be seen as a justified protest against the plethora of 'establishment' images ... Lau rediscovers the erotic and the fetishistic and removes them from the political wilderness. By doing so, she reinstates them as reputable artistic forms. She takes up issues which have been abandoned both by feminists and by the radical left. Her photographs explore ideas of eroticism with particular reference to pornography and fetishism, long-time taboos of radicals and conservatives alike. Like Miller and Durrell and Anais Nin before her, Grace Lau attempts to reinstate pornography as a reputable means of exploration. Like them, she uses a combination of humorous devices, odd juxtapositions and traditional narrative to render pornography harmless. The work of Grace Lau ... is not so much an excursion into 'adult' territory, but rather a re-encounter with the myths and stories which litter childhood. In Lau's photographs there are goblins and chains, dungeons and masked jailers – fairytales re-invented to suit an older audience, with their central core of pursuit and escape, morality and retribution left unaltered.

Lau retells many familiar stories using time-honoured characters – peroxided princesses accosted by goblins, beaked invaders capering through arched doorways, warriors in metallic armour. One photograph shows a chorus-line of leather-clad legs and combines peculiar connotations of end-of-the-pier entertainment with taboo notions of violence and pain. ... Lau may be dealing with profound issues of sexuality, but she is also exploring a tradition of dressing-up that is rooted in English popular culture.

The photography of eroticism has been pushed to the margins of the medium. Its associations with violence, oppression and exploitation have made it an obvious target for attack. Its undoubted power has come not just from the disturbing qualities of its own images, but also from the depth of feeling of those who oppose it.

Lau's work does much to demarginalise pornography, and to return the picturing of eroticism to its established place within British photography. Lau proves, too, that a woman's pornography does not have to be parodying or satirical, and that there are no areas of imagination which feminists must avoid.

Photography like Grace Lau's which portrays and supports a particular subculture is important, too, in that it radicalises something which is frequently consigned to the tatty fringes of commercialism. Removed from its niche of sexploitation, pornography becomes not only art but also a coherent political position. Lau's own strongly defined stance as a woman artist – within a fetishistic subculture – marks her out as an important interpreter of a very particular sexual politic.

Val Williams, 'Taboo Territory – A Review of MASKED PASSIONS', *New Statesman and Society* (1989)

One of the titles originally suggested for this collection was 'Just Looking?' The act of looking, however, is loaded – with power, with desire, with guilt and with hope – and takes place within a complex and dynamic web of social rules and behaviour. In particular, the look is embedded in relations of power. Historically, this power has belonged to men; consequently, they have, for far too long, dictated our right to look, both in public and in private. Since they possess economic control of the sex industry, they control the visual images; they have so far denied women the right to be creative in this field and the right to produce their own erotica.

Now, at last, a timely and indignant reaction to the traditional and male-monopolised industry is struggling to emerge. I am enormously inspired by all the recent activity among my female colleagues. We are exploring and expressing our sexuality and extending our sexual horizons – albeit not as freely as we would like, given the British censorship laws. There is a healthy and fervent buzz as we share the platform in open debates and discuss our needs and fears. Our unique power lies in our ability to communicate freely among ourselves – a strength that is sadly lacking in many of our male colleagues. Their fear of being seen as vulnerable is frequently a handicap in their communication with us and with each other. As a photographer of erotic images, I am obviously involved in the question of 'looking' and in the current debates concerning pornography and censorship. While I do not wish to analyse these issues in detail here, I want to express my dismay at the general lack of imagination and curiosity on the part of many feminists – or is it their lack of courage? Although we have an open attitude to discussion, too much time is still devoted to words and not enough is given over to action.

True, we are fragmented in our attempts to explore sexuality, which is already so fraught with personal and intellectual anxieties. True, we need a strong cohesive voice rather than so many differentiated, muted whispers or Dworkin-type roars. But what we really need to do is to leave the debating platform and experiment in the sphere of creative practice. We need to be as prolific as possible and to produce work motivated by our gut feelings in order to mount a challenge to the male-dominated sex industry. We must show the world that we want – and need – erotica, but

Photo copyright © Grace Lau

that we don't necessarily like the tacky and tedious top-shelf offers currently imposed on the indiscriminating public.

At every interview – either with professional journalists or with students researching sexual imagery – I am asked the same question: 'What are your definitions of pornography and erotica?' This question always exasperates me because, of course, there are no definitive answers. Personally, I prefer images that conceal, rather than those that reveal all. Most men, however, need to be re-educated to appreciate images that stir the imagination, rather than those which assault the senses. Susan Sontag encapsulates the issue in 'The Pornographic Imagination' (1967): 'The issue is not, whether pornography, but the *quality* of pornography.'

I would like to talk now about my own work and how I progressed from looking sideways at sexual imagery to being a complete scopophiliac. Ten years ago, as part of my degree thesis, I started to explore the concept of creating erotic photography for women. At that time it was generally unacceptable for women to be the consumers of sexual images, let alone to take an active part in their production. Furthermore, men were fearful of losing their power over these images and so guarded it fiercely. Women reinforced this status quo by regarding sexual exploration as a problem and not as a pleasure. Carol S. Vance articulates these difficulties in a recent article:

> Heirs to a Victorian cultural tradition that regarded sexual pleasure with profound suspicion, we greet explicit images of sexuality with anxiety and an underdeveloped history of looking. ... Our unease often increases if the sexual acts depicted are unfamiliar or unconventional or stigmatised, as the moment of viewing becomes tinged with judgment, and erotophobic and homophobic prejudice. Female viewers may scan the images for signs of sexism and danger, contrasting the seemingly conventional, even ubiquitous female nude with her less frequently seen male counterpart. And although we admire the power of photographic images to arouse feeling and emotion, we remain uneasy, sometimes ashamed, when those feelings are sexual.[1]

Undaunted by these handicaps and driven by my voracious curiosity, I shed my inhibitions behind my protective camera equipment while my male models shed their clothes. But to my dismay, my initial pictures turned out to be uninspiring, flat and apologetic. Far from being 'turned on', my female friends either laughed or felt embarrassed, but they did encourage me to continue. I haunted the gyms, the dance classes, and used my friends' reluctant boyfriends as models. I even advertised. Then, as I became progressively bolder, I looked at male nudes less furtively, with less guilt and with more pleasure.

Despite the fact that my models were all gay – straight men felt threatened in this role-reversal situation – I started to admire the male physique with female eyes while my rigid social conditioning evaporated. I felt a real erotic frisson during my photo sessions and, whilst I needed to maintain

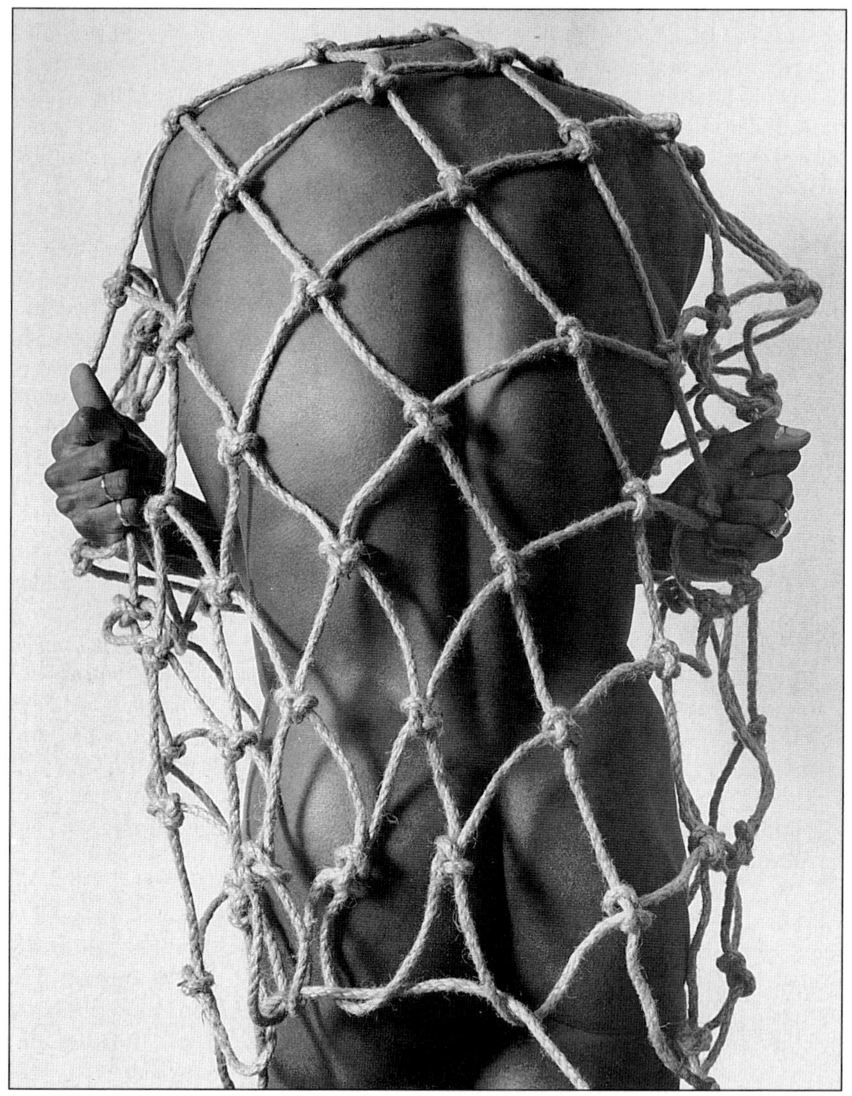

Photo copyright © Grace Lau

Photo copyright © Grace Lau

Photo copyright © Grace Lau

professional control, I was simultaneously exulted by being able to command my models. It was a loaded experience; it was power, and such power was highly stimulating. There was an erotic tension in the relationship between the undressed model and the clothed photographer – me. Perhaps my camera symbolised my new phallic power, my phallic tool. I attempted to convey this tension through my images to my audience, and this was the beginning of my success.

During my recent work, I have learnt that many women are able to enjoy being both exhibitionists and voyeurs; they also enjoy looking at images of both men and women. They have a more fluid imagination, having been denied previous blueprints, cutouts or stereotypes of sexuality. I have worked well with female models without the sort of discomfort or friction that straight male photographers would experience when photographing male nudes. I also enjoy and admire the work of my lesbian photographer friends, such as Della Grace and Jill Posner. We share mutual respect, and are able to move across gender and prejudicial barriers. We look, we communicate and we do not compete as men would do in a similar situation.

My most subversive work is the work I do for the *Skin Two* scene. This taboo territory covers fantasies and fetishism, involving adult games of bondage, sadomasochism and other theatrical rituals. Despite the obvious theatricality of these images, there is nevertheless a popular misconception that these games involve acts of violence against women. I have seen more blood shed between young children playing war games, which to me have a far more insidious influence than that involved in the acting out of sexual fantasies between consenting adults. Furthermore, I believe that such magazines as *Combat* and *Survival*, sold at W.H. Smith on the next-to-top shelf, encourage far more violence than *Skin Two*-type magazines.

Another area of subversive or taboo imagery lies in the 'gender bender', the transvestite, transsexual or androgynous person. Not all women object to the male transvestite; he is, after all, paying them a compliment through imitation. It is usually the heterosexual male who finds it utterly abhorrent that another man should wish to demean himself by donning female clothes and wearing make-up. It lets down the patriarchal side. Such transgression of social boundaries threatens stability and the status quo. I believe that a man who prefers to wear stockings and a dress is far less dangerous than one who lusts after a military uniform and a gun.

'Your fantasies and fetishes photographed by Grace Lau,' runs my advertisement in *Skin Two*. I have been enormously rewarded through meeting many fascinating people. During the initial years of working as house photographer and taking private portrait commissions, I used the basement 'dungeon' in a large North London house where Tim Woodward, the editor, lived and worked. To ensure my health and safety, he installed a baby-alarm hearing device through to his office above the dungeon, in case I needed rescuing. Having advertised my services as the 'house photographer for fetishes and fantasies', I was prepared to encounter all manner of perversions. Contrary to initial expectations, however, nearly all my male clients had a similar fantasy – that of being a submissive female. Consequently, they brought with them suitcases full of delectable underwear, brand-new sheer stockings, elaborately boned corsets, wigs, five-inch heels and a variety of other ultra-feminine clothes. It was interesting that their particular vision of the ideal woman tended to replicate a 1950s image – well-coiffured and slightly tarty – certainly not the casual self-presentation of the 80s feminist. Their icons are Joan Crawford and Joan Collins, and, dressed as perfect clones, they are not in the least threatening to anyone – rather the reverse, since their teetering heels and tightly laced bodies present a distinctly conformist, passive, pre-liberated image of women.

So while Tim listened anxiously to the alarm system, all he heard were gruff masculine voices pleading, 'Please help me lace up this girdle, Grace', or enquiring, 'Are my seams straight?' One of my favourite clients was a retired marine. Well-built, a fitness freak and seemingly macho in attitude, he was actually a sweet and gentle man who enjoyed wearing satin negligees - and who also taught me how to tie intricate marine knots. When he first appeared at the *Skin Two* basement studio, I felt a tinge of apprehension, until he hesitantly opened his case and tenderly unfolded a pale pink, frilly, size 18 satin negligee, protected in tissue paper and followed by a roll of tough fibre rope. He timidly explained that none of the professional dominatrices he visited were able to bind him tightly enough. So we spent an hour patiently practising marine knots, and then he carefully donned his satin robe; I duly roped him up, following his detailed and explicit instructions. All this preparation took more than an hour. The actual photography took fifteen minutes. Some weeks later, he called to thank me for the pictures; the only complaint he had was that the satin material of his negligee did not reveal sufficient 'rope stress' marks in the photograph. I am still puzzling over this observation.

My most rewarding job was in response to a discreet request from a gentle lady in her forties, sadly stricken with a terminal illness, who wanted to give her husband a keepsake of herself. They had a happy and sensuous relationship, adored each other, and she wanted him to remember her as a healthy sexual woman. We worked hard for an entire day, creating erotic images, and there was a poignant urgency about our task because her physical deterioration was becoming increasingly noticeable to her. A few weeks later she called to say how pleased her husband had been to receive what was, perhaps, his last gift from her and to tell me how grateful they both were for my efforts. I have not heard from her again.

The job which I most enjoyed was that of recording a wedding anniversary which was celebrated at 'Westward Bound', a bed, breakfast and bondage hotel in Devon, run by devotees of the *Skin Two* scene. The energetic couple had decided to have their night of hedonistic delights photographed for their album and fully intended to sample every device on offer in the well-equipped dungeon-playroom. We started the photo-narrative in the early evening, when they put on suitable attire – he slipped

Photo copyright © Grace Lau

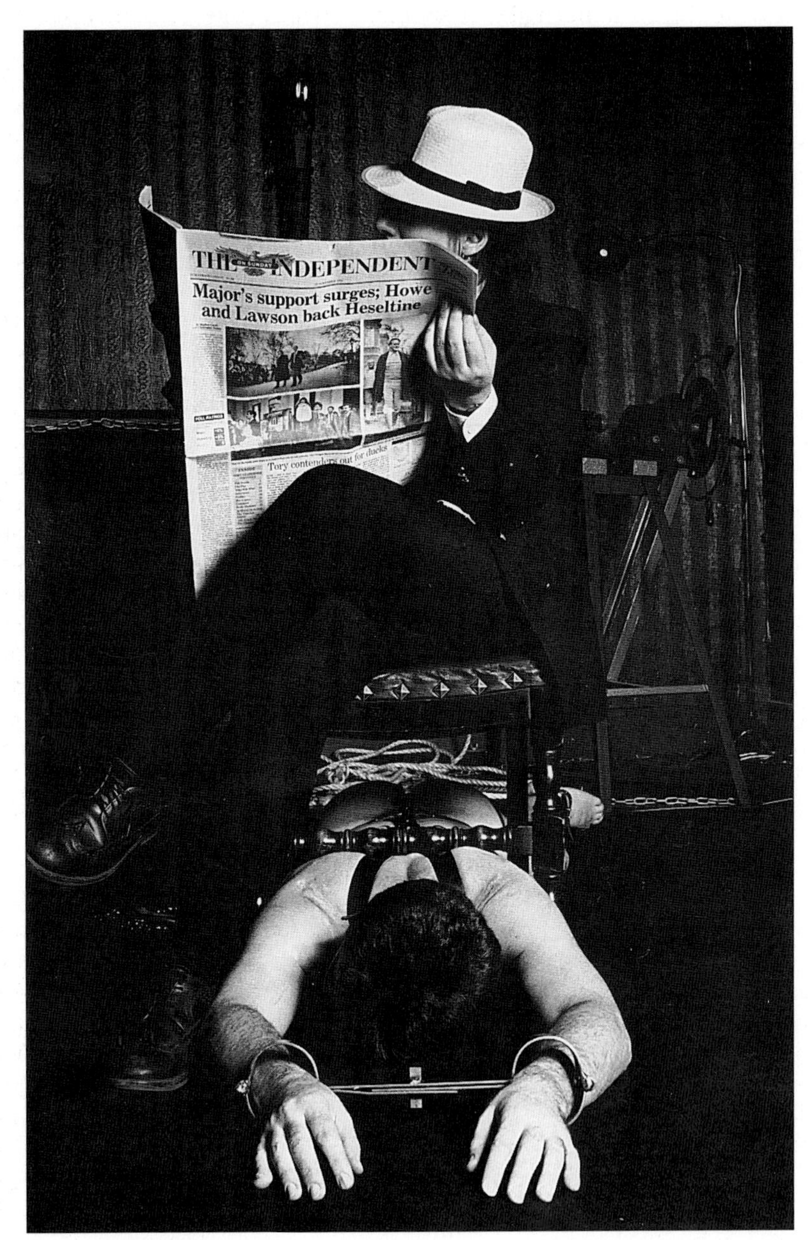

Photo copyright © Grace Lau

into a sexy maid's uniform and she donned a man's suit, complete with trilby hat. I set up my studio-flash, focused my camera and we set off to test the torture equipment, amid giggles and champagne bubbles. From the roasting spit to the electric chair to the spinning cage, I dragged my photographic paraphernalia after them, whilst they tirelessly experimented with each and every toy, even changing costumes and munching sandwiches during short breaks. What pleasure these playthings provided – it was Disneyland for perverts. Amid the tangle of chains, whips, films, light-leads, underwear and other items of both pain and pleasure, we managed to produce some half-dozen rolls of film. I was utterly exhausted by midnight, but they still frolicked among the hardware while I crept up to bed. Next morning at breakfast, the welcoming host and hostess informed me that the celebratory couple were still active at dawn. I shall not forget their anniversary.

Despite the unusual aspects of my *Skin Two* work, I have so far neither experienced any fear nor been placed in an obviously dangerous situation. I do, of course, take certain elementary precautions – such as asking my clients for their telephone numbers and then calling them to check that the number does in fact exist. I have had very few requests which I found so repugnant that I had to turn them down. Those which I have refused involve either a demand for my personal participation in acts of sexual gratification, or the enactment of dangerous or violent games. Whilst I am not averse to helping a client create an authentic bondage image by the use of ropes and chains, I once had to object when a man requested thirty-five different bondage poses, knowing full well that his allotted one roll of film contained thirty-six exposures. The client – who never in fact collected his prints – was more interested in employing me as a dominatrix than as a photographer. At times, Tim, my self-appointed protector, would pick up on his hearing device the pleading tones of a client: 'Please, Grace, can't you tie me up tighter – for a more realistic photograph?' I often wonder whether I should have charged these gentlemen for the extra services.

During the 1980s, female desire became lucrative business, including the appearance of a number of Athena-type cards and posters. But very few women artists exploited this fact – most feminists were still talking, not acting. However, at long last things are changing; I think that, for the first time, we are being seen and heard. The issue of female erotica is definitely on the agenda, and is – finally – a subject for serious consideration. I hope that the images I create will help make the public less uneasy when confronted with fantasy – I want to disturb, but not to repel. Sarah Kent, reviewing an exhibition in which some of my work was shown, commented: 'Upfront and erotic, Lau is able to represent fetishistic interest without prurient voyeurism, without violent overtones and without calling on stereotypical images of domination and submission.' I would like to think that this is true.

A quotation from Roland Barthes would provide a suitable coda to this essay. He is, as I have said elsewhere, my guru, and these particular words could be my mantra: 'Photography is subversive not when it shocks or repels, but when it is pensive – when it thinks.'[2]

Notes

1. Carol S. Vance, 'Photography, Pornography and Sexual Politics', from 'The Body in Question', *Aperture* (USA), no.121, Autumn 1990.
2. Roland Barthes, *Camera Lucida: Reflections on Photography*, trans. Richard Howard (New York: Hill and Wang, 1981; London: Fontana, 1984).

ANNE McCLINTOCK

Maid to Order

Commercial S/M and Gender Power

In *Sex*, Madonna has her wits, if not her clothes, about her. The scandal of *Sex* is the scandal of S/M: the provocative confession that the edicts of power are reversible. So the critics bay for her blood: a woman who takes sex and money into her own hands must – sooner or later – bare her breasts to the knife. But with the utmost artifice and levity, Madonna refuses to imitate tragedy. Taking sex into the street, and money into the bedroom, she flagrantly violates the sacramental edicts of private and public, and stages sexual commerce as a theatre of transformation.

Madonna's erotic photo album is filled with the theatrical paraphernalia of S/M: boots, chains, leather, whips, masks, costumes and scripts. Andrew Neil, editor of the London *Sunday Times*, warns ominously that it thus runs the risk of unleashing 'the dark side' of human nature, 'with particular danger for women'.[1] But the outrage of *Sex* is its insight into S/M as high theatre.[2] Demonising S/M confuses the distinction between unbridled sadism and the social sub-culture of consensual fetishism.[3] To argue that in consensual S/M the master has power, and the slave has not, is to read theatre for reality; it is to play the world forwards. The economy of S/M is the economy of conversion: slave to master, adult to baby, pain to pleasure, man to woman, and back again. S/M, as Foucault puts it, 'is not a name given to a practice as old as Eros; it is a massive cultural fact which appeared precisely at the end of the eighteenth century, and which constitutes one of the greatest conversions of Western imagination: unreason transformed into delirium of the heart.'[4] Consensual S/M 'plays the world backwards'.[5]

In *Sex*, as in S/M, roles are swiftly swapped. At the Vault, New York's amiable S/M dungeon, the domina Madonna archly flicks her whip across the glistening leather hips of a female 'slave'. The domina's breasts are bare; the slave is armoured. Contrary to popular stigma, S/M theatrically flouts the edict that manhood is synonymous with mastery, and submission a female fate. Further into the album, a man genuflects at Madonna's feet, neck bound in a collar, the lash at his back. But the domina's foot is also bound, and the leash straps her hand to his neck. The bondage fetish performs identity and power as twined in interdependence, and rebuts the Enlightenment vision of the solitary and self-generating individual. The lesbian with the knife is also the lover; scenes of bondage are stapled to scenes of abandon, and *Sex* makes no pretence at romantic profundity but flaunts S/M as a theatre of scene and surface.

Hence the paradox of consensual S/M. On the one hand, it seems to parade a servile obedience to conventions of power. In its clichéd reverence for formal ritual, it is the most ceremonial and decorous of practices. S/M is 'beautifully suited to symbolism'.[6] As theatre, S/M borrows its decor, props and costumery (bonds, chains, ropes, blindfolds) and its scenes (bedrooms, kitchens, dungeons, convents, prisons, empire) from the everyday cultures of power. At first glance, then, S/M seems a servant to orthodox power. Yet, on the contrary, with its exaggerated emphasis on costume and scene S/M performs social power as *scripted*, and hence as permanently subject to change. As a theatre of conversion, S/M reverses and transmutes the social meanings it borrows, yet also without finally stepping outside the enchantment of its magic circle. In S/M, paradox is paraded, not resolved. This essay is pitched at the borders of contradiction.

Against Nature: S/M and Sexology

In 1885, the sexologist Richard von Krafft-Ebing coined the terms sadism and masochism, and medicalised them both as individual psychopathologies of the flesh.[7] Sadism, for Krafft-Ebing, was an aberrant and atavistic manifestation of the 'innate desire to humiliate, hurt, wound or even destroy others in order thereby to create sexual pleasure in one's self.'[8] Nature was the overlord of power, that had, in its wisdom, seen fit to ordain the aggressive impulse in men, not women. 'Under normal circumstances man meets obstacles which it is his part to overcome, and for which nature has given him an aggressive character.'[9] 'Normal' sexuality thus merely enacts the male's 'natural' sexual aggression and the female's 'natural' sexual passivity: 'In the intercourse of the sexes, the active or aggressive role belongs to man; woman remains passive, defensive. It affords man great pleasure to win a woman, to conquer her.'[10] Yet women, for Krafft-Ebing, are indirectly to blame for male sadism, for their very shyness provokes male aggression: 'It seems probable that this sadistic force is developed by the natural shyness and modesty of women towards the aggressive manners of the male.'[11] Happily, however, Nature designed woman to take a refined pleasure in man's rough victory: 'Woman no doubt derives pleasure from her innate coyness and the final victory of man affords her intense gratification.'[12]

The task for medical sexology was to police a double boundary: between the 'normal' culture of male aggression and the 'abnormal' culture of S/M, and between 'normal' female masochism and 'abnormal' male masochism. The first contradiction – between 'natural' heterosexuality and the 'unnatural' perversions – was primarily managed by projecting the 'perversions' onto the invented zone of race. Sexologists like Krafft-Ebing demonised S/M as the psychopathology of the atavistic individual, as

Action in an early eighteenth-century flagellant brothel; frontispiece of the 1718 London edition of Meibom's treatise. Note the voyeurs at the window. Courtesy of the British Library Board.

a blood-flaw and stigma of the flesh. S/M, like other fetishisms, was figured as a regression in time to the 'prehistory' of racial 'degeneration', existing ominously in the heart of the imperial metropolis – the degeneration of the race writ as an individual pathology of the soul.

Thus for Krafft-Ebing, decent doses of male aggression are a *fait accompli* of nature. Genuine sadism, however, exists in 'civilised man' only in a 'weak and rather rudimentary degree'.[13] While sadism is a natural trait of 'primitive' peoples, atavistic traces of sadism in 'civilised man' stem, not from environment or social accident, but from a primordial past: 'Sadism must ... be counted among the primitive anomalies of the sexual life. It is a disturbance (a deviation) in the evolution of psychosexual processes sprouting from the soil of psychical degeneration.'[14]

Like Krafft-Ebing, Freud agrees that the aggressive impulse is 'readily demonstrable in the normal individual'.[15] Again, the 'normal individual' is male: 'The sexuality of most men shows an admixture of aggression, of a desire to subdue.'[16] For Freud, the difference between aggression and sadism is one of degree, not of kind: 'Sadism would then correspond to an aggressive component of the sexual instinct which has become independent and exaggerated and has been brought to the foreground by displacement.'[17] Masochism, however, presents a more subtle riddle. For Krafft-Ebing, since it is simply Nature's way of saying that women are destined for a passive role in society, masochism is natural to women but not to men. Freud, however, sees the 'most striking peculiarity' of sadomasochism as the fact that 'its active and passive forms are regularly encountered together in the same person.'[18] Male masochism, moreover, is by no means an uncommon phenomenon. Freud, however, manages this contradiction by identifying male masochism as, more properly speaking, 'feminine'.[19] The heterosexual distribution of 'male' aggression and 'female' passivity is sustained, if precariously.

By contrast with unbridled sadism, however, consensual and commercial S/M is less a biological flaw or pathological variant of natural, male aggression and natural female passivity, than it is a historical sub-culture that emerged in Europe alongside the Enlightenment. Far from being a primordial manifestation of racial 'degeneracy', S/M is a sub-culture organised primarily around the symbolic exercise of social risk. Indeed, the outrage of S/M is precisely its hostility to the idea of nature as the custodian of social power: S/M refuses to read power as fate or destiny. Since S/M is the theatrical exercise of social contradiction, it is self-consciously *against* nature, not in the sense that it violates natural law, but in the sense that it denies the existence of natural law in the first place. S/M *performs* social power as both contingent and constitutive, as sanctioned neither by fate nor by God, but by social convention and invention, and thus open to historical change.

Consensual S/M insists on exhibiting the 'primitive' (slave, baby, woman) as a *character* in the historical time of modernity. S/M stages the 'primitive irrational' as a dramatic script, a communal performance in the heart of Western reason. The paraphernalia of S/M (boots, whips, chains, uniforms) are the paraphernalia of state power, public punishment converted to private pleasure. S/M plays social power backwards, visibly staging hierarchy, difference and power, the irrational, ecstasy, and the alienation of the body as at the centre of Western reason, thus revealing the imperial *logic* of individualism, but also irreverently refusing it as *fate*. S/M manipulates the *signs* of power in order to refuse their legitimacy as *nature*. Hence the unstinting severity of the law in policing commercial S/M.

Nothing to Use but Your Chains: Fetishes in the Land of Fem-Dom

Some feminists demonise heterosexual S/M as the sanctioned exercise of male tyranny: 'Patriarchy and heterosexuality attempt to freeze power, to make one side always passive. ... It is the origin of masochistic and sadistic positions.'[20] For other feminists, even lesbian S/M is 'self-debasement on all levels that renders wimmin unable to execute truly feminist goals.'[21] Kathleen Barry in *Sexual Slavery* denounces S/M as 'a disguise for the act of sexually forcing a woman against her will.'[22]

It is also commonly thought that men who pay for commercial S/M pay to indulge in the sadistic abuse of women. Yet the testimony of dominatrixes reveals precisely the opposite. By far the most common service paid for by men in heterosexual S/M is the extravagant display of submission. In most commercial B & D (bondage and discipline), men are the 'slaves', not women. As the dominatrix Lindi St Clair says, far from being the vicious unleashing of male dominance, S/M is typically 'the other way round'.[23] Allegra Taylor agrees:

> Amber can call on the services of a couple of 'submissive' girls who themselves enjoy being beaten, to service the needs of the few 'dominant' men who want to dish it out rather than take it, but the majority of her clients come and pay a lot of money in order to submit, to relinquish themselves, to suffer.[24]

Who are these men? 'Proper gentlemen who know how to behave.' Amber's regulars include 'solicitors, Harley Street doctors, senior police officers, business executives and churchmen. They come to be punished, humiliated, frightened and tormented to the limits of their endurance.'[25]

Kelly, an Australian B & D specialist, claims her clients are 'mostly businessmen, middle-age upwards. They were all well dressed, you wouldn't pick them in the street, they could be your boss at work. B & D seems to attract that kind of clientele, as though people in authority want that taken away from them.'[26] As Lindi St Clair testifies:

> An awful lot of men ... want to dress up in what we call rubber-wear, or leather, or they want to be tied up, and put into bondage, or spanked, or caned, or they want to dress in ladies' clothing, or they want to be urinated on, or they want to be abused by a dominant female ... and none of this involves straight sex. ... All these men are married, with families. ... They'd never admit it to anyone.[27]

Far from male sadism being the norm, she says: 'There's a few of what are called 'masters', who want submissive girls, but I've never come across that. It's very, very small. It's the other way round.'[28] Bonnie, an Australian prostitute writes: 'In New Zealand and here it's much the same, usually they're guys who want to get a beating.'[29] Says Kelly: 'There are those who are just happy grovelling around the floor begging for mercy.'[30] This verdict is confirmed again and again: 'In the world of the sadomasochist, there is nothing "abnormal" about a male being passive and submissive.'[31] Indeed, male passivity is by far the most common phenomenon. What is the meaning of this conversion?

The Domestic Slave

Prostitutes testify that men frequently enact scripts framed by the 'degradation' of domesticity: paying large sums of money to sweep, clean, launder and tidy, under a female regime of verbal taunts and abuse:

> 'Domestic' slaves want to be drudges and set to work cleaning, shopping, ironing, etc. ... One elderly gentleman of seventy does the best domestic work I have ever seen. Another slave tried to get rid of him, and they would bicker over who would wash up, peel the potatoes, or sweep the floor.[32]

Some dominas keep 'pets', who pay regularly to do their housework for them. During her trial in 1987, Madame Cyn Payne calmly confessed to the court: 'Well, I've had one or two slaves. It's someone who does all the housework and painting and decorating, and in return he likes a little bit of caning, insults and humiliation.'[33]

Similar testimonies abound. Lisa, an Australian prostitute, remembers a domestic 'slave' who liked nothing so much as 'to crawl around the floor doing the vacuum with a cucumber up his bum.'[34] Kelly remembers: 'Another guy came around each week and paid to do our laundry.'[35] Another paid to empty the bins of condoms and tissues. The eighteenth-century prostitute, Ann Sheldon, records in her memoirs 'a person of very gentleman-like behaviour' who had a fancy for being roundly beaten with dishcloths while doing the washing up:

> Looking over the kitchen-door, I saw the good man, disrobed of his clothes and wig, and dressed in a mob cap, a tattered bed-gown, and an old pettycoat belonging to the cook, as busy in washing the dishes as if this employment had been the source of his daily bread, – but this was not all; for while he was thus occupied, the mantua-maker on one side, and the cook on the other, were belabouring him with dish-clouts; he continuing to make a thousand excuses for his awkwardness and promising to do the business better on a future occasion.[36]

What are we to make of these rituals, belonging as they do in the realm of the fetish?

In their secret society of the spectacle, male 'slaves' enact with compulsive repetition the forbidden knowledge of the power of women. In cultures where women are the child-raisers, an infant's first identification is with the culture of femininity, which enters the child's identity as its first structuring principle. But in these same societies, boys are tasked with identifying away from women, that is, away from a founding dimension of their own identity, towards an often abstracted and remote masculinity – identity not through recognition, but through negation. Masculinity thus comes into being through the ritualised disavowal of the feminine, predicated on a host of male rites of negation. Nonetheless, identification with the culture of women survives in secret rites – taboo and full of shame.

By cross-dressing as women or as maids, by paying to do 'women's work', or by ritually worshipping dominas as socially powerful, the male 'slave' relishes the forbidden, feminine aspects of his own identity, furtively recalling the childhood image of female power and the memory of maternity, banished by social shame to the museum of masturbation. In Freudian psychoanalysis, as in Western culture at large, male identification *with* the mother figure is seen as pathological, perverse, the source of arrest, fixation and hysteria, rather than as an inevitable aspect of any child's identity. For Freud, the mother is seen as an object the child must try to possess and control, rather than a social ideal *with whom* to identify. For boys, active identification is allowed only with men, thus splitting complex, dynamic patterns of identity into two distinct, gendered categories. For men, the disjunction between women as object-choice and women as desirable to identify *with* is split and unresolved, policed by social shame and stigma.

It is not surprising, then, that cleaning rituals figure so often in the land of Fem-Dom (Female Domination). Male floor-washing, laundering, foot-licking and boot-scrubbing rituals fill the fantasy columns of Fem-Dom magazines such as *Mistress, F-D Xtra* and *Madame in a World of Fantasy*. Perhaps these expiation rituals symbolically absolve the 'slave' of sexual and gender shame, in elaborate absolution scenes that are replete with Christian overtones. Sex can be indulged if guilt can be atoned for, through the ritual washing of floors, feet and lingerie – 'masochism as expiation for the sin of sexuality'.[37]

The domestic fetish brings into crisis the historic separation of the 'male' sphere of the market and the 'female' sphere of the home. By paying handsomely to perform household services that wives are expected to perform for free, male 'slaves' stage, as outrageous display, the social contradiction between women's paid work and women's unpaid work in the home. If the middle-class cult of domesticity disavowed the economic value of housework, and exalted the home as the space for the elaborate display of leisure and consumption, domestic S/M does the opposite. In the ritual exchange of cash and the reversal of gender roles, domestic S/M stages women's work as having both *exhibition* and *economic* value. The social disavowal and *undervaluation* of domestic work is reversed in the extravagant *overvaluation* of women's dirty work, and the remuneration of *women* for the supervision of *men's* labour.

The domestic-slave fetish – inhabiting as it does the threshold between private and public, marriage and market – embodies the trace of both historical and personal memory, exhibiting, without resolution, the social contradiction between the historical disavowal of women's labour and the personal memory of women's power. Male 'slaves' throw into question the liberal separation of private and public, insisting on exhibiting women's work, women's *value* in the home: that space putatively beyond both slave labour and the market economy. Exhibiting their 'filth' as value, they give the lie to the disavowal of women's work and the middle-class denunciation of sexual and domestic 'dirt'. At the same time, the slave-band brings into the bourgeois home the memory of empire: the clanking of chains and the crack of the whip. The fetish slave-band, mimicking the metal collars worn by black slaves in the homes of the imperial bourgeoisie, enacts the history of industrial capital as haunted by the traumatic and ineradicable memory of slave imperialism.

Male TV (transvestite) 'slavery' thus veers between nostalgia for female power, embodied in the awful spectacle of the whip-wielding domina, and the ritual negation of female power, embodied in the feminised male 'slave' as the nadir of self-abasement. In the process, however, the spectacle of the male 'slave' on his hands and knees, naked as a newt and scrubbing the kitchen floor, throws radically into question 'Nature's' edict that differences in gender entail natural divisions of labour.

Some men play the submissive role only when dressed as women, doing 'women's work' costumed as housemaids or nannies. A question then arises: do men indulge in submission only when dressed as women and slaves, dogs and babies? Would heterosexuality be flung into confusion if men performed domestic work in Dacron suits and Leonard From Paris ties? After the *via dolorosa* of the S/M session, the domina bears witness to the resurrection of manhood: 'Finally, it was all over. ... Dennis got up and gingerly put his pants on. He was instantly transformed into a normal, confident, assertive man. ... We all stood around chatting and having a cup of tea.'[38] Is the heterosexual male thus left finally unimpaired, to be reassembled again in boardroom and bedroom?[39]

Yet not all 'slaves' cross-dress when doing domestic work. As one writer grumbled in *Madame in a World of Fantasy*: 'Dear Candida, I know you like to give all tastes a share in your magazine, but the portion given to those interested in men that are feminised is way over the top.'[40] Many 'slaves' retain their male persona and perform domestic work as an elaborate reversal of gender *agency*, but not of gender *identity*. It is therefore important to stress that S/M does not constitute a single sub-culture, but rather comprises a cluster of circulating genres, some of which are distinct, some of which overlap.

In S/M, social identities shift libidinously. In her ground-breaking book *Vested Interests*, Marjorie Garber invites us to take transvestites on their own terms, not as one sex or gender but as the enactment of ambiguity itself: not even so much a 'blurred sex', as the embodiment and performance of social contradiction.[41] She contends that the 'specter of transvestism' throws into question the very notion of a fixed and stable identity, challenging any easy binarity of 'female' and 'male'. The cross-dresser represents the 'crisis of category itself'. Garber thus sets herself against the 'progress narrative' theory of cross-dressing, which attempts to uncover a 'real' desired identity, either 'male' or 'female' beneath the transvestite mask. Rather, the transvestite is the figure that inhabits the borderland where oppositions are permanently disarranged.

Cross-dressing celebrates the peculiar freedoms of ambiguity, rather than the fixity of one identity. For many, the allure of transvestism is not the transformation of man-to-woman, or woman-to-man, but the subversive parade of man-*as*-woman, woman-*as*-man. Cross-dressers often desire, not the security of a perfect imitation, but rather the delicious impersonation that belies complete disguise: the hairy leg in the lace suspender, the bald pate in the bonnet. In 'tranny' (transvestite) publications such as *The World of Transvestism*, a man's hirsute calf protrudes beneath the silken skirt, the shadow of an erection is pressed against the lacy lingerie. One TV writes:

> I agree with what you have said, Brian, about contrast – male with female. Long black fishnet stockings, frilly suspender belts, pretty frocks and finally see-through panties that when one raises one's frock, the big erect penis bulging through the silky flimsy material can clearly be seen.[42]

The Dirt Fetish

Domestic S/M is organised in complex and repetitive ways around the fetish of 'dirt'. Why does 'dirt' exert such a compulsive fascination over the S/M imagination?

The dirt fetish embodies the traces of both personal and historical memory. Dirt may recall, as personal memory, punishment during toilet training for being out of control – of one's faeces, one's urine, one's erections and ejaculation, one's wandering, desirous fingers. Faecal dirt smeared by children on themselves, their walls, their cots or their siblings can embody a variety of inchoate passions: rage, curiosity, an attempt to reach out and influence the world, frustration and loneliness. If unaccountably punished for such acts, the emotion may be arrested, destined to recur compulsively for ritualistic re-enactment. In the dirt fetish, the fetishist takes control of perilous memory, playing memory backwards, in an excess of desire, and disarranging the social compact between sexual transgression and dirt. If fetishists, as children, were punished for being out of control of their 'dirt', in the rebellious circus of fetishism they re-enact, in reverse, an *excess* of control over 'dirt'. If, as children, an obscure logic of parental rebuke equated erotic pleasure with 'filth' and 'smut', meriting swift retribution, then, as adults, the S/Mers invert the logic, equating dirt with an exquisite excess of erotic pleasure, re-enacting 'toilet training' in an exhibitionist parody of the domestic economy of pleasure and power.

S/M also embodies a historical memory trace. Since the nineteenth century, the sub-culture of S/M has been denounced by reference to the bestiary and the iconography of 'filth'. But nothing is inherently dirty; dirt expresses a relation to social value and social disorder. Dirt, as Mary Douglas suggests, is that which transgresses social boundary. A broom in a kitchen closet is not 'dirty', whereas lying on a bed it is. Sex with one's spouse is not 'dirty', whereas the same act with a prostitute is. Boxing is not 'dirty', but S/M is.

During the nineteenth century, the iconography of 'dirt' became deeply integrated in the policing and transgression of social boundary. In Victorian culture, the bodily relation to 'dirt' expressed a social relation to labour. The male middle class – seeking to dismantle the aristocratic body and the aristocratic regime of legitimacy – came to distinguish itself as a class in two ways: it earned its living (unlike the aristocracy), and it owned property (unlike the working class). Unlike the working class, however, its members, especially its female members, could not bear on their bodies the visible evidence of manual labour. Dirt was a Victorian scandal, because it was the surplus evidence of manual work, the visible residue that stubbornly remained after the process of industrial rationality had done its work. Dirt is the counterpart of the commodity; something is dirty precisely *because* it is void of commercial value, or because it transgresses the 'normal' commercial market. Dirt is what is left over after exchange value has been extracted. Dirt is by definition *useless*, since it is that which belongs outside the commodity market.

If, as Marx noted, commodity fetishism exhibits the *overvaluation* of commercial exchange as the fundamental principle of social community, then the Victorian obsession with dirt marks a dialectic: the fetishised *undervaluation* of human labour. Smeared on trousers, faces, hands and aprons, dirt was the memory trace of working-class and female labour, unseemly evidence that the production of industrial and imperial wealth lay fundamentally in the hands and bodies of the working class, women and the colonised. In this way dirt, like all fetishes, expresses a crisis in value, for it contradicts the liberal dictum that social wealth is created by the abstract, rational principles of the market, and not by labour. For this reason Victorian dirt entered the symbolic realm of fetishism with great force.

As the nineteenth century drew on, the iconography of dirt became a poetics of surveillance, deployed increasingly to police the boundaries between 'normal' sexuality and 'dirty' sexuality, 'normal' work and 'dirty' work, and 'normal' money and 'dirty' money. 'Dirty' sex – masturbation, prostitution, lesbian and gay sexuality, S/M, the host of the Victorian 'perversions' – transgressed the libidinal economy of male-controlled, heterosexual reproduction within monogamous marital relations (clean sex which has *value*). Likewise, 'dirty' money – associated with prostitutes, Jews, gamblers, thieves – transgressed the fiscal economy of the male-dominated, market exchange (clean money which has *value*). Prostitutes stood on the dangerous threshold of work, money and sexuality, and came to be figured increasingly in the iconography of 'pollution', 'disorder', 'plagues', 'moral contagion' and racial 'filth'.

Men Babies in the Land of Fem-Dom

S/M is haunted by memory. By re-enacting *loss* of control in a staged situation of *excessive* control, the S/Mer gains symbolic power over perilous memory. By reinventing the memory of trauma, S/M affords a delirious triumph over the past, and from this triumph an orgasmic excess of pleasure. But since the triumph over memory is symbolic, however intensely felt in the flesh, resolution is perpetually deferred. For this reason, the fetish, the scene, will recur for perpetual re-enactment, and compulsive repetition emerges as a fundamental structuring principle of S/M.

By many accounts, babyism is a common fetish in commercial S/M. As Allegra Taylor says: 'There's a whole area of deviant behaviour called Babyism where the client likes to dress up in a nappy, suck a giant dummy or one of her [the domina's] breasts and just be rocked.'[43] In trade parlance, a 'babyist' or 'infantilist' pays large sums of money to be bathed, powdered, put in nappies, sat in playpens, or wrapped tightly in swaddling clothes. The fem-dom magazine *Fantasy* explains: 'We often have requests for stories of poor (un)willing creatures who wish to return to the beginning of their existence and be completely babyfied, dominated entirely.'[44] Ann Sheldon's eighteenth-century gentleman who fancied being beaten while doing the dishes liked the two women who beat him then 'to skewer him up tight in a blanket, and roll him backwards and forwards upon the carpet, in the parlor, 'till he was lulled to sleep.'[45]

Enough men like to be rocked and 'nursed' to give dominas a steady trade. As St Clair attests: '"Babyists" need mummy Lindi to dress them in nappies, bibs, bonnets and booties, to powder their bottoms and breast-feed them.'[46] Another domina runs a two-storey building: at lunchtime, businessmen arrive, discreetly take off their clothes, don giant-size nappies with giant-size nappy pins, and spend large sums of money to sit for an hour in giant-size playpens, sucking bottles, before redressing and returning to the hurly-burly of high finance.

Babyist scenes in F-D magazines feature grown men in outsize frilly baby wear, strapped into baby cots, or gazing wide-eyed at the camera from behind their dummies. A typical magazine fantasy runs as follows:

> He began to feel, not just his mummy's child, but his total dependency on her. ... He sighed contentedly. Babba had been his childhood name. ... Now he was to be Babba again. ... From the next day, all baby hair was removed. Mummy bathed him, dried him, put baby-oil between his legs. ... Bobby, at home, has become a baby again.[47]

Male babyism holds up to society a scandalous, accusatory hybrid: not so much man-into-baby but man-*as*-baby, baby-*as*-man. Contradictions are exhibited but not resolved. In these scenes, men surrender deliriously to the memory of female power and their own helplessness in their mother's or nurse's arms. If men are socially tasked with upholding the burden of rational self-containment, perhaps in the babyland of fem-dom they can fleetingly relinquish their stolid control, surrendering responsibility and authority in an ecstatic release of power.

Babyism may also grant men retrospective control over perilous memories of infancy: nightmares of restraint, rubber sheets, helplessness, inexplicable punishments, isolation and grief. The rubber fetish seems associated, for some, with inchoate memories of rubber diapers, wet beds and mortification. F-D magazine fantasies reveal aching images of childhood as a bewildering limbo of denial, discomfort, parental rage and neglect. One babyist muses:

> The problem probably stemmed from my early childhood. I was an only child and my mother left home. ... My father was away fighting the war ... and I was thus brought up by an aunt. ... She would cuff me round the ear at the slightest excuse.[48]

Another fetishist recalls:

> But in the depths of my mind there lurked a more sinister side of myself, an obsession to be dominated and humiliated as a child, forced back to the cradle by beautiful, cruel women, normally nurses or nannies.[49]

This writer's masochism began at boarding school, when he was ridiculed for bed-wetting. When punishment failed to cure him, the school nurse subjected him to a public circus of mortification:

> She gathered all the boys around ... while she removed my shorts and underpants. With a captive audience, she pinned me into a bulky nappy. ... 'There,' she beamed, 'baby has a nappy on at last.' ... My humiliation was complete.[50]

Now, however, as an adult, in his F-D theatre of conversion, the babyist converts the *incapacity* to control body functions and the failure to preserve the boundaries between child and adult into the *imperative* to lose control, and to blur the boundaries between adult and child. Through the control frame of cash and fantasy, perilous memory of *loss* of control is re-enacted under circumstances of a scrupulous *excess* of control.

In their secret nursery for Goliaths, babyists ritually indulge in the forbidden, nostalgic spectacle of the power of women. The land of Fem-Dom is frequently described by men as a 'feminist' utopia, a futuristic paradise in which women are 'fully liberated and universally recognized as the Superior Sex'.[51] The voices of martinets, scolds and governesses crack through the pages of these magazines: "This is exactly what you *deserve*, my boy. A good smacked *bottom*!," she said sternly, *just* like a strict governess.'[52] The Agony Aunts of F-D columns are similarly vituperative: 'Disgusting creature though you are, you have my permission to write again,' snaps one.[53] 'You sound a miserable worm to me ... and deserve all you get,' barks another.[54]

The 'naughty husband' fantasy, in which callous men are punished for various domestic infringements, appears frequently. A STRICT BOTTOM SMACKING WIFE writes: 'A little wifely discipline is often necessary. I am sure that many wives have often felt like turning a misbehaving young husband over a knee and smacking his bottom – the thing is to do it.'[55] 'I am a firm believer,' writes another 'wife', 'in petticoating and nursery treatment as a means of reminding a troublesome husband that he is still subject to maternal rule.'[56]

Perhaps in these expiation rituals, men pay not only to surrender gender responsibility, or to gain control of perilous memories, but also to be symbolically absolved of guilt for the everyday abuse of women – only to resume their authority once more as they return restored from babyland. As Gebhard suggests: 'The masochist has a nice guilt-relieving system – he gets his punishment simultaneously with his sexual pleasure or else is entitled to his pleasure by first enduring the punishment.'[57] Moreover, the 'feminist' utopia exalted by these men is a paradise arranged and organised for male pleasure. In the private security of fantasy, men can indulge secretly and guiltily their knowledge of women's power, while enclosing female power in a fantasy land that lies far beyond the cities and towns of genuine feminist change.

Criminal Justice: The Policing of S/M

On 28 January 1987, at the height of the celebrated trial of Madame Cyn Payne, Sergeant David Broadwell dragged into court a large plastic bag and exposed to the titillated courtroom the taboo paraphernalia of S/M: whips, belts, chains, a dog collar, and assorted sticks and leather items.[58] For days, police and witnesses described the 'naughtinesses' at Payne's party: spankings, lesbian shows, elderly gentlemen cross-dressed in women's evening clothes, policemen in drag, and lawyers, businessmen and even a Peer of the Realm waiting in queues on the stairs for sex.

The sex trial, conducted in a blaze of publicity, exposes its own structuring paradox, staging in public, as a vicarious spectacle, what it renders criminally deviant outside the juridical domain. Ordering the unspeakable to be spoken in public, the sex trial takes shape around the very fetishism it sets itself to isolate and punish. Through the prostitution trial, transgressions in the distribution of money, pleasure and power are isolated as *crimes*, and are then performed again in the theatrical ceremony of the trial as *confession*. The judiciary is a system of ordered procedures for the production of 'Truth'. It is also a system for disqualifying alternative discourses: the disenfranchised, feminists, prostitutes, fetishists. By being obliged to speak 'forensically' in the courtroom about their illicit activities, prostitutes rehearse, as spectacle, the taboo body of the woman who

" I'M AFRAID THERE'S A QUEUE ON THE STAIRS AGAIN, OLD BOY ! "

receives money for sex. The more she speaks of her actions in public, however, the more she incriminates herself. But in its obsessive display of 'dirty' pictures, filmed evidence, confessions and exhibits, the sex trial reveals itself as deployed about the archival exhibition of the fetish. Under his purple robes, the judge has an erection.

The sex trial and the flagellation scene mirror each other in a common liturgy. There is, first of all, the Chamber. In the trial, this is the Court; in S/M it is the Vault, the Dungeon, or the Schoolroom. The first rite is exposure – in the trial, the accused is exposed before the crowd; in the flagellant scene the 'slave's' buttocks are bared. The Judge, like the Dominatrix, is theatrically costumed, while the judge's wig, like the prostitute's wig, guarantees the separation between self and body, and thereby the 'impartiality' of the trial. Both Judge and Dominatrix are paid money to exercise the right to punish, while fetish elements are common to both: theatrical costumery, stage, gavels, whips, handcuffs. The second rite is restraint: the accused is penned in the dock, the 'slave' is tied, or bent over the block. The third element is the charge, for which it is also necessary that there be spectators, voyeurism being an indispensable element in both scenes. Next, it is crucial that both accused and 'slave' participate verbally in their trial, in the plea, the interrogation, denials and confession. Warnings are given, sentence is pronounced, and execution takes place. Only then is the logic of pleasure and punishment reversed: the trial displays illicit pleasure and power for punishment; S/M displays illicit punishment for pleasure and power. The trial exists to produce the sentence of rational Truth, while in S/M Truth becomes orgasm, and the word is made flesh. S/M thus emerges as a private parody of the public trial: public punishment converted to private pleasure.

If the sex trial isolates 'deviant' sexual *pleasure* for *punishment*, commercial S/M is the dialectical twin of the trial, organising the *punishment* of sexual deviance for *pleasure*. If the sex trial redistributes illicit female money back into male circulation through fines, commercial S/M enacts the reverse, staging women's sexual work as having economic value, and insisting, strictly, on payment.

Consensual S/M brings to its limit the liberal discourse on consent. In 1990, the notorious Spanner investigation became an estimated £2.5 million showcase for the policing of gay S/M in Britain. On 19 December 1990, fifteen men were sentenced at the Old Bailey by Judge James Rant for willingly and privately engaging in S/M acts with each other for sexual pleasure. Eight of the men were given custodial sentences ranging up to four and a half years. On 19 February 1992, five of the men failed to have their conviction overturned by the Court of Appeal.[59] The presiding Lord Chief Justice, Lord Lane, ruled that the men's consent and the privacy of their acts were no defence, and that S/M libido did not constitute causing bodily harm 'for good reason'.

By contrast, activities such as boxing, football, rugby or cosmetic surgery apparently constitute, in the eyes of the law, well-recognised cases of licit, consensual bodily harm, for they are conducted for 'good reason', that is, for the profitable, public consumption of 'natural' female vanity, 'natural' male agression and the law of male, market competition – for the proper maintenance, that is, of heterosexual difference. In violent contact sports, men touch each other in furious and often wounding intimacy, but the homoerotic implications are scrupulously disavowed.

Perhaps even more revealingly, Feminists Against Censorship, the gay rights group Outrage, Liberty (formerly the National Council of Civil Liberties), and others, have pointed out that the sentences meted out by Judge Rant for consensual S/M exceed, in many cases, those for the violent, non-consensual rape or battery of women or for cases of lesbian and gay bashing. As Alex Kershaw notes: 'In 1988, for example, a man was fined £100 at Carlisle Crown Court for sado-masochistic assaults on women.'[60] Suzanne Moore sums it up: 'In other words when a heterosexual woman says "no" she really means "yes", but when a homosexual man says "yes", the law says that is not good enough.'[61] The Spanner trial throws radically into question the law's putative impartiality in the adjudication of consent.

The outrage of consensual S/M is multiple. It publicly exposes the possibility that manhood is not *naturally* synonymous with mastery, nor femininity with passivity. Social identity becomes commutable, and the boundaries of gender and class open to invention and transfiguration. Men touch each other for pleasure and women wreak well-paid vengeance. Perhaps most subversively of all, eroticism is sundered from the rule of procreation: the erotic body expands beyond the genitals to include non-procreational sites – ears, feet, nipples – of life-saving potential in the era of AIDS.[62] At the same time, the power dynamics and erotic implications of social ritual are visibly and flagrantly explored. As Califia says: 'In an S & M context, the uniforms and roles and dialogue become a parody of authority, a challenge to it, a recognition of its secret, sexual nature.'[63] In S/M's house of misrule, woman is judge and jury, man is penitent, the master does the slave's bidding, and the sacred is profane.

S/M is the most liturgical of forms, sharing with Christianity a theatrical iconography of punishment and expiation: washing rituals, bondage, flagellation, body-piercing and symbolic torture. Like S/M, the economy of Christianity is the economy of conversion: the meek exalted, the high made low. Mortifying the flesh exalts one in the eyes of the Master. Through humility on earth, one stores up a surplus stock of spiritual value in heaven. Like Christianity, S/M performs the paradox of redemptive suffering, and like Christianity, it takes shape around the masochistic logic of transcendence through the mortification of the flesh: through self-abasement, the spirit finds release in an ecstasy of abandonment. In both S/M and Christianity, earthly desire exacts strict payment in an economy of penance and pleasure. In S/M, washing rituals and the pouring of water effect a baptismal cleansing and exoneration of guilt. These are purification rituals, a staged appropriation of Christian pageantry, stealing a delirious, fleshly advance on one's spiritual credit – a forbidden taste of what should properly be exaltation in the hereafter.

The Right to Punish

The historic sub-culture of S/M emerged within the Enlightenment, alongside what Foucault has identified as a new technology of the power-to-punish.[64] During the Enlightenment, as Foucault argues, penal reform shifted the right-to-punish from the whimsical, terrible vengeance of the sovereign to the contractual 'defence of society'.[65] The spectacle of punishment no longer lay in the sumptuous rage of the monarch, which had taken effect as a series of ostentatious mutilations of the criminal's flesh – floggings, brandings, beheadings, flayings, quarterings and so on. Punishment now lay in the visible *representation* of an abstract, bureaucratic power, which took effect as a series of ritual restraints – detention, incarceration, regulation, retraining, restrictions, fines, and, in some cases, rationalised and limited corporal punishment. An array of techniques was devised for adjusting punishment to the new social body, and a host of new principles was laid down for refining the art of punishing.[66] In the hands of an elite bureaucracy, punishment became legitimised, not as personal revenge, but as civic prevention. Punishment became the rationally calculated, causal *effect* of the crime, and the administrators of punishment were figured as no more than the dispassionate ministrants of rational law.

Penal reform, as Foucault sees it, had the centrifugal effect of multiplying and dispersing punishment as an 'art of affects': the penalty must have its most intense effects on those who have not committed the crime.[67] The link between crime and punishment must be publicly *seen* to coincide causally with the operation of rationally administered Truth. The Enlightenment technology of punishment thus had two aims in view: to get all citizens to participate in the 'contractual' punishment of the social enemy, and to render the power to punish 'entirely adequate and transparent to the laws that publicly define it'.[68] Punishments became less ritual marks violently gouged into the flesh, than *tableaux vivants* designed to be witnessed by the general public as representative of the mechanics of natural law.

Under this regime, schools came to serve as miniature penal mechanisms, with forms of discipline borrowed directly from the juridical model: solitary confinement, flagellation, petty humiliations and an extravagant attention to rule. Public mortification was meted out according to a theatrical liturgy of floggings, restraints and deprivations, with the undeviating precision of machinery.

The scandal of S/M, however, is that it borrows directly from the juridical model, while radically disarranging the right-to-punish. S/M stages the right-to-punish, not for the civic prevention of crime, but for pleasure, parading a scrupulous fidelity to the *scene* and costumery of the penal model while at the same time interfering directly with the rules of *agency*. Hence the intolerable affront embodied in the dominatrix and her client. How can punishment be established in the minds of the public as a logical calculus of criminal *cause* and penal *effect* – the rational execution of Truth – if members of the general public can take up, on whim, the birch, the rod, the handcuffs, the whipping block, and declare sentence not for the prevention of crime, but for the delirious excess of pleasure? For it is as subversive of the modern penal economy to commit an unpunished crime as it is to enjoy a punishment without having first committed a crime.

Hence the unstinting severity of the law in policing consensual S/M. Penal reform, despite its egalitarian, civic-minded cast, placed the restricted exercise of the penal right in the hands of a few elect institutions and a few elect actors: judges, prison warders, schoolteachers, army courts, and parents, as proxies of natural law. Whatever else changed, however, punishment remained a male right: the judge, the jury, the prison governor, and the executioner were, until very recently, all men. Wives of elite men might punish slaves, servants and children, but only as proxies of male law.

By contrast, heterosexual, commercial S/M flagrantly subverts the gendered economy of the right-to-punish, putting the whip and the money in the woman's hand, and exhibiting the man on his knees. With even greater effrontery, lesbian and gay S/Mers parade punishment, not as the dutiful exercise of civic prevention, but as a recreational theatre of power, denying the state its penal monopoly and provocatively exposing the right-to-punish, not as Reason's immutable decree, but as the irregular product of social hierarchy.

The legal denunciation of consensual S/M flies out, then, not as a human cry from the heart, a refined shrinking from the infliction of pain and the spectacle of torment, but as the jealous wrath of the penal bureaucracy challenged in its punitive monopoly. In sentencing S/Mers to bondage and discipline, floggings and ritual humiliation in Houses of Correction, the law, far from exhibiting defined disgust at the exhibition of pain, is merely asserting its jealous right over the penal regime.

S/M as a Theatre of Social Risk

Most consensual S/M is less 'the desire to inflict pain', as Freud argued, than what John Alan Lee calls 'the social organisation of sexual risk'.[69] One can also call S/M the *sexual* organisation of *social risk*, for one of S/M's characteristics is the eroticising of scenes, symbols, contexts and contradictions which society does not typically recognise as sexual: domestic work, infancy, boots, water, money, uniforms and so on. Contrary to Robert Stoller's notion that S/M sex is the 'erotic form of hatred', a great deal of S/M involves neither pain nor hatred.[70] The ritual violations of S/M are less violations to the flesh than symbolic re-enactments of social violations to selfhood, which can take a myriad of shapes and emerge from a myriad of social situations. S/M publicly performs the failure of the Enlightenment idea of individual autonomy, staging the dynamics of power and interdependency for personal pleasure. As such, S/M rituals may be called *rituals of recognition*. In these rituals of recognition, participants seek a witness – to trauma, pain, pleasure or power. As Lee puts it: 'Each partner served as an audience to the other, and in the process, *contained* the other.'[71] The prevalence of voyeurism and spectators comes to represent a transposed desire for social recognition. In commercial S/M, the domina acts as an official, if forbidden, witness – to private anguish, baffled desires and the obscure deliriums of the flesh.

In many respects, S/M is a theatre of signs, granting temporary control over social risk. By scripting and controlling the circus of signs, the fetishist stages the delirious loss of control within a situation of extreme control. For many S/Mers, *loss* of control as *memory* is mediated by a show of *excess* of control as *spectacle*. As a result, S/Mers depend deeply on what Goffman calls 'control frames', by which to manage the staging of social risk.[72] In an important article, John Alan Lee explores the ways in which gay S/M culture attempts to limit the 'great potential dangers involved' in S/M: through the screening of partners, the shared understanding of costume signals, colour coding, the reciprocal negotiation of scenarios and ground rules, scripting, the use of signal words or 'keys' to indicate limits, and the confirming of consent during the scenario.[73] Mastering the control frame – the scene, the script, the costume, the magazine, the fantasy, the exchange of money – is indispensable to the sensation of mastery over what might otherwise be terrifying ambiguities.

Indeed, it is often not so much the *actuality* of power or submission that holds the S/Mer in its thrall but the *signs* of power: images, words, costumes, uniforms, scripts. The self-styled sexual therapist Sara Dale says her clients want often only to hear the snap of her whip through the air.[74] Lindi St Clair writes: 'Men wanting a fantasy liked to be in kinky "theme rooms" and "pretend": for example they would *talk* about certain props or scenarios, although in reality they wouldn't be interested in *doing* such things at all.'[75] Many clients are helplessly fascinated by fetish images of authority – handcuffs, badges, uniforms – and most dominas have rackfuls of costumes: '"Uniformists" desire to wear or be serviced by someone wearing uniform – military, medical, police, traffic warden, or any other persuasion. The most popular are schoolgirl's and French maid's.'[76] Allegra Taylor, visiting a Dungeon, recalls:

> I was still amazed by the sheer volume of props and costumes. It was like a theatre warehouse or a film set. Hanging on pegs on all the walls and corridors were hundreds of outfits – nurse's and policewomen's uniforms, gymslips, black rubber knickers, dozens of pairs of boots ... anything you can imagine having a fetish about.[77]

Other clients are enthralled by the verbal *representation* of desire, and like nothing so much as to send their 'literary Mistresses' letters, fantasies and scripts: 'Dear Madam Candida, If you find you have the space, would you kindly print the following humble letter. ... Madame, may long you reign.'[78] In one Fem-Dom magazine, large white spaces are left beneath photographs of male 'slaves', accompanied by the schoolmarmish instruction: 'I am asking you to write beneath each photo what you imagine

Madame Sheena is saying to her slave.'[79] Here, does the voyeur identify with Madame Sheena, her slave, or both? Identity shifts libidinously.

Hence the importance of scripts and initiation rituals in consensual S/M. Far from being the tyrannical exercise of one will upon a helpless other, consensual S/M is typically collaborative, involving careful training, initiation rites, a scrupulous definition of limits, and a constant confirmation of reciprocity.[80] As Paul Gebhard writes: 'The average sadomasochistic session is usually scripted. ... Often the phenomenon reminds one of a planned ritual or theatrical production.'[81] Clients and dominas typically agree on key words, which the 'bottom' uses to intensify, change or stop the action. Many S/M fetishists claim that it is thus the 'bottom' who is in control.

Havelock Ellis was the first to point out that much S/M is motivated by love. Since S/M involves the negotiation of perilous boundaries, mutual fidelity to the pledge of trust can create intimacy of a very intense kind. The bond of collaboration binds the players in an ecstasy of interdependence: abandonment at the very moment of dependence. Far from ruthlessly wreaking one's sadistic will upon another, 'the sadist must develop an extraordinary perceptiveness to know when to continue, despite cries and protests, and when to cease.'[82] Here, 'enslavement' is ceremonial rather than real, a symbolic gift that can be retracted at any moment. For this reason, Pat Califia calls S/M 'power without privilege'.[83]

Yet at the same time, any violation of the script is fraught with risk. If, at any point, control is lost, or the rules of the game transgressed, either of the players can be plunged into panic or rage. Dominas therefore stress the emotional and physical skill, as well as the dangers, involved in commercial S/M: '[It] does take a special kind of person who can do B & D properly because it can get right out of control. You have to keep your cool all the time.'[84] Untoward changes in the script or collapse of the control frame can plunge clients into extreme distress or ferocious rage. The magic spell can be violently broken, and at such moments dominas face great danger.

For this reason, I remain unconvinced by the libertarian argument that all S/M lies in a cloud-cuckoo land safely beyond any real abuses of power. The libertarian view all too easily conflates sexual repression with political oppression in a Reichian celebration of unlimit. But as Califia says, 'I do not believe that sex has an inherent power to transform the world. I do not believe that pleasure is always an anarchic force for good. I do not believe that we can fuck our way to freedom.'[85] S/M's theatre of risk inhabits the perilous borders of transgression, power and pleasure, where emotions can slip, identities shift, inchoate memories surface out of control, or everyday inequities be imported unexpectedly into the scene. As Sophie, a prostitute, says:

> People need to be pretty sure what they're doing. I don't want to make it sound like an elitist pastime, but you're dealing with such deep and potent forces that there is a risk of getting out of your depth. This hap-

pened with my previous lover. The sex we had brought up loads of stuff for her about being abused as a child which would have been a lot better coming through slowly and gently in therapy. I don't begin to have adequate resources to deal with that with a lover. I think S/M sex is good and it can be great, but I'd only want to do it with someone who has extensive self-knowledge.[86]

To recognise the theatrical aspect of S/M does not diminish the risks that may be involved. S/M inhabits the anomalous border between the theory of mimesis and the idea of catharsis, neither replicating social power nor finally subverting it, veering between polarities, converting scenes of disempowerment into a staged excess of pleasure, caricaturing social edicts in a sumptuous display of irreverence, but without substantially interrupting the social order.

In my view, the extreme libertarian argument that S/M *never* involves real anger or hate runs the risk of disavowing the intense emotional voltages that can be S/M's appeal.[87] Some dominas confess to potent expressions of feminist anger, outrage and power when they work: 'In bondage you have the power and control,' says Zoe, a parlour and escort woman, 'and it's quite refreshing to be in that position of total power getting a little anger out and let(ting) your expression out, and it wasn't threatening to the guy asking for it. ... I gained a lot of confidence out of it.'[88] Kelly explains that she became a bondage specialist because she 'enjoyed beating up men'. Some dominas, she said,

like inflicting pain perhaps because they have been hurt in their private lives, or where they are suppressed in their home life it is a role reversal, just like the guys the other way around. It is a reversal of the patriarchal system in which they have been suppressed all their lives; they are home doing the washing and ironing for their husbands in the day and they go out of a night and whip guys, and get paid for it.[89]

While such emotions may be unrepresentative, they cannot be wholly dismissed.

An important theoretical distinction therefore needs to be made between *reciprocal* S/M for mutual pleasure, and *consensual* S/M organised as a commercial exchange. Whatever else it is, commercial S/M is a labour issue. While all S/M is deeply stigmatised and violently policed, the criminalising of sexwork places dominas under particular pressure. Sexworkers argue that the current laws punish rather than protect them. In Britain, if a domina shares a flat with a friend, she can be convicted for running a brothel. If she pays towards the rent or upkeep of her flat, her friend can be convicted for living off immoral earnings. Yet working alone can be fatal. Moreover, where sexwork is a crime, a domina cannot seek police or legal aid if she is raped, battered or robbed. Clients know this, so commercial S/M's theatre of risk can, at times, become risky indeed, losing some of the collective safeguards that characterise much reciprocal

S/M. Nonetheless, sexworkers insist that it is not S/M or the exchange of cash that endangers them, but the laws and the context in which the exchange is made. Whatever else it does, commercial S/M throws into question the myth of all sexworkers as unambiguous victims. Dominas, like all sexworkers, are calling internationally for the decriminalising of their profession, so that they can collectively organise to transform the trade to meet their own needs.[90]

On its own, then, S/M does not escape its own paradoxes. Within its magic circle, social and personal contradictions can be deployed or negotiated but may not be resolved, for the sources and ends of these paradoxes lie beyond the individual, even though they may be lived with exquisite intensity in the flesh. S/M thus brings to its conceptual limit the libertarian promise that individual agency alone can suffice to resolve social dilemmas. In order to understand more fully the myriad meanings of S/M, it is necessary to distinguish between the social cultures from which it takes its multiple shapes, and against which it sets itself in stubborn refusal. The sub-culture of collective fetishism is an arena of contestation and negotiation, which does not teach simple lessons in power and domination.

Notes

1. Andrew Neil, Channel 4, 16 October 1992.
2. In this paper, I use the term S/M in its broad sense, to refer to the general sub-culture of organised fetishism. The term S/M thus includes a wide variety of fetishes: B and D (bondage and discipline), CP (corporal punishment), TV (transvestism), babyism, Scat, body piercing, foot fetishism and so on. These fetishes should be seen as sometimes overlapping, sometimes distinct sub-genres in a general sub-culture of collective fetish ritual. Moreover, within these genres there may be distinct forms: there are different forms of transvestism, for example, and different forms of B and D. Indeed, understanding and negotiating these distinctions serves as a crucial source of the pleasure, intimacy, identity and communality that can be engendered by consensual S/M.
3. The sub-culture of S/M is not synonymous with the non-consensual inflictions of violence, pain, abuse or terror. A man does not usually don leather gear, fetish costumes and make-up before battering his wife. At times, however, the boundaries may blur and distinctions falter.
4. Michel Foucault, *Madness and Civilisation: A History of Insanity in the Age of Reason*, trans. Richard Howard (London: Tavistock Publications, 1965).
5. Erving Goffman, *Frame Analysis* (New York: Harper and Row, 1974), quoted by Thomas S. Weinberg in 'Sadism and Masochism: Sociological Perspectives', in Thomas S. Weinberg and G.W. Levi Kamel, *S and M: Studies in Sadomasochism* (Buffalo, NY: Prometheus Books, 1983), p. 106.
6. Paul H. Gebhard, 'Sadomasochism', in Weinberg and Kamel, *S and M.*, p. 39.
7. Richard von Krafft-Ebing, *Psychopathia Sexualis*, trans. Franklin S. Klaf (New York: Stein and Day, 1965). See Jeffrey Weeks, *Against Nature: Essays on History, Sexuality and Identity* (London: Rivers Oram Press, 1991), and Jonathan Dollimore, *Sexual Dissidence: Augustine to Wilde, Freud to Foucault* (Oxford: Clarendon Press, 1991), for analyses of the discourses on 'perversion'.
8. Krafft-Ebing, *Psychopathia Sexualis*, p. 53. Quoted in Weinberg and Kamel, *S and M*, p. 17.

9. Ibid., p. 53. Quoted in Weinberg and Kamel, *S and M*, p. 27.
10. Ibid.
11. Ibid., p. 25.
12. Ibid., pp. 25-6.
13. Ibid., p. 26.
14. Ibid.
15. Sigmund Freud, *The Basic Writings of Sigmund Freud*, trans. and ed. A.A. Brill (New York: Modern Library, 1938), p. 569. Excerpted in Weinberg and Kamel, *S and M*, p. 30.
16. Ibid.
17. Ibid.
18. Ibid., p. 31.
19. 'I have been led to recognise a primary erotogenic masochism from which there develop two later forms, a feminine and a moral masochism.' Freud, 'Das Ökonomische Problem des Masochisten', Int. Zeit. f. Psa, 10, 121, 1924. Translated in *Collected Papers* (London: Hogarth Press, 1953-74), vol. 2, p. 255. Quoted in Weinberg and Kamel, *S and M*, p. 32.
20. Juicy Lucy, 'If I Ask You To Tie Me Up, Will You Still Want To Love Me?' in Katherine Davis *et al.* (eds.), *Coming to Power, Writings and Graphics on Lesbian S/M* (Boston: Alyson Publications, 1983), p. 32.
21. Vivienne Walker-Crawford, 'The Saga of Sadie O. Massey', in Robin Ruth Linden *et al.* (eds.), *Against Sadomasochism: A Radical Feminist Analysis* (San Francisco: Frog in the Well, 1982), p. 149.
22. Kathleen Barry, *Female Sexual Slavery* (New York: New York University Press, 1979), p. 209.
23. Interview with Anne McClintock, London, 3 July 1991.
24. Allegra Taylor, *Prostitution: What's Love Got to Do With It* (London: Macdonald Optima, 1991), p.42.
25. Ibid., p.41.
26. Roberta Perkins and Garry Bennett, *Being a Prostitute: Prostitute Women and Prostitute Men* (Sydney: Allen and Unwin, 1985), p. 127.
27. Interview with Anne McClintock, London, 3 July 1991.
28. Ibid.
29. Perkins and Bennett, *Being a Prostitute*, p. 142.
30. Ibid., p. 128.
31. Thomas S. Weinberg and G. W. Kamel, 'S/M: An Introduction to the Study of Sadomasochism', in Weinberg and Kamel, *S and M*, p. 21.
32. Lindi St Clair with Pamela Winfield, *It's Only a Game: The Autobiography of Miss Whiplash* (London: Piatkus, 1992), pp. 65, 74.
33. Gloria Walker and Lynn Daly, *Sexplicitly Yours: The Trial of Cynthia Payne* (London: Penguin, 1987), p. 66. One slave, Payne explained, came every Monday and let himself in with his own key, setting about his housewifely chores wearing only a wristwatch.
34. Perkins and Bennett, *Being a Prostitute*, p. 87.
35. Ibid., p. 128.
36. Quoted in Neil Philip, *Working Girls: An Illustrated History of the Oldest Profession* (London: Albion Press, 1991), p. 112.
37. Gebhard, 'Sadomasochism', in Weinberg and Kamel, *S and M*, p. 37.
38. Taylor, *Prostitution*, p. 45.
39. See Weinberg and Kamel, *S and M*, p. 109. Also Leyvoy Joenson, '"Erotic Blasphemy": The Politics of Sadomasochism', unpublished paper.
40. *Madame in a World of Fantasy*, vol. 15 no. 8, p. 19.
41. Marjorie Garber, *Vested Interests: Cross-Dressing and Cultural Anxiety* (New York: Routledge, 1992), pp. 11, 10. See my essay 'The Return of the Female Fetish and the Fiction of the Phallus', forthcoming in *New Formations*, for a sympathetic critique of Garber's theory of fetishism.
42. *The World of Transvestism*, vol. 1 no. 5, p. 10.

43. Taylor, *Prostitution*, p. 39.
44. *Madame in a World of Fantasy*, vol. 14 no. 10, p. 5.
45. Philip, *Working Girls*, p. 112.
46. St Clair, *It's Only a Game*, p. 64.
47. *Madame in a World of Fantasy*, vol. 15 no. 8, p. 49.
48. Ibid., p. 51.
49. *Madame in a World of Fantasy*, vol. 14 no. 10, p. 7.
50. Ibid., p. 9.
51. *Mistress* 28, p. 48 (n.d.)
52. *Madame in a World of Fantasy*, vol. 15 no. 8, p. 61.
53. *Mistress* 28, p. 47.
54. Ibid.
55. *Madame in a World of Fantasy*, vol. 15 no. 8, p. 17.
56. Ibid., p. 37.
57. Gebhard, Sadomasochism', in Weinberg and Kamel, *S and M*, p. 37.
58. See Walker and Daly, *Sexplicitly Yours*, p. 66.
59. See Clare Dyer, 'Sado-masochists Guilty Verdict Upheld,' *Guardian*, 20 February 1992. Also Alex Kershaw, 'Spanner in the Works', *Guardian Weekend*, 8–9 February, 1992, pp. 12–13; and Kershaw, 'Love Hurts', in *Guardian Weekend*, 28 November 1992, pp. 6–10.
60. Kershaw, 'Spanner in the Works', p. 13. See also Helena Kennedy, *Eve Was Framed: Women and British Justice* (London: Chatto and Windus, 1992), for a searing account of the miscarriage of justice.
61. Suzanne Moore, 'Deviant Laws', in *Marxism Today*, February 1991, p. 11.
62. Anthony Brown, one of the men sentenced in the Spanner case, suggests: 'Perhaps there's a tendency for S & M activity to have increased, particularly among homosexual men, as a result of the threat of AIDS. To a degree it's a displacement activity.' Quoted in Kershaw, 'Spanner in the Works', p. 13.
63. Pat Califia, quoted in Kershaw, 'Love Hurts', p. 7.
64. Michel Foucault, *Discipline and Punish: The Birth of the Prison*, trans. Alan Sheridan (London: Penguin, 1977).
65. Ibid., p. 91.
66. Ibid., p. 81.
67. Ibid., pp. 93, 95.
68. Ibid., p. 129.
69. John Alan Lee, 'The Social Organisation of Sexual Risk', in Weinberg and Kamel, *S and M*, pp. 175–93. Freud, *Three Essays on the Theory of Sexuality* (New York: Basic, 1962), p. 23.
70. Robert Stoller, *Perversion: The Erotic Form of Hatred* (New York: Dell, 1975).
71. Lee, 'The Social Organisation of Sexual Risk', p. 189. See also Goffman, *Frame Analysis*, p. 135.
72. Goffman, *Frame Analysis*.
73. Lee, 'The Social Organisation of Sexual Risk', p. 178.
74. Interview with Anne McClintock, London, October 1992.
75. St Clair, *It's Only a Game*, p. 64.
76. Ibid.
77. Taylor, *Prostitution*, p. 38.
78. *Madame in a World of Fantasy*, vol. 15 no. 8, p. 18.
79. Ibid., pp. 42-3.
80. As Weinberg and Kamel argue: 'S & M scenarios are *willingly and cooperatively* produced; more often than not it is the masochist's fantasies that are acted out'. Weinberg and Kamel, *S and M*, p. 20.
81. Gebhard, Sadomasochism', in Weinberg and Kamel, *S and M*, p. 37.
82. Ibid.
83. Pat Califia, 'Unravelling the Sexual Fringe: A Secret Side of Lesbian Sexuality', *The Advocate*, 27 December 1979, p. 22. Quoted in Jeffrey Weeks, *Sexuality and Its Discontents: Meanings, Myths and Modern Sexualities* (London: Routledge, 1985), p. 238.

84. Kelly, 'It's Not a Right or Wrong Issue, It's Up to the Individual', in Perkins and Bennett, *Being a Prostitute*, p. 130. ('Kelly' is a working pseudonym.)
85. Pat Califia, *Macho Sluts: Erotic Fiction* (Boston : Alyson Publications, 1988), p. 15.
86. Quoted in Taylor, *Prostitution*, p. 31.
87. See Donald McRae's brilliant account of the power struggle between a domina and a client in *Nothing Personal: The Business of Sex* (Edinburgh: Mainstream, 1992).
88. Zoe, 'The Only Way I Can Be Independent', in Perkins and Bennett, *Being a Prostitute*, p. 108.
89. 'I had by this stage recognised myself as a lesbian. I was also on a male hate trip and I thought all men were useless at that stage of my life.' Kelly, quoted in 'It's Not a Right or Wrong Issue', in Perkins and Bennett, *Being a Prostitute*, pp. 127, 130. For others, the imaginative demands are fatiguing, and they prefer the greater detachment that comes with giving brisk sexual services. As Margaret, an Australian prostitute says, 'I did bondage sometimes, but it was so damn exhausting I would prefer to do sex than bondage. Some of them wanted to be hit hard and that took it out of me physically and mentally.' In *Being a Prostitute*, p. 121.
90. See my expanded analysis of the legal issues facing sexworkers in Anne McClintock, 'Screwing the System: Sexwork, Race and the Law', in *Boundary 11*, Fall 1992.

Index